Digging Up Devils

The Search for a Satanic Murder Cult in Rural Ohio

By Jack Legg

For the Scapegoats

Table of Contents

Foreword

On September 08, 2023, only one day prior to the writing of this preface, the City of Louisville, KY agreed to pay $20.5 million to two men wrongfully convicted of "Satanic ritual" murder in 1992 and incarcerated for over two decades before their release in 2016. Jeffrey Clark never identified as a Satanist. Keith Hardin, unlike most of those convicted during the anti-Satanist moral panic of the 1980s and 90s, did identify as a Satanist, helplessly noting that his religion actually forbade the practice of blood sacrifice.

Diminished standards of evidence that allowed for "recovered memories" to be treated as credible eye-witness accounts had created an environment in which deranged conspiracy theories were assumed validated. More recent investigation has concluded that authorities had fabricated evidence and even threatened Clark with a gun when he refused to implicate Hardin. Fabricating Satanic crimes was relatively easy in an era in which authorities were swayed by conspiracy theorists who assured law enforcement that a lack of substantial evidence could be taken as evidence of a well-organized plot.

$20.5 million is a nominal fee for the loss of over 20 years of one's life, and ever since the proclaimed "end" of the Satanic Panic – generally placed by journalists and academics around 1995 – a slow trickle of similar stories have come to light, indicating that we will likely never appreciate the full depth and breadth of the destruction that this irrational uproar has wrought.

Despite having studied the Satanic Panic for most of my adult life, I was unaware of the plight of Hardin and Clark until their release, and there are surely many others who languish in prison today – first as victims of false Satanic crime convictions, later as victims of cruel bureaucrats. Former Massachusetts Attorney General Martha Coakley was one such cruel bureaucrat, having fought to deny the 2004 release from prison of one Gerald Amirault, who had been falsely accused of Satanic cult crimes and incarcerated for 18 years prior to his release. Coakley asserted that there was no new exculpatory evidence in the case, despite the fact that the man was convicted on the merits of no credible evidence at all.

Disgraceful politicians like Coakley, corrupt law enforcement officers, and true believers in Satanic cult conspiracies themselves "conspired" to ruin the lives of an untold number of victims in the modern-day witch hunt that we now refer to as the Satanic Panic, for which there has still been remarkably little institutional introspection with a mind toward ensuring that such ugly events do not happen again. Only about a year after the Salem witch trials, a judge publicly apologized for his role in the witch hunt, while no such apologies would manifest even after a general recognition of the illegitimacy of punishments meted out during the 80s and 90s in response to imaginary Satanic crimes.

Mental health care professionals have generally remained silent toward the ongoing use of "recovered memory therapies" by their pseudoscientific peers who utilize a variety of techniques, including hypnosis and sodium amytal interviews, to draw forth "repressed memories" of traumatic abuse, long known to create confabulatory false memories of non-existent events. Despite these techniques being equally suited, and utilized, to draw forth "memories" of extraterrestrial abductions and "past lives," organizations like the International Society for the Study of Trauma and Dissociation (ISSTD) still advocate for their use, simply ignoring the horrors of the Satanic Panic and their therapeutic model's role in it. Some of the prominent figures in the ISSTD were active propagators of the Satanic Panic at its peak, leading vulnerable mental health consumers to embrace crippling false memory-based paranoid delusions that shattered families and endlessly haunt those who believe in them.

"Occult Crime" specialists still offer their consultations to police departments, some government websites still contain informational packets for law enforcement agents that reference "Satanic Ritual Abuse." Many of the most deranged lectures and literature from the Satanic Panic, propagated by its most unhinged proponents, have found a new audience among the QAnon faithful today. Interviewers often ask me if I see parallels between QAnon and the Satanic Panic of the 80s and 90s, but in reality, the one is just a continuation of the other. And as this next wave of Satanic

Panic captures the imaginations of conspiracists, opportunists, and the gullible paranoid, we still sift through the wreckage of the last wave hoping to finally bring a more widespread understanding to what went wrong, and what we can try to avoid in the future.

The journalistic profession, which naturally played the largest role in mainstreaming and normalizing Satanic Panic conspiracy theories, today shows little general understanding of what the Satanic Panic was, or the gravity of its impact on the lives of millions. Today, when top 40 musicians provoke public conservative Christian outrage by incorporating devilish imagery, this is invariably reported as a "Satanic Panic," all but completely denying the magnitude of what the term suggests academically. Worse, there now exists a popular genre of retrospective reports about the Satanic Panic that take a very narrow and minimizing view of the panic, focusing on the laughable elements, such as the obsession with backward messaging in music and the alleged demonic influence of Dungeons & Dragons.

Something these reports tend to hold in common is that they assert that the Satanic Panic was strictly the result of Moral Majority conservative conspiracism. The uncomfortable truth is that the Satanic Panic managed to insinuate itself into our institutions and law enforcement agencies because of the bipartisan political support it received. While evangelicals saw a literal Satan guiding an occult conspiracy and hiding subliminal messages in films, books, and music, their erstwhile opposition came to support the notion that no claim of abuse was too outlandish to be disregarded; and, in fact, any such claims need be taken at face value in recognition of a "culture of denial" that had persisted to that point. Then, as now, conspiracists learned that framing their battle as one in which they acted as defenders of victims of Satanic childhood sexual abuse allowed them to denigrate skeptics as defenders or denialists of pedophilia.

Political polarization creates a rife environment for moral panics, becoming all but unstoppable if an irrational common ground is found… and polarization has seldom been as extreme and apparent as it is now. Polarization can also blind us to the extent of irrationality that fueled the Satanic Panic, if we turn a blind eye to the evidence that we feel implicates our political tribe.

If those who fail to confront history are condemned to repeat it, this is exactly the kind of motivated ignorance that can prevent confrontation with the facts in even the more educated analysts.

Digging Up Devils tells the previously untold tale of an imaginary cult dreamed up by conspiracists in rural Ohio, and the subsequent devastation that followed. Author Jack Legg has compiled original interviews and previously unreleased documentary evidence to tell a story that is both unique and indicative of the larger moral panic at the same time. For those familiar with Satanic Panic literature to date, this book is an excellent addition. For those with little familiarity with any particular cases of Satanic Panic, this is as good a place as any to start. May it help us to better navigate the rough waters ahead.

Lucien Greaves,
Co-Founder of the Satanic Temple

Initiation

I've always been a sucker for a good horror story.

As a kid, I was fascinated by all things mysterious and spooky. Ghosts. Monsters. Demons. UFOs. I'd even dabble in the occasional Bigfoot story. If there was a thin veil between this realm and the next, I wanted to be the one to pull it back.

I came by it honestly. Growing up in a fundamentalist Baptist church, I heard countless warnings about Satan and his work. I learned there was an invisible world of spirits all around us. I heard there were satanic messages in certain types of music and television shows. They told me I could open a portal to Hell if I played with a Ouija board or that demons could get into my house if I watched movies with occult-related themes. And they told me that some people, no matter how nice they seemed on the outside, might be working for the Devil.

One autumn, when I was in junior high, I sat in a revival meeting while a traveling evangelist warned that a satanic group had infiltrated the highest ranks of a well-known Bible publisher. He also told us the government was planning to insert microchips under our skin, which would later become the Mark of the Beast. As we sang our closing hymn, I remember looking around the sanctuary with eyes as wide as saucers, wondering why no one else was panicking.

Subsequently, I took great interest in the so-called "Satanic Panic" era of the 1980s and 1990s. During this time, there was widespread concern among parents and religious leaders across the United States regarding "the occult" and satanic influences in society. For more than a decade I collected books, articles, videos, and podcasts on the topic.

When I stumbled across a footnote which mentioned a 1985 incident in Toledo that had involved a sheriff-led search for a mass grave of sacrificial cult victims, I had to find out what happened. This book is a product of that quest.

I am deeply indebted to the dozens of hardworking journalists who thoroughly documented the events in question, often with more skepticism than they're given credit for. I am eternally grateful for the contributions of Deputy Trilby Cashin, who took time out of her busy schedule to talk about the case. I am also grateful to Dr. G. Michael Pratt for sharing his keen insights about archaeology and forensic anthropology, as well as his own personal recollections of the Spencer Township incident.

Finally, this book would not have been possible without the assistance of Detective Jason Langlois of the Lucas County Sheriff's Department. From my first tentative phone call to our final email exchange, he shepherded this amateur historian through the case files with courtesy and professionalism, offering insightful observations along the way. From one researcher to another: thank you, Detective.

For any Satanists, pagans, witches, or Wiccans who may be reading, I'd like to offer a disclaimer. This book describes allegations made against a secret cult. Accusers often described these alleged cult members as Satanists, witches, or devil worshipers. Wherever possible, I have preserved the phrasing used by those who made the claims, but it should be noted that these labels are imprecise and often inaccurate. Please know that the labels used in this book are not intended to represent modern day practitioners or practitioners of that time, nor are they intended to represent any reader's personal experience, values, or beliefs. Thank you for your grace. The devil, as they say, is in the details.

Finally, I'd like to offer a sensitive content warning: this book includes descriptions of various unproven allegations of murder, violence, and sexual assault at the hands of a satanic cult. Reader discretion is advised.

Part One:

Scratching
the Surface

1. Stop the Presses
Thursday, June 20, 1985
7:00am

By the time Sheriff James Telb convened his early morning press conference, investigators were already combing the woods.

At first, the searchers drew little attention. It was just after sunrise, around 6:00 am, when deputies converged on a garbage-strewn wooded area in the southeastern corner of Spencer Township, Ohio and many residents were still sleeping. Those early risers who did notice the investigators were little more than bemused.

That was before the sheriff told everyone about the satanic murder cult.

In neighboring Springfield Township, just a few minutes down the road from the search location, reporters gathered at the modest Sheriff's Department substation near the intersection of King and Angola Roads. James Telb, forty-two years of age and only six months into his first term as Sheriff, stepped in front of the cameras and ignited a media frenzy.

A local girl was missing, said the sheriff, and she had not been seen in over two years. Officers would be executing a search warrant at a home in the area, where they expected to find weapons, drugs, and other paraphernalia. But this was no standard kidnapping.

After a three-month investigation, the sheriff told reporters he had reason to believe the missing child had been murdered by a cult. They suspected the girl's grandfather, who had already been charged with child-stealing, was the leader of a Devil-worshiping cult and that he had slaughtered his granddaughter in a satanic ritual sacrifice.[1]

The search warrant also indicated that officers expected to find evidence of cult practices, including robes and occult paraphernalia. Later in the press conference, an officer would display a hand-drawn map of the search area, identifying a specific property as the "cult house."[2]

The sacrificial murder of a local child at the hands of her own grandfather was shocking enough, but the sheriff was just getting started. When it came to devilish dealings in Spencer Township, he had barely scratched the surface.

According to the sheriff's sources, this satanic cult had been active in the area for sixteen years, since 1969. The cult had more than two

1

hundred members, most of whom lived in the county and throughout the surrounding area. The nefarious group met in fields, forests, and abandoned properties throughout Spencer Township. They believed Satan was all-powerful. They mutilated animals. They took drugs and had sex.

And they sacrificed humans. After cult members had their way with the body, hapless victims were "carved to death" in the ultimate act of service to Satan.[3]

As reporters listened with rapt attention, the sheriff went on to characterize the cult as a splinter group of a non-traditional cult. "Traditional cults use animals. Non-traditional cults sacrifice children and human beings," he said.[4] A key informant claimed to have witnessed witches and Satan worshipers administering their unholy practices.

Telb said his investigation had uncovered a satanic calendar which prescribed sacrifices on certain dates. Using this information, the sheriff estimated that the cult had murdered an average of five people every year. Most of these victims were said to be children and infants. They expected to uncover fifty to sixty bodies.[5]

Sheriff James Telb speaks at press conference.
© *The Toledo Blade*.

They needed to act fast. According to the satanic calendar, the next human sacrifice was scheduled to take place on the summer solstice: the very next day, June 21. Sheriff Telb had accelerated his investigation in hopes of subverting the cult's plans and saving future victims.[6]

If anyone doubted the seriousness of the situation, the Sheriff punctuated his remarks with a stern reproach for any cultists who may be listening in.

"I don't think it's a game," he said.[7]

Within hours, the eyes of the world would be focused on Spencer Township, Ohio.

In July of 1984, nearly one year before Sheriff Telb announced his cult investigation in Spencer Township, *The Columbus Dispatch* printed a multi-page profile on a police officer from Tiffin, Ohio named Dale Griffis. At the time, the man was just beginning to gain national notoriety for his research into satanism and the occult. The article, entitled "Sympathy for the Devil," profiled Griffis and his work, but also recounted several strange and horrifying tales of murder and mayhem around Ohio and across the nation.[8]

Griffis shared the shocking story of a twenty-four-year-old woman from Fairfield County who had allegedly come face-to-face with pure evil. The woman agreed to tell her story to a reporter from *The Dispatch*, but only on the condition of anonymity. She went by the name "Jane."

Jane said she grew up in an upper-middle class home in Columbus, Ohio. When she was eleven, her father suddenly became ill and passed away. One day at school, Jane remembered falling to the ground and crying about her circumstances, but she received no comfort.

"I said my dad just died, and everybody just laughed."

About two weeks after her father died, a mysterious stranger approached Jane as she walked down the street. The strange man looked her in the eye and said, "How would you like to have everything you ever wanted?" According to Jane, this was her first contact with a Satanist.

Jane began attending satanic meetings, which were held in private homes in her neighborhood. During these meetings, anonymous strangers wore black robes, chanted, and burned black candles. Jane was quick to insist there were no sexual perversions during these ceremonies. "They were purists," she explained. Unfortunately for Jane, things would soon take a dark turn.

Over time, the cult members gradually introduced Jane to the ritual slaughter of animals, including pigs and goats. The rituals involved killing the animals, mutilating their bodies, and drinking their blood. She said, "It was different. It was weird. I suppose there was a rebellion factor. And everything was brought on so gradually, it was not repulsive when they got to the killing and stuff."

Jane admitted it was difficult to remember all the details, because she had been high on drugs most of the time, but she still shuddered as she reflected on the experience. "I don't think any of it registered with me until after it was all over," she said.

One fateful summer night, about a year after she joined the cult, Jane was taken to a remote field somewhere in northern Ohio. There, she witnessed the cult's darkest ritual to date. She did not recall the exact date or location of the incident, but she knew she was thirteen years old at the time.

Shortly after she arrived in a large, open field, Jane witnessed the unimaginable. "This one lady was being initiated, and they told her to go home and get her baby," she said. After the woman had left and returned with an infant, the leader of the ritual commanded her to hand over the child. Jane said the woman became docile and compliant with the cult leader, as if in a trance. "She was like a zombie. She stared straight ahead."

Jane watched in horror as the cult leader pulled out a knife and cut the baby's throat.

Aside from turning to flee in terror, Jane could not remember anything else that happened that night. The next thing she knew, she was waking up safely in her own bed, with no knowledge of how she got back to her home in Columbus. She never saw or heard from any cult members again.

Occult expert Dale Griffis acknowledged that with stories like Jane's, it can be difficult to separate fact from fiction. He noted, however, that the story could be true. Griffis told *The Dispatch*, "There are indications throughout the United States that there have been babies used for sacrifice, but I would call this a high exception."

Eleven years after the alleged event, fears still lingered for Jane. "I still have nightmares. I don't feel safe. These people believe you take the life force of anything you sacrifice. And it's a lot more widespread than people think it is."

2. Search and Seizure
Thursday, June 20, 1985
7:00am

Patricia Litton was at home with her children when deputies burst through the front door. Armed with a search warrant issued by a Lucas County Common Pleas judge, twenty deputies swiftly swarmed the premises, fully armed with shotguns.[1] The shocked mother of five had no advance warning and she had no idea why the officers were there.

Situated at the corner of Angola and South Crissey Roads, the Litton house was no more than two miles from the sheriff's department substation where James Telb had held his morning press conference. Although the search for human remains would eventually center on Spencer Township, the Litton residence was located on the western edge of Springfield Township.

Deputies were searching for a man named Leroy Freeman, who had already been charged with child-stealing and unlawful flight to avoid prosecution. When deputies raided the Litton residence, neither Leroy nor Charity Freeman had been seen for over two years.[2]

Based on the word of unnamed informants, the Litton family was believed to be harboring the fugitive.[3] Some reports claimed that Freeman was a member of a satanic cult;[4] others claimed he was the leader of the cult.[5] Regardless of his ranking among the devil worshipers, authorities believed Freeman had abducted the child for the express purpose of murdering her in a ritual sacrifice.

Unbeknownst to the Litton family, their house had been under surveillance for three months. In addition to Freeman himself, the deputies expected to find deadly weapons, including up to half a dozen shotguns, along with marijuana and other drugs. The search warrant indicated the house may also contain evidence of child-stealing, abuse, and murder, including robes and other cult materials.[6]

Not only did the police believe seven-year-old Charity Freeman had been murdered by a cult, but they had reason to believe there were more child victims from Ohio and other surrounding states. Investigators from Michigan had been brought into the investigation.[7]

As deputies peppered her with questions, Patricia Litton was at a loss. She did not know who Leroy Freeman was and she certainly had no

5

knowledge of a satanic cult. "I have no idea who this person is or have any idea what this is about," she told deputies.[8]

Patricia and her five children would be detained in their home for the next two and a half hours.

There is no question that Charity Freeman was missing. When the Lucas County Sheriff's Department executed their search warrant at the Litton residence, they were reacting, in part, to an actual disappearance. This part of the story was no mere rumor.

But the story in Spencer Township went beyond one documented case of a missing child. The allegations grew to include the ritual slaughter of fifty to seventy-five innocent victims, most of whom were children and infants, at the hands of dangerous devil worshipers. According to the sheriff, there were people in their midst who wanted to steal children. They wanted to hurt children. Given the opportunity, these people would kill the children.

And somehow, the parents had failed to notice.

Spencer Township was not the only community grappling with such ideas. Throughout the 1980s and early 1990s, there was a resurgence of fears related to the safety and well-being of children. In some communities, these shared anxieties bubbled over into full-blown rumor-panics. Where did these fears come from, and what made such rumors so alluring?

In 1962, the identification of "battered child syndrome" by pediatric psychiatrist C. Henry Kempe brought the issue of child maltreatment into the mainstream. While professional inquiry into this topic focused mainly on the physical abuse of children, the general discourse led to a growing emphasis on protecting child victims. Over time, this protection grew to include neglect, emotional abuse, sexual abuse, and exploitation.[9]

In the 1970s, the study of child abuse emerged as an area of academic study in the United States. This led to a significant increase in the number of social workers, researchers, and mental health professionals who devoted their time and attention to helping child victims. An organized and increasingly robust child-protection apparatus began to emerge.[10]

By the late 1970s, a few self-appointed spokespeople began promoting claims that American children were gravely in danger of prostitution rings and pornographers. Author Robin Lloyd claimed to know about an international prostitution ring which involved hundreds of thousands of male minors. Law enforcement professionals repeated this claim during a Congressional hearing on child safety. Judianne Denson-Gerber later doubled Lloyd's original estimate to account for female victims. Later, she arbitrarily doubled it again. By 1977, NBC News reported, "It's been estimated that as many as two million American youngsters are involved in the fast-growing, multi-million-dollar child pornography business."[11]

This rhetoric played up the idea that American families were menaced on all sides by dire threats. In 1984, Senator Arlen Spector tapped into this fear when he said, "the molestation of children has now reached epidemic proportions."[12] By the mid-1980s, millions of American preschoolers were attending Good Touch/Bad Touch educational programs. Studies later found that many children had misunderstood the content of this training, sometimes taking normal activities such as bathing to be inappropriate.[13]

Several widely publicized incidents gave rise to a movement focused on recovering missing children. In 1979, six-year-old Etan Patz disappeared after leaving his house to go to school. He became one of the first missing children to be pictured on a milk carton. President Ronald Reagan went on to designate the date of Etan's disappearance, May 25, as National Missing Children's Day. In 1981, six-year-old Adam Walsh disappeared from a shopping mall and was later found murdered. Both cases received widespread media attention, and the Walsh case was dramatized in a television movie in 1983.[14]

The National Center for Missing and Exploited Children was formed in 1984. By 1986, fears of child abduction were on the rise. One public opinion poll in Illinois found that 89 percent of parents believed children being kidnapped by strangers was a very serious concern.[15] Public information campaigns began emphasizing potential threats to children, with some reports claiming that over fifty thousand children were abducted by strangers every year.[16] Best estimates from law enforcement officials at that time put the true number of abductions at two or three hundred per year.[17]

Popular urban legends from this time also reflected deep-seated anxieties about child safety. Some communities warned parents about drug dealers who loitered on playgrounds, distributing Mickey Mouse stickers laced with LSD. One popular story told of a young girl who was lured away from her parents in a shopping mall. According to the legend, mall security guards were able to seal off the building and recover the girl, but not before the perpetrators had changed her clothes and cut and dyed her hair to disguise her appearance.[18] Other whispered warnings from the 1980s included boys being lured into public restrooms to be castrated, kidnapped babies from department stores, girls being abducted by "white slavers," and lick-on tattoos being laced with hallucinogenic drugs.[19]

During the Halloween season of 1970, *The New York Times* ran an article about the danger of razor blades being hidden inside apples distributed to trick-or-treaters. In the decade that followed, similar stories popped up across the nation, warning parents about harmful items hidden in Halloween candy. When researcher Joel Best scoured newspaper reports and other records from this time, he could only find two cases of death or injury related to tampered-with Halloween candy. Both cases were perpetrated by a member of the victim's own family.[20]

In 1974, noted conspiracy believer and author John Todd began promoting the idea that satanic cults were actively stealing children across the nation to use them in ritual sacrifices.[21] By the mid-1980s, numerous experts and officials had lent credibility to this notion. At one point, Officer Mitch White of the Beaumont, California police department openly declared that ninety-five percent of all missing children were victims of occult-related abductions.[22]

Kidnapping was not the only concern. Widespread fears of sexual abuse and molestation at the hands of devil-worshipers rose to prominence during the infamous McMartin Preschool case, beginning in 1983. One parent involved in the case claimed that over one thousand children had been abused in their city alone. Most of these children were said to be the victims of satanic cults.[23]

On the heels of McMartin, and the outbreak of similar cases which followed, child-saving movements began to address a brand-new type of child victimization: ritual abuse. Coined in 1985, the term ritual abuse came to denote abuse which occurred "in a context linked to some symbols or group that have a religious, magical, or supernatural connotation, and where invocation of these symbols or activities, repeated over time, is used to frighten and intimidate the children."[24]

Fears of ritual abuse in preschools and childcare centers marked an escalation in the nature of the threat. Not only were devil-worshippers "out there," somewhere, seeking to kidnap our children; they had infiltrated our neighborhoods, taken over our institutions, and were actively using their positions of intimate familiarity to harm the most vulnerable among us. This escalation of fears corresponded with significant societal changes, particularly in family life.

According to the Bureau of Labor Statistics, the percentage of women in the workforce grew from 39 percent in 1970, to 49 percent in 1978, to 56 percent in 1988. Between 1978 and 1988, the percentage of working women who had children increased from 53 to 65 percent, a fivefold increase since 1950. This rapid change in the workforce contributed to a growing demand for childcare.[25]

As working parents left their homes and joined the labor force, many had significant concerns about entrusting their children into the care of strangers. Public opinion polls indicated that men and women in the age group most likely to need childcare from a provider outside the family considered this change to be worse than the conditions of their parents' generation. Fully one-third of women surveyed said they would be afraid to leave their child in a daycare facility.[26]

With common themes of blood, sacrifice, defilement, and cannibalism, historical myths often find their locus in children. Late medieval art portrays the Devil devouring live victims, and even witches presenting the Horned God with children they have stolen or conceived through an incubus as an offering. In the mid-nineteenth century, white residents of New Orleans had persistent fears that "every small child that vanished had become a Voodoo sacrifice."[27] Charges of ritual mistreatment of children can be found throughout history, from the pre-Christian era to modern times.

One function of demonologies, or beliefs about satanic cults, is that they can distract us from the immediate, daunting problems around us. As it became increasingly necessary to expose children to influences outside the home, parents feared they were losing control of the socialization process. Satanic subversion narratives gave a human shape to this sense of vulnerability. Fears of child abduction and ritual abuse in the 1980s coincided closely with the sharp increase of women with young children in the workforce and the growing need for childcare, further illustrating the tension between family and economy.[28]

These rumors of satanic ritual abuse may not have been deliberately created by parents and leaders, but there are certain groups who are more likely to believe and disseminate such rumors, particularly in times of great change, social disorganization, or socioeconomic pressure.[29] In essence, parents were asking, "Who is taking care of my children? Can they be trusted? Are other religious options safe? And how widespread is the horror of abuse?"[30]

Of course, real-world dangers exist. It is not irrational for parents and caregivers to take precautions, promote safety, and avoid potential threats. But when it comes rumors of secret cults and satanic conspiracies, Jeffrey Victor reminds us, "Bizarre stories of animal sacrifice, child kidnapping, ritual torture, infanticide, blood drinking, and cannibalism must be interpreted symbolically, in terms of culturally inherent symbolic meanings. The origin of these stories can be found in the collectively shared anxieties which they arise."[31]

3. Tight Knit
Thursday, June 20, 1985
9:30am

Spencer Township, Ohio was only about ten miles from Toledo, but many considered the area to be "out in the country." With a population of 1,744, the majority of whom lived in a single development called Oak Grove Estates, most of the people knew each other by name. An amalgam of private property, automotive junkyard, and densely forested land, Spencer Township was no thriving metropolis. One longtime resident characterized the place as a close community which stayed "pretty quiet most of the time."[1]

When news began to spread that the sheriff had uncovered a two-hundred-member cult in their midst, many residents were incredulous. As more investigators arrived on the scene, people began to congregate near the search location on Meilke Road. Bewildered by the burst of sudden activity in their quiet corner of Lucas County, few residents believed the search would uncover any bodies.

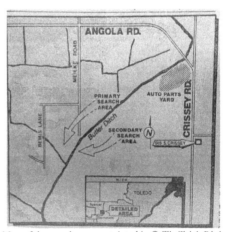

Map of the search area, as printed in © *The Toledo Blade*.

Mack Robinson lived on Meilke Road. Looking over the search area, he told reporters he had never seen anything unusual. Before investigators arrived, he had never seen the earth disturbed. According to Robinson, "There was nothing but junk back there."[2]

11

Leonard Dubon, who had also lived in the area for years, said, "I've been all through these woods – winter and summer – hunting, and I've never seen anything out of the ordinary, certainly no devil worshipers." In the spirit of civic responsibility, he concluded, "I'd have shot 'em if I had seen any."[3]

For some, rumors about night rituals and human sacrifice made no sense in such a tight-knit community. A group of devil worshipers would need secrecy to operate. In a close community like Spencer Township, such secrecy would only be possible if the cult and their activities were completely invisible. Either that, or every resident had joined a conspiracy of silence. Neither option seemed plausible.

"Two hundred people chanting is pretty hard to miss," said longtime resident Oliver Ennols. Later that morning, the media would set up camp on his front lawn to observe the proceedings. "That area is sort of a lovers' lane and dumping ground, but we haven't heard anything strange out there."[4]

Although some expressed doubt, Sheriff Telb insisted the investigation was merited. He had heard persistent rumors about the cult for months. The sheriff also claimed that his deputies had carried out surveillance operations, even managing to observe and record a devil-worshiping service in the area. Deputies claimed to have seen around one hundred people entering and leaving a home where chanting could be heard. There were no signs of violence that night, but Telb maintained the threat was imminent.

"They moved these sacrificial places around, so we couldn't take a chance. We had to make our move now," he said.[5]

The alleged devil-worshiping ceremony was not the only strange occurrence. Two days before the search in Spencer Township, nearby Wilkins Methodist Church had been vandalized. The minister arrived at the church that morning to find strange symbols written in soap on the altar and stained-glass windows. These symbols were said to be satanic. He also found a baby doll near the altar, with its dress pulled up over its head. Someone had also burned a Bible.[6]

Spencer Township resident Eli Bias, who had lived in the area since 1956, told reporters he would not be surprised if the investigation turned up something significant. "Since I've been out here, there have been some strange activities that's not quite kosher," he said. "It has always been talked of. They always just say people were seeing ghosts out here. Well, some people don't believe in ghosts, and they were seeing something."[7]

4. On Portents and Being Earnest

The residents of Spencer Township may have been shocked at reports of a satanic cult, but at least they weren't alone. As Sheriff Telb launched his investigation, ominous signs and devilish rumors had already surfaced elsewhere in Ohio.

About ninety miles south of Toledo, in rural Union County, someone had been killing animals and mutilating them beyond recognition. As investigators explored possible connections between a series of deaths among domestic and farm animals, ripples of speculation spread throughout the community.

In December 1984, a Union County man contacted the sheriff to report that someone had cut off the head and front legs of his pet Doberman Pinscher. The perpetrator had also killed four puppies and three more were missing. Two days later, someone left twenty-four dead cats in the driveway of a residence in Plain City. One cat had been decapitated and several others had been killed by blows to the head or broken necks. In August, seventy-six chickens had been found dead at a local farm, their necks wrung.[1]

On December 22, 1984, a man returned home to find two Poodle puppies dead. One puppy showed no apparent signs of violence, but all that remained of the other was four paws, its tail, and a badly mutilated head.[2] This was the only known case of animal mutilation which occurred inside a house; the owner found the remains of one puppy in the kitchen and the other in the living room.[3]

As the reports of dead animals spread, so did the rumors. Some theorized that the killings may have been revenge for some perceived injustice. The dead cats, for example, had been left in the driveway of an official from the local Humane Society. Perhaps these were thrill-killings, perpetrated by juveniles trying to get their gruesome kicks. Or maybe the animal slayings were the work of some mentally disturbed individual.

Union County Sheriff John G. Overly had his own theory: these slayings were ritualistically carried out by an organized, satanic cult. The sheriff told the media he had personally studied the matter himself.

"I'm not saying it definitely is cult-related, but I can't say it isn't either," Overly told reporters.[4] He went on to list several clues which pointed to satanic activity.

14

First, the sheriff said occult groups often used black animals and chickens as live sacrifices. Some of the incidents had occurred on the night of a full moon, a significant time for devil-worshipers. When he put the locations of animal slayings on a county map, Sheriff Overly said the points could be connected to form a star-shaped pattern.

Overly said he had once discovered mysterious symbols engraved on the hearth of an empty house. Unknown persons had attempted to unearth a Civil War-era grave in a remote area several months prior. The perpetrator had dug within inches of the coffin.[5] Because some cults drink animal blood from human skulls, Overly said the attempted grave-robbing may have been connected to the animal mutilations.

"We feel that we do have cults practicing in this county, but the whole thing is something new to us," he said. "It's something you'd think of being in a city like Cleveland or Los Angeles or Chicago."[6]

Sheriff Overly appointed Deputy John Lala to launch a probe into the animal deaths. In addition to finding the perpetrators, they intended to stop the slayings before they escalated to human sacrifices. They also wanted to prevent Satanists from capturing local children.

"I think they are watching the kids who are loners," said Lala. "I feel they are possibly singling out some people to try to recruit. I believe some of these groups actually watch a child grow up – and influence growth – to the point where the child is easy prey. They get kids so deeply involved they have no choice but to continue." Once they were in the cult, warned the officer, the only way out was disbandment of the group or death.[7]

"I think what we've got to do is help these younger kids not to get involved in it. We have to get across to them that satanic worship is not what they are led to believe it is," said Deputy Lala in April 1985. He said his research had found that cult members tortured lambs, dogs, and other animals before sacrificing them in rituals. They would also eat the flesh of these animals and drink their blood.[8]

Deputy Lala told reporters he had uncovered five groups of devil-worshipers in Union County alone. He had spoken with some group members and had even photographed occult books in area homes. Some of the titles he'd found included *The Encyclopedia of Ancient and Forbidden Knowledge*, *The Anatomy of Witchcraft*, and *Magicks and Ceremonies*.

"In some of these homes, you're talking about thousands of dollars' worth of books. To me, that's more than curiosity," said Lala.[9] *The*

Columbus Dispatch printed photos showing Overly and Lala standing next to the Civil War grave, as well as various amulets, jewelry, and figurines that were said to be cult related.[10]

Weeks before Sheriff Telb launched his own investigation in Lucas County, Deputy Lala told reporters that he had uncovered a vast network of cult members throughout Ohio. Lala said the devil worshipers gathered in small groups called covens. Each group was composed of up to thirteen members. They met in abandoned houses, fields, barns, and wooded areas to carry out their dark deeds.

Lala said cult members came from all walks of life and ranged in age from fifteen to fifty-five.[11] In later interviews, Lala said cult members were as young as thirteen.[12] The deputy also told reporters that many of the cult members were homosexual.[13]

Apparently, the cult flocked to Union County because the rural setting provided many remote areas where they could practice their rituals without being seen. One Satanist allegedly boasted of a massive group with more than one thousand devil worshippers.

"At first, we believed this number was too high, but as we progress into the investigation and come up with new information, we are realizing there are a lot more people involved than we thought," said Lala.[14]

According to Deputy Lala, cult members would deliberately leave signs of their presence to advertise their presence. He had found trees with paint on them, which he believed to be cult markings. An area realtor had found "666" written on the wall of an abandoned house, along with an inverted star carved into the mantel.[15]

Between December of 1984 and June of 1985, Deputy Lala estimated that he had spent over one thousand hours on the investigation, including his interviews with local Satanists. In that time, investigators claimed to identify two hundred animal mutilations which they believed were connected to cult activity.[16]

Lala said rituals coincided with fifty different sacred dates and holidays, usually tied to cycles of the moon. During these rituals, the high priest or priestess would slice open animals and remove their internal organs. Participants would then drink the blood or consume the flesh. Lala also said the ultimate goal of some non-traditional satanic rituals was to have a woman impregnated by the high priest. The resulting child would be considered the offspring of Satan and would later be slaughtered.

"Sex and drugs play a heavy part in this," said Lala. "We were told 1,500 people had come into Union County over a period of time. We think we've uncovered only the tip of the iceberg."[17]

When it came to prosecution, Lala said his hands were tied. There was little to no prosecutable evidence in most cases. He also claimed Satanists were shielding themselves behind an Ohio law which exempted religious animal slaughter from prosecution as long as the perpetrator owned the animals they killed.

Despite the lack of results, some residents praised officers for taking the investigation seriously.

"Only a few agencies handle the matter as professionally and diligently as they have in Union County," Tiffin Police Captain Dale Griffis told the press.[18] "When the case is finished, it can be used as a primer for other agencies to review."[19]

The president of the county Humane Society offered a $500 reward for any information leading to the arrest of the perpetrators. He told reporters, "When you find a dog with its head and legs cut off, there has to be something more to it. But I'm not familiar with cults and most of us in a small town like this don't know what to look for."[20]

Sheriff Overly conceded that there was no physical evidence for the alleged crimes and, if they were able to find any perpetrators, misdemeanor charges of trespassing and cruelty to animals may be all that could possibly come from the case.

This did not stop adults in the community from issuing somber warnings to area youth. Deputy Lala visited schools throughout Union County, lecturing about the dangers of satanic cults. Tom Wedge, a youth counselor from Bellefontaine, sometimes accompanied Lala. Wedge had spent over seven years studying the occult and he offered lectures on the topic in the surrounding region.

"It's real. And it's not a thing that's just developing. They're coming out of the woodwork now," said Wedge. "These people, once they get exposed, get out. And the one thing I'd like to see is for them to get out of Ohio."[21]

The Union County case prompted at least a few responses from area Satanists. In response to their coverage of the investigation, *The Columbus Dispatch* received two anonymous letters, complaining that the case was giving Satanists a bad name. "Satanism, like Christianity, comes in many flavors," wrote the unnamed correspondents. "It has its extremists

17

who hide behind a label in order to achieve ends which are strictly their own."[22]

In the Kenmore area of Akron, one hundred thirty miles east of Toledo, residents had discovered several dead animals over several years. Concerned citizens, religious leaders, and civic figures came to believe these animals had been tortured and killed by human hands.

Residents claimed they remembered numerous cases of animal mutilation in recent years, but police had no record of reports prior to March 1985, when a dead cat had been found by the crossing guard at Highland Park Elementary School.[23] Since then, there had been three other cases, most of which had been reported by children to the same crossing guard. By June of 1985, some parents claimed they could recall approximately one dozen incidents of animal mutilation over the past four years.[24]

As rumors stoked fears, and fears turned to public uproar, several members of the community took it upon themselves to plan an informational meeting.[25] Reverend Dale Smith of Sherwood Baptist Church in Kenmore arranged a gathering in the gymnasium in Highland Park Elementary School. Although Smith acknowledged there had been no cult activity in the area, apart from the alleged animal mutilations, he felt the meeting was necessary due to parents' concerns that the cult might begin targeting children.[26]

On June 10, 1985, just ten days before Sheriff Telb would hold a press conference about satanic activity in his county, several hundred Kenmore residents filled the Highland Park school gymnasium. A photograph which appeared in local newspaper coverage of the event shows attendees packed side by side, both seated and standing, filling the entire gymnasium from wall to wall.[27]

To coordinate the meeting, Reverend Dale Smith worked with Cult Watch, an Akron-based group of former cult members and concerned citizens. The group's mission was to educate the public about cults of any kind, protect against manipulation and mind control, and warn of the possible dangers posed to youth by Satanist organizations. David Eid, the founder of Cult Watch, and Eric Fetterolf, a member of the group, were among the speakers at the meeting.

Eid said his organization offered training seminars to bring visibility to the issue. According to him, unsavory cults could sometimes flourish because few people took the threat seriously. "Everyone laughs about it," he told reporters.[28]

Speaking to the audience, Eid explained, "A cult is any group that psychologically manipulates its members and allows no room for personal expression. Cults can be any kind of group, not only satanic, that has a charismatic leader, a totalitarian society, and easy answers to complex questions. They destroy family relationships, teach fear and hatred of society, demand a full-time commitment and use deception and peer pressure to attract members."[29]

Cult warning is sounded in Kenmore

Animal mutilations spur information session

By Yalinda Rhodes
Beacon Journal staff writer

Satan worshipers may be in the Kenmore area and parents are concerned that their children are in danger of becoming victims of sacrifice or cult members.

Cult Watch, an Akron group of former cult members, conducted an informational meeting Monday at Highland Park Elementary School on West Waterloo Road.

The meeting was called as a result of recent animal mutilations in the area believed to be acts of sacrifice by a satanic cult.

Residents crowded into the school gymnasium to listen to David Eid and Eric Fetterolf, Cult Watch members, discuss how to recognize the development of a cult.

"A cult is any group that psychologically manipulates its members and allows no room for personal expression," Eid said.

"Cults can be any kind of group, not only satanic, that has a charismatic leader, a totalitarian society and easy answers to complex questions," he said. "They destroy family relationships, teach fear and hatred of society, demand a full-time commitment and use decep-

Several hundred Kenmore residents turned out Monday to hear about possible Satan worship in their area

Hundreds gather in Kenmore for cult informational meeting. © Ted Walls, Akron Beacon Journal – USA TODAY NETWORK

Eid said Cult Watch had interviewed several former cult members who admitted to carrying out ritual sacrifices alongside groups of two hundred followers. "It is a kind of mentality that is sweeping the country," Eid said, adding that heavy-metal music and popular entertainment promoted demons and sorcery among young people.[30]

As area residents listened carefully in the overstuffed gymnasium, Eid and Fetterolf explained how satanic groups sacrificed animals during their dark rituals. Sometimes, the men warned, these cults use small children. They went on to screen a portion of a recent *20/20* television program, which had aired one month earlier. The segment was called "The Devil Worshippers," and it detailed the alleged spread of satanic cult activity across the country.

Reverend Smith told attendees that he firmly believed a cult was active in the area, although he did acknowledge some of the incidents may have been the work of pranksters.[31] Smith also speculated that teenagers may be involved in the suspicious animal deaths. Many residents also raised concerns about Lisa Ann Park on Ivor Street. Whether their behaviors were connected to Satan or not, some parents claimed the park served as a teen hangout where delinquents gathered to drink and do drugs.[32]

As the informational meeting came to an end, some believed it had raised more questions than answers. The content of the presentation had certainly done little to assuage the fears of concerned parents. Some attendees left the meeting unconvinced, while others remained uncertain. The meeting organizer, however, knew it was time to take decisive action.

On June 17, 1985, Reverend Dale Smith held a second community meeting, this time at Sherwood Baptist Church in Kenmore. Approximately forty people attended to hear from cult experts, school staff, and city officials.

William Laughard, director of the Humane Society of Greater Akron, told the audience that his investigators had identified six cases of likely animal mutilation in the past six months. Akron City Councilman Dan Brode said he knew of four animal mutilations in the Kenmore area, which "couldn't have been done by other than human hands." Both Brode and Laughard went on to say that no pets had been targeted.[33]

Lieutenant James Buie of the Akron Police Department and Akron Deputy Mayor Anthony O'Leary assured citizens that the police were taking the mutilations seriously as well as the rumors about cult activity. Lt. Buie asked for patience while officers worked to bring the perpetrators to justice.[34]

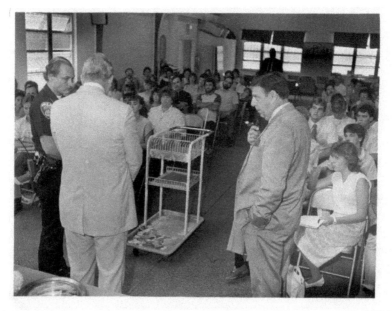

Rev. Dale Smith leads community meeting at Sherwood Baptist Church. © Lew Stamp – USA TODAY NETWORK

The principal of Kenmore High School, Harry Jordan, reiterated that even if someone knew who the perpetrators were, officials had no way of forcing them to share information. "A couple of kids who live near Lisa Ann know more than they're willing to tell me, but I'm not an investigator," he said, referencing Lisa Ann Park, a suspected problem location.[35]

Some residents worried that the rumors were stirring up fear. George Henry, who lived near the park in question, said, "We're blaming kids too much – they have nowhere else to go." Henry was in favor of forming community "watch groups" to keep police informed, but he had concerns about troubling reports of men from the community patrolling the area with baseball bats, trying to catch perpetrators in the act.

About these self-appointed vigilantes, Henry continued, "Maybe they'll jump on someone and hurt them when there's no excuse for it. It's no answer to carry a ball bat around and ask people what they're doing in the park. They have no right. We're not going to condone people getting hurt."[36]

Elsewhere in Summit County, the sheriff's department reported that an Ohio Edison employee had discovered a dead pig attached to a

21

wooden cross behind a Coventry Township church. The police quickly determined that this was not the work of cultists, but a prank inspired by the recent news coverage.[37]

This quotation appeared, in large, bold font, at the top of the page in *The Akron Beacon Journal* on June 23, 1985: "When the daylight begins to fade, the neighborhood children go inside, and fears emerge."[38]

Police did all they could to calm these fears. "As far as we can determine, a cult is not mutilating animals in Kenmore," said Lieutenant James Hubbell, who had been assigned to the investigation. The police believed the acts in question had been perpetrated by teens, who might enjoy the havoc they had created by watching adults "run wild on the evening news shows."[39]

For city councilman Dan Brode, proof that an actual cult existed was beside the point. He knew the rumors themselves were enough to cause an uproar. "It's a perceptual problem. If you perceive a cult that will hurt your children, you will change your ways because of that. You act according to what you perceive is true... It doesn't matter whether what you see is really true or not," he said.[40]

Reverend Smith of Sherwood Baptist Church, who had now held multiple meetings for the public, had no doubts about the existence of a cult. He claimed a former cult member had spoken with him, who had been permitted to leave the group after participating in a ceremony where he was made to drink blood and eat raw flesh. The reverend declined to give the name of this individual to police.

"I have a responsibility to the community, the larger community outside my congregation," said Smith. He went on to praise the police for taking the investigation seriously, but faulted investigators for prematurely implicating typical teenagers in the alleged crimes.[41]

Reverend Smith wasn't the only one who resented this implication. Fourteen-year-old Kim Thoma told reporters, "The kids are blamed who hang around Lisa Ann Park, but I know they wouldn't do anything like that." She went on to say that she knew kids who "say they worship the devil, but it's sort of a front. They get cult information from hard rock, heavy metal, and know signs and stuff, but they don't do it. If it's someone doing it, it would be someone older."[42]

Area teens felt targeted for good reason, especially since the meetings at Smith's church had included some tough talk by men who claimed Lisa Ann Park was being "taken over" by older children. In the weeks that followed, some grown-ups confronted teens in the park, accusing them of assorted sins, including drug use, drinking, sex, vandalism, and ritual animal mutilation.[43]

Police told parents that interpersonal conflict between older and younger children was common. Every park had bullies, they maintained, and Lisa Ann Park was no different. Frustrated by this response from the police, some area residents took matters into their own hands.

Kenmore resident Jim Palmer formed a group called the Kenmore Protective Organization. Palmer insisted that none of his eighteen members intended to hurt anyone, but their insistence on patrolling the area with baseball bats had raised concern on numerous occasions. After police and city officials spoke to them several times, the group disbanded because of adverse publicity.

Palmer claimed their motives had been pure. "We'd just tell them that if they want to smoke dope or drink beer to get out. Before we started going around, there was punks everywhere. Now there is none. But if they want the punks back, that's the way it will be. We are disbanding."[44]

As a result of the widespread concern, police increased their presence in the park. Lt. James Hubbell even went out to talk with neighborhood teenagers himself. He concluded, "They may be punks, they may be jerks, but we've become convinced they didn't mutilate any animals."[45]

As the uproar gradually died down, the Kenmore community came to terms with the situation. Councilman Brode conceded that, even if there were Satanists in Akron, there was little he could do about it. "It is difficult for me to say this, but I guess they do have a right to exist. There are organized satanic churches that have every right to exist, as deplorable as I might think that is."[46]

It wasn't all bad. After the neighborhood meetings, a group of neighbors banded together and vowed to clean up the park and scrub graffiti off the jungle gym.

The events in Union and Summit Counties were not the first involving animal mutilations, nor were they the first to provoke a public uproar. A few days before Halloween in 1983, the Fairfield County

Sheriff's Department found a dead dog, pierced with an iron rod, lying within a five-pointed star inside an abandoned farmhouse near Lancaster, Ohio. Photos of the pentagram and the surrounding symbols later appeared in the newspaper. Belmont County Sheriff Richard Stobbs called occult expert Dale Griffis for consultation when investigators found candles, a pentagram, and a slab in the vicinity of an area where chickens were slaughtered.[47]

Two incidents in Shelby County, which featured dead animals, were also frequently cited as evidence of occult activity. In one case, someone dumped six dead lambs in a dumpster behind a local supermarket. Four days later, six more dead lambs turned up in a dumpster behind a Sidney motel.[48]

In August 1976, the city of Logan, Ohio faced a problem of their own. After the discovery of several dead animals, rumors began to spread about a "bizarre religious sect that operates in the area by night." Stories began to circulate about black-robed figures gathering in the woods. A campsite, later pictured in the newspaper, was thought to be cult-related because it featured a ring of stones with a cow's skull in the center.[49] Gun sales skyrocketed, with some vendors reporting that their sales increased four to five hundred percent.[50]

One area resident, whose son's rabbits had been mysteriously killed, said, "These rumors are creating a panic. Most of my friends are calling frequently now with rumors and telling me they will not go outside at night anymore."

To the consternation of local police, a group of men began patrolling the area after dark, hoping to catch the devil-worshipers in the act. One man even said he would gladly pay bail for any of his colleagues who happened to shoot a cult member.

One weekend, the group of vigilantes chased down a van, which they believed to be full of men and dogs. The night before, they spotted what appeared to be a burning cross through the trees. The armed men got out of their vehicles, crept through the woods, and surrounded the group of devil-worshippers.

They soon realized they had surrounded members of a local Lutheran church, who were hosting a social gathering around a bonfire.

5. Raiders of the Cult House
Thursday, June 20, 1985
9:45am

Two hours after officers first arrived at the Litton residence, the search inside the house was winding down. Patricia Litton and her children had been thoroughly questioned by the police, but the search had turned up no evidence connecting the family to the accused, Leroy Freeman.

"I can't be mad because they were just doing their job," Mrs. Litton later told reporters. "But I was a little surprised when they came in." She said the police later apologized for the inconvenience.[1]

Alvin Litton, Patricia's husband who worked as a truck driver, returned home to find his family in the national spotlight. He was angry to learn his family had been held on house arrest, finding the accusations of cult activity to be absurd.[2]

"It was a big mistake, is what it was. They raided the wrong place. I've never even heard of Freeman. I wonder if my lawyer could have fun with this," Mr. Litton said to reporters.[3] He was particularly upset that the deputies had not explained their actions. "They don't explain nothing, they just take."[4]

Photo of the Litton residence on the morning of the raid. Photo courtesy of Lucas County Sheriff's Dept.

None of the items listed in the search warrant were found on the premises. There were no deadly weapons, no drugs, and no sacrificial knives or cult apparel. Despite the lack of expected evidence, deputies confiscated several items from the house. According to the Littons, there were perfectly reasonable explanations for everything the officers examined.

In the back yard, investigators found a large hole in the ground, about five feet wide and eight feet long. Officers examined the hole closely and asked a series of questions, believing there were two underground tunnels, for the purpose of hiding Leroy Freeman.[5] Alvin Litton explained that he had dug the hole himself as a footer for a family room he planned to build onto the house.[6]

Police also found a bone inside the house, which they took into evidence. Patricia Litton said her inquisitive son had brought the bone inside after he found it while digging in the backyard. Mrs. Litton also vouched for their pet goats, which officers had eyed suspiciously. She assured deputies that the animals were innocent and had no connection to satanic practices.[7]

This photo was taken by investigators on the day of the raid,
showing one of two goats in the backyard. Photo courtesy of Lucas County Sheriff's Dept.

Officers also questioned the Littons about reports that Leroy Freeman had been seen coming and going from the house. Mrs. Litton reiterated that she did not know who Mr. Freeman was or what he looked like. Investigators said they had reason to believe the suspected cult leader may have altered his appearance to hide from authorities.[8] Based on their description, Mrs. Litton realized that witnesses must have seen her father, Erwin, and mistaken him for the fugitive.[9]

Although they had failed to recover any of the items listed in the search warrant, Alvin Litton said officers seized military dog tags which belonged to him and his father. They took a round piece of wood and two blank cassette tapes. Inexplicably, they also seized the family Bible.[10] Chief Deputy Tom Wilson characterized these items as "some cult-type materials that were lying out in view."[11]

Police seized a piece of wood and a Bible during the raid. Photos courtesy of Lucas County Sheriff's Dept.

Investigators were looking for red flags. Omens. Clues pointing to occult practices. That's why, before they left the house, deputies also seized the most chilling items of all: two albums by rock musician Ozzy Osbourne and a poster depicting scenes from the film *Indiana Jones and the Temple of Doom.*[12]

As the 1980s gave rise to various campaigns to protect children from abuse, abduction, and exploitation, there was also renewed interest in protection against the damaging influence of movies, television, music, fantasy games, and other forms of popular entertainment. Heavy metal music was an obvious target because it was immensely popular with young people, but also because several well-known artists and bands included devilish and macabre imagery in their work.

With songs like "Dead Babies," "Halo of Flies," and, "I Love the Dead," popular rocker Alice Cooper embraced some of the symbols which frightened "traditional" America the most. Sometimes he performed on stage wearing women's clothing, or with a boa constrictor around his neck. He skewered baby dolls with swords in front of the audience, performed

27

amidst giant spiders and live snakes, and even appeared to hang or decapitate himself on stage.[13]

After leaving Black Sabbath in 1979, Ozzy Osbourne launched his solo career, branding himself as rock and roll's "Prince of Darkness." His 1980 album *Blizzard of Ozz* included such songs as "Crazy Train," and the controversial "Suicide Solution." Osbourne also became famous for his antics, on and off stage, including biting the head off a live dove and a bat, and urinating on the Alamo in 1982.[14] The track "Mr. Crowley," drew significant concern from parents. Named for the famous occultist Aleister Crowley, the 1980 song was said to glorify dark themes, magic, and devil worship.[15]

In a rapidly growing market, most bands did not need good publicity and they often found that bad publicity worked in their favor. A rumor began going around that the letters in the name of the rock band KISS stood for "Knights in Satan's Service." Guitarist Ace Frehley called the rumor "complete and utter bullshit," but such an idea added to the band's allure. According to some detractors, AC/DC allegedly stood for "Anti-Christ/Down with Christ."[16]

When MTV launched in August of 1981, rock music gained increased visibility and a much wider audience. As this style of music became more popular, FM radio stations began devoting more airtime to rock and heavy metal, broadening the audience even further.[17] Rock music had long been the target of conservative Christians, but the 1980s marked a notable change in thinking. For the first time, concerned adults were treating rock music as an "occult threat," linked to a large-scale criminal conspiracy of Satanists.[18]

As if the overt references were not troubling enough, many became concerned about subliminal messaging hidden in popular music. This idea was fueled by several best-selling books on the topic, written by Wilson Bryan Key between 1974 and 1989. Key endorsed the idea that the Beatles' "Hey Jude," was secretly about drug use, and that Simon and Garfunkel's "Bridge Over Troubled Water," was really "a drug user's guide to withdrawal into a syringe-injected hallucinatory drug experience – most probably heroin." These were not just songs, according to Key; these were concerted efforts at cultural conditioning.[19]

Police photographed these heavy metal albums, by Quiet Riot and Twisted Sister, during the raid of the Litton home. Photos courtesy of Lucas County Sheriff's Dept.

This belief gave rise to another popular rumor: when played backward, most popular rock albums would reveal hidden satanic messages. Backmasking, or the process of recording sounds backward onto a track that is meant to be played forward, was not a new practice. Although the practice gained popularity with the Beatles' use of backward instrumentation in 1966's *Revolver*, there are early examples of backmasking dating back to 1959. While artists may intentionally backmask messages for artistic or comic effect, messages found through phonetical reversal can often be completely unintentional. One such unintentional message resulted in the infamous "Paul is dead" urban legend of the early 1970s.

At first, fans were the ones searching for hidden messages, but soon various religious and anti-rock groups were leading the charge. In 1981, Christian DJ Michael Mills claimed that Led Zeppelin's "Stairway to Heaven" contained hidden satanic messages designed to enter the unconscious mind of the listener. When the song was played in reverse, one could allegedly decipher the message, "There is no escaping/ Whose path will make me sad, whose power is Satan/ He will give you 666/ Here's to my sweet Satan."[20]

In 1982, Paul Crouch of the Trinity Broadcasting Network hosted a show which argued that rock stars were cooperating with the Church of Satan to hide subliminal messages on records.[21] This led to various record-burning or record-smashing events around the country. In 1982, Minnesota

29

DJ Chris Edmonds helped popularize the concerns by playing "backmasked" clips on his radio station and deciphering the phrases he believed he heard.[22]

Most often, the listener's own suggestible, pattern-seeking mind was the culprit, but not every message was imagined. Some artists truly had embedded easter eggs in their albums. After facing allegations of backmasking, the Electric Light Orchestra intentionally parodied the panic. The ELO album *Fire on High* contains the message, "The music is reversible, but time is not. Turn back, turn back, turn back."[23] In his 1984 album, Weird Al Yankovic used the technique of backmasking to boldly declare, "Satan eats Cheez Whiz."[24]

In 1985, a group of Washington political spouses formed the Parents' Music Resource Center (PMRC) to advocate the use of warning labels on albums said to contain pornographic, violent, or satanic material. Tipper Gore, one of the central figures of the movement, drew connections between music and satanism in her 1987 book *Raising PG Kids in an X-Rated Society*.[25] She wrote, "This childhood fascination with the occult has led to one of the most sickening marketing gimmicks in history. Just as some in the music industry emphasize sex or violence in their songs, others, specifically heavy metal groups, sell Satan to kids… Many kids experiment with the deadly satanic game, and some get hooked."[26]

Music was not the only concern. Throughout the late 1960s and early 1970s, there was a resurgence of interest in the occult in popular books, films, and television shows. Some of this interest came on the heels of major motion pictures, such as 1968's *Rosemary's Baby*, 1973's *The Exorcist*, or 1976's *The Omen*. A 1972 issue of *Time* magazine even christened the moment "The Occult Revival."[27] Author George Case observed, "In hindsight, it was obvious that much of the satanic panic was an unintentional consequence of the occult boom of the sixties and seventies. The satanic panic was not a sudden eruption of irrationality but a natural and probably inevitable result of a media saturation that was by then so deep that few were still noticing it."[28]

Fantasy role-playing games became suspect, most notably Dungeons & Dragons, for their alleged promotion of satanic themes. When her son died by suicide in June of 1982, Patricia Pulling launched a moral crusade against D&D, believing her son's involvement in fantasy gaming had directly contributed to his death.[29] Pulling formed a public advocacy organization called Bothered About Dungeons & Dragons (BADD).

Beginning in 1983, BADD circulated warnings about the dangers of fantasy games, claiming they promoted demonology, witchcraft, murder, rape, suicide, insanity, homosexuality, satanic rituals, perversion, and various other potential dangers. Speaking at a conference for law enforcement officers, Pulling said, "Those D&D players who irretrievably cross the imaginary line between reality and fantasy sometimes act out torture and killing with deadly results… Family values are attacked… [the symbols in the game] are used in real sorcery and conjuration of demons."[30]

Conservative Christian leaders launched similar crusades against various books, films, and television series. In his 1986 book *Turmoil in the Toy Box*, Phil Phillips warned parents of the dangers lurking in their children's favorite programming. The list of dangerous occult media included *He-Man and the Masters of the Universe, Care Bears, Star Wars, E.T., Cabbage Patch Kids, Barbie, G.I. Joe, ThunderCats, Gremlins, The NeverEnding Story, Star Trek III*, and many others.[31]

Phillips wrote, "Unknowingly, youngsters will ally themselves with demons and become willing disciples and slaves of Satan. In fact, Americans are glorifying Satan and promoting his war against the church by going to see movies that feature occult philosophies and phenomena and by buying children toys and t-shirts, portraying devilish human mutations and creatures that are featured in the movies."[32]

Phillips also warned against *Indiana Jones and the Temple of Doom*, which was at the time, the most recent entry in the film franchise depicted on the poster seized by deputies from the Litton residence in Spencer Township.

Training seminars for police officers and social workers amplified these concerns. Detective Gary Sworin from the Luzerne County, Pennsylvania described the slippery slope of satanic cult involvement when he said, "Participation could mean starting out with just listening to some heavy metal rock music, starting to read satanic bibles, starting to be involved in a ritual, satanic ritual, and then gradually lead to bigger and so-called, in their perspective, better things. … And then, all of the sudden, it starts to progress, and all the contributing factors we listed come together and finally something happens.

LUCAS COUNTY SHERIFF DEPARTMENT

INVENTORY AND RECEIPT FOR PROPERTY SEIZED BY SEARCH WARRANT

DATE 6-20-85

TIME 20 15 hrs.

FROM: 915 S Crissey

PERSON OR PLACE

INVENTORY OF PROPERTY SEIZED WAS MADE IN THE PRESENCE OF:

Det Pam Crum

Det. Bobbie Leist

Warrant Applicant: Name: Alvin + Patricia Litton

Address: 915 S. Crissey

Other Credible Person:

Name:

Address:

Possessor of Seized Property:

Name: Alvin + Patricia Litton

Address: 915 S. Crissey.

INVENTORY

1. 1 Beck - Computer Tape.
2. 1 Holy Bible white in color
3. 1 Tape unknown type
4. 2 Dog Tags US (Service)
5. Bone - unknown type.
6. 1 Poster - (Mola Kam)
7. 1 Tape for cassette
8. 1 Round Piece of woods w/ markings
9. 1 Brown Note Book.
10. Picture Frame with Ezzy Bank At the moon
11. Drawing - Book

The above seized property inventoried by the undersigned officer

At 915 H. to cry to Lcc
Grey os Bruca

Det. Pam Crum

A copy of the Search Warrant and a receipt has been given to the person from whom it was taken.

Copy to Clerk of Courts

Copy to be placed with seized property.

Inventory of items seized from Litton residence. Courtesy of Lucas County Sheriff's Dept.

6. Breaking Ground
Thursday, June 20, 1985
10:00am

One mile from the Litton residence, in eastern Spencer Township, a backhoe had arrived on the scene. The sheriff's department had arranged to borrow the heavy earth-moving equipment from Lucas County along with an operator.[1]

Investigators began digging along Meilke Road at the south end of Bemis Lane, about three miles northeast of the Toledo Express Airport. The search location was situated just west of an auto parts salvage yard, known by locals at the time as Spud's junkyard. Deputies had originally planned to dig south of Butler Ditch, which runs across the area, but around 9:00 am, they moved their equipment north of the ditch and started digging there instead. At the time, investigators gave no reason for this change in plans.[2]

Deputy Trilby Cashin watches as Joe Inman, from the coroner's office, digs for remains. © *The Toledo Blade*.

The area mostly consisted of an overgrown open field surrounded by woods. There was some garbage and miscellaneous junk scattered about, along with a dilapidated, abandoned house. The sheriff said the property was owned by an out-of-state resident.[3]

One of the abandoned structures near the dig site. Photo courtesy of Lucas County Sheriff's Dept.

By 10:00am, there were about ten deputies on the scene, accompanied by a small mob of neighbors and reporters. As the day wore on the crowd would continue to grow. The news had spread quickly after the press conference and everyone in the immediate vicinity knew what investigators expected to unearth: fifty, or sixty, or maybe even seventy-five dead children.[4]

Soon, Sheriff Telb arrived on the scene. In addition to supervising the dig, the sheriff and his staff would spend most of the day answering a relentless barrage of questions hurled at them by the gathering throng of reporters.

Standing at the excavation site, Telb indicated that the dig was the culmination of months of investigative work, which had been corroborated by three separate informants. These informants had confirmed the presence of the cult in Lucas County and verified the location of their victims. In addition to these unnamed sources, Telb reiterated that the department had carried out its own reconnaissance.

"We don't have any witnesses to a human sacrifice," said Telb, but he acknowledged that he had consulted with the FBI.[5]

Trilby Cashin, one of three deputies assigned to the case, spoke to reporters on the scene. She estimated that more than two thousand staff hours had been put into the case. On April 30, deputies hid in a wooded area and observed a two-hour ceremony with approximately one hundred participants, officers alleged. The officers were able to hear chanting coming from inside the house, which they managed to capture on tape recorder. They observed no sacrifices, human or otherwise.[6]

Lt. Kirk Surprise, who had also spoken at the sheriff's press conference, was one of the officers who carried out the surveillance. He told reporters he had personally observed what he believed to be a satanic ritual in progress. From his vantage point in the woods, Surprise could see numerous people entering the house. He could also hear male voices chanting. Unfortunately, the deputies were unable to get close enough to the house to see what was happening inside. Surprise declined to elaborate further but acknowledged that the incident on April 30 had not occurred at the excavation site currently under investigation.[7]

As the world waited with bated breath, the digging commenced.

During the 1970s, religious fundamentalism became a powerful political and economic force in the United States. Founded by Reverend Jerry Falwell in 1979, the Moral Majority movement positioned religious leaders to exert their influence in new ways. Capitalizing on their strength in numbers, faith communities registered thousands of new voters and became active in political campaigns.

Fundamentalists of the Protestant, Catholic, and Mormon traditions realized they had common ground when it came to key social issues. By banding together, they could exercise their considerable influence to form a united front against heavy metal music, the content of schoolbooks, and satanism.[8] By the mid-1980s, the fundamentalist Christian ideology emerged to frame modern anxieties. Societal ills were framed as signs of the "last days," driven by the hidden cosmic realities of satanic conspiracy and demonic attack.[9]

Changes in social structure also rankled conservative leaders. As more women joined the workforce, the conception of the "traditional" family continued to morph, with an increase in single-parent households, cohabitation, second or third marriages, and same-sex households.[10] Pat Robertson attacked feminism as "a socialist, anti-family political movement that encourages women to leave their husbands, kill their children, practice witchcraft, destroy capitalism, and become lesbians."[11]

Lawmakers fueled these anxieties by introducing legislation designed to protect the traditional family.[12] In 1980, the influential book *Michelle Remembers* pointed the finger squarely at women. As Alexandra Heller-Nicholas notes, "These women, the book implies, are aligned with Satan by rejecting traditional roles as mothers. [The author] at times interchanges references to 'all those mommies' with witches... consolidating the book's dedication to its central depiction of the monstrous feminine."[13]

As religious groups became increasingly organized, it became much easier to disseminate information through their vast network of organizations, publications, and television and radio broadcasting. As the fundamentalist Christian apparatus grew, it also became easier to weaponize messaging against political opponents, competing groups, or conflicting ideologies.

The resurgence of religious fundamentalism in America also had a measurable effect on satanic cult beliefs. National survey data at the time showed an increase in belief in a literal Satan, corresponding with the rise of religious fundamentalism. Many believed it was their Christian duty to push back against anything which might further Satan's hold on society, and to warn others of impending danger.[14]

The social changes of the 1960s gave rise to many new religions and spiritual movements which emerged with the youth counterculture. Fundamentalist organizations launched counter-propaganda efforts aimed at opposing these new religious groups. Some of the earliest targets of the anti-cult movement included the Unification Church (the Moonies), the Krishna Consciousness movement (the Hare Krishnas), and the Children of God. Coverage of the word "cult" became more critical in the wake of the Manson murders and reached irredeemable status after the events in Jonestown in 1978.[15] Fears of Satanism quickly became an extension of the anti-cult movement.[16]

The Cult Awareness Network became the largest anti-cult organization with about fifty different affiliates around the nation at the height of their activity. The group was mostly composed of local volunteers including youth workers, parents, social workers, and clergy. Driven by the belief that "lost" children were being "taken" by new religions, anti-cult advocates began to lobby politicians, spread information, and present their concerns to the press.[17] The American Family Foundation carried out similar work, with a focus on academia and mental health professionals.

The satanism scare was to the 1980s and 1990s what the religious cult scare was to the 1970s.

Christian lecturers and performers toured the country, warning against the dangers of satanism. One such example is Mike Warnke, an evangelist and Christian comedian who claimed to have committed numerous crimes in his former life as a satanic high priest. In 1973 he wrote an autobiography called *The Satan Seller*, which sold millions of copies across the country. Warnke also became a frequent guest on television talk shows where he was cited as an authority on satanism.[18] Bob Larson Ministries' Dr. James Dobson's Focus on the Family, and other outlets shared Warnke's story extensively.[19]

Warnke quickly became one of the most loved talents on the religious circuit. A typical Warnke program included preaching, comedy, music, and graphic stories about satanic violence against children. At the end of the proceedings, there was often an appeal for fundraising, inviting attendees to contribute to the fight against ritual abuse at the hands of devil worshipers.[20]

Warnke was actively touring in the months leading up to the Spencer Township dig. In 1984, Warnke filled the Anderson Arena at Bowling Green University in Bowling Green, Ohio, approximately twenty-five miles south of Toledo.[21] Two months before the dig, Warnke was performing in Pennsylvania.[22] And two months after the dig, Warnke appeared at Wellsville High School, about an hour from Akron.[23] When a Warnke associate gave a two-day seminar in Steubenville, Ohio in 1988, many parents kept their children home from school to protect them from satanic cults, prompting the local sheriff to hold a press conference to address devil worship among teenagers.

7. Media Circus
Thursday, June 20, 1985
11:00am

Using the county-owned backhoe, investigators turned over the earth in Spencer Township. As they meticulously sifted through the soil in search of human remains, they photographed each layer.[1] Investigators were not the only ones taking photographs.

Robert Whalen had climbed aboard the backhoe that morning expecting nothing out of the ordinary. He certainly did not expect to become the focus of national media attention. A reserved and mild-mannered Lucas County employee, Whalen had been asked to operate the digging equipment on behalf of the sheriff's office. As soon as he mounted the backhoe, he found himself surrounded by ten television cameras and seven press photographers.[2]

As Mr. Whalen began to dig, reporters shouted questions at him, shoving microphones in his face. Hours after the dig, Whalen was still shaken by the ordeal. He said, "You get a little nervous. You keep thinking, 'Boy, if I hit one of these reporters, I'm in real trouble.'"[3]

Thanks to his skillful maneuvering, Mr. Whalen did not run over any reporters, but it certainly would have been easy to do so. The place was swarming with journalists. From locations as far as Chicago, Cincinnati, Detroit, and Fort Wayne, Indiana, reporters had descended on Spencer Township with remarkable speed.[4] Representatives of more than a dozen Ohio and Michigan newspapers were on the scene, along with correspondents from national publications including *Time* magazine, *Newsweek*, *The Associated Press*, *Reuters*, and *United Press International*.

Reporters from various radio and television stations were also present. These crews represented local stations from all over the region, many of whom were passing along tapes and film to larger networks. Television reporters came from Detroit, Cleveland, Cincinnati, and Columbus. Various national networks were also on the scene, including reporters from ABC and the Cable News Network (CNN).[5]

Late in the day, a pair of photographers from *The National Enquirer* arrived. Although such topics rarely overlapped with the interests of mainstream journalists, rumors of evil conspiracies and human sacrifice were well within the wheelhouse of a supermarket tabloid. One of the men from the *Enquirer* cheerfully greeted his colleagues from the fourth estate by shouting, "Hey, this is a mainline story for us!"[6]

For most of the day, the press had free rein of the area. With no clear plan in place to disseminate information to the media in an organized fashion, the search location quickly descended into chaos. Numerous outlets began broadcasting live from the dig site. Frenzied journalists trailed behind investigators, tripping over bundles of electrical cables and jostling against bystanders in pursuit of a scoop.[7] At times, the scene took on what some described as a "carnival atmosphere."[8]

News vans and other vehicles clogged the nearby roads, and even the airspace over the site became crowded. From as far as Columbus, nearly 150 miles away, television stations rerouted their traffic-spotting airplanes and sent them barreling toward Toledo. Some stations rented airplanes and helicopters to get to the scene as quickly as possible. Explaining why he had taken to the air, the news director of a Columbus-area radio station said, "When you hear they've got sixty bodies and a satanic cult, that's enough to convince me I'd better get in a plane and go."[9]

Oliver and Juanita Ennols, who lived a few hundred yards from the digging site, stepped outside to find a radio station broadcasting live from their front yard. As they surveyed the fleet of trucks and camera crews in front of their home, they were shocked. "All this was here when I woke up this morning," said Mrs. Ennols. "I couldn't believe it. I still don't."[10]

Another person stunned by the turnout was Sheriff Telb. Having vastly underestimated the potency of his initial press conference, the sheriff found himself surrounded at one point by more than forty news people. Telb can be seen in photographs from that morning, fielding questions before a gaggle of reporters while standing between a county-owned truck and a discarded washing machine.

"I don't have time to find out what's going on before they ask me questions," Sheriff Telb lamented during a break in the questioning. "I guess if I had known it was going to turn out like this, I might have done things differently."[11]

The initial lack of direction among the press led to some wild goose chases. When a Detroit television reporter noticed three sheriff's deputies jump across a small ravine and wander into the woods, she grabbed her cameraman and rushed after them. Seeing a competitor jump into action, six other news crews quickly followed. A few minutes later, they all came back through the marsh, slogging through mud and water in their ready-for-primetime clothing. "Nothing," said one of the cameramen. "The cops just went to eat lunch."[12]

Sheriff James Telb surrounded by television reporters. © *The Toledo Blade*.

Despite hours of downtime, most of the crews stayed all day. If the story broke, no one wanted to miss it. Reporters ran from site to site following investigators, occasionally checking in with Sheriff Telb for updates. They also traded information between themselves. As the day wore on, reporters became increasingly skeptical. Some began to characterize the incident as the type of story where "no one was injured when the car failed to crash."[13]

Even without a notable discovery, the nationwide news coverage had an immediate effect. Police departments began receiving dozens of phone calls from concerned parents. Some asked questions about the cult.

Others wondered if the sheriff had uncovered information about their missing children.

Ken Perry, chief deputy for administrative services at the Lucas County Sheriff's Department, said the calls were overwhelming. "We didn't have a contingency plan for that," he said. "We just never imagined the impact the media would have."[14]

In just a few hours, the inauspicious search of a vacant lot had spiraled into a media sensation. Investigators could feel the mounting pressure. Chief Deputy Tom Wilson commented on the atmosphere, saying "There's this sense somehow that we're letting them down. You feel you're somewhat under siege, like, 'Gosh, we've got to find a body for the six o'clock news.'

"But how can you be disappointed in not finding sixty bodies?"[15]

✪

In the eighteen months leading up to the Spencer Township investigation, media coverage related to satanism skyrocketed, both in local markets and at the national level. By the time Sheriff Telb initiated his dig, every television viewer, radio listener, or newspaper reader in the Toledo area would have been exposed to frequent tales of devilish mayhem on any given day of the week.

In 1984, a teenager named Gary Lauwers was killed by two young acquaintances in Northport, New York. The primary perpetrator, Ricky Kasso, stabbed Lauwers to death during an argument. Jimmy Troiano, another acquaintance, was also charged. In the extensive news reports that followed, police and commentators emphasized the young men's interest in heavy metal bands Black Sabbath, Led Zeppelin, and AC/DC. One witness later alleged that Kasso had commanded his stabbing victim, "Say you love Satan!"[16]

Although Kasso had been under the influence of drugs at the time, and although the stabbing occurred during a heated argument, most media coverage left little room for doubt regarding the alleged satanic nature of the crime. The lead detective on the case told *Newsday*, "This was a sacrificial killing. It was pure satanism." Kasso's own father later told the *Associated Press*, "We learned that he was very deeply involved in Satan, along with a number of boys." Statements like these drove further press coverage about the hidden threat of satanic cults.[17]

In 1984 and 1985, Richard Ramirez, also known as the Night Stalker serial killer, rapist, and kidnapper, had become active in California. He left pentagrams and satanic writing at some of the murder scenes, fueling media speculation about the killer's involvement in the occult. When he was later apprehended and tried in 1988, he famously displayed a pentagram on the palm of his hand during his first court appearance and shouted, "Hail Satan!" Although Ramirez was epileptic, a heavy drug user, and a sadist with a childhood history of intense trauma, most media coverage focused on his self-proclaimed satanism instead of his various pathologies.[18]

Also in the press was the McMartin Preschool trial, which included allegations of child molestation, abuse, and bizarre satanic rituals at the hands of a secretive cult. Although the first allegations occurred in 1983, the story did not receive widespread media coverage until February of 1984, when Wayne Satz of KABC Channel 7 in Los Angeles aired his first report on the case. Many similar stories followed.

In 1990, *The Los Angeles Times* reflected on the significance of these initial reports, saying, "it was Satz's early coverage that triggered a feeding frenzy in the media, both locally and nationally. Los Angeles television reporters in particular were immediately under pressure from their superiors to match, or surpass, the exclusive McMartin stories Satz was broadcasting night after night." Ross Becker of KCBS added, "There was hysteria in the newsroom."[19]

After the longest and most expensive trial in United States history, all charges were ultimately dropped in the McMartin case because prosecutors failed to provide evidence for the alleged crimes, and because testimony given by children had been gathered using coercive methods. Still, media coverage of the trial almost universally presented the allegations of satanic ritual abuse as if they were factually true.[20]

Throughout the 1980s, there was a sharp uptick in headlines containing words like "grotesque," "horrifying," "nightmarish," "chilling," "bizarre," and "mind-blowing."[21] Sensational atrocity stories were appealing to the media because they often drew a large audience, captured ongoing attention, and helped outlets stand out against competitors. Media coverage helped spread rumors of satanic crime from one area to another. In the wake of the first news broadcast about McMartin Preschool, eight other local preschools faced similar accusations; within days, over one hundred allegations had appeared throughout the country.[22]

The Los Angeles Times later completed a detailed analysis of press reports, including their own coverage. Their scathing conclusions could have easily applied to many other cases of the era. They wrote, "McMartin at times exposed basic flaws in the way contemporary news organizations function. Pack journalism. Laziness. Superficiality. Cozy relationships with prosecutors. A competitive zeal that sends reporters off in a frantic search to be the first with the latest shocking allegation, responsible journalism be damned. A tradition that often discourages reporters from raising key questions if they aren't first brought up by the principals in the story.

"In the early months of the case in particular, reporters and editors often abandoned two of their most cherished and widely trumpeted traditions – fairness and skepticism. As most reporters now sheepishly admit – and as the record clearly shows – the media frequently plunged into hysteria, sensationalism..."[23]

The news media is often a convenient scapegoat for satanic rumor-panics, but basic chronology suggests they should not get all the blame. These stories did not originate from news outlets. In most cases, the rumors were up and running long before reporters arrived on the scene. But by broadcasting unsubstantiated claims, the media helped amplify concern, taking fears from the paranoid fringe and transmitting them into the mainstream.[24]

In addition to nightly news programs, satanic cult crusaders soon found an abundance of new platforms. The growth of cable and satellite television increased the number of channels available. The demand for original content grew. Talk shows were reasonably popular and inexpensive to produce and they could easily fill time slots in one-hour increments. As a result, talk shows proliferated.

A talk show that aired every weekday, like *Donahue* or *The Sally Jessy Raphaël Show*, would require up to two-hundred fifty topics per year. By the late 1980s, there were enough syndicated talk shows with an appetite for fresh topics that almost any group or movement could gain time in the spotlight to share their views.[25] Between 1985 and 1989, many programs aired episodes devoted to satanic cults, including Larry King, Oprah Winfrey, and Sally Jesse Raphaël. Geraldo Rivera devoted at least three television specials to the topic of satanism.[26]

The emergence of religious cable broadcasting led to a growth in religious programming and televangelism. Due to the ease of production and relatively low cost, many religious broadcasters quickly adapted the talk show format. This provided additional forums for theological, social, and political topics, many of which welcomed anti-satanism messages of any kind.[27]

Within Christian publishing companies, exposés on satanism became a big industry. Dozens of books were released with titles containing the word "Satan," most of which spun alarmist theories about the dangers of ritual abuse or murder at the hand of secretive cults. Many religious books warned parents about alleged threats targeting their children. Often, the claims in such books resulted in the spread of fear, blame, and harm against real-world individuals, all accused of committing unspeakable acts in service to the Devil.[28]

On Thursday, May 16, 1985, a pivotal news broadcast aired during prime time on network television, sending shockwaves across the nation. Just one month before the Spencer Township dig would make its public debut, the national news program *20/20* aired a stunning segment produced by Ken Wooden and Peter Kunhardt which would greatly influence the public discourse about satanism for years to come. The fateful piece was entitled, "The Devil Worshippers."

Although it was only twenty-three minutes in length, the *20/20* segment is historically significant because it lent credibility to claims which had previously been nothing more than local or regional rumors. The journalists' uncritical acceptance of the claims gave an air of authenticity to the story. In the years that followed, the *20/20* segment was frequently cited as "documentation" or "proof" that secretive satanic cults existed.[29] For example, when town hall meetings were held in the Kenmore area of Akron, Ohio in response to alleged cases of satanic animal mutilation, local leaders played a video recording of "The Devil Worshippers."[30]

The broadcast illuminated many of the key talking points of anti-satanism activists of the time. The segment also served as the satanic exposé template which would be reiterated and repurposed by many others throughout the following decade.[31] Watching the program now, it is easy to see why so many reacted so strongly.

"The Devil Worshippers" begins in the studio, with a somber Hugh Downs looking into the camera from behind a desk. Behind him, the image of a dark-robed figure looms over the segment title, which appears in a spooky red and white font. Downs somberly intones, "Now, police have been skeptical when investigating these acts, just as we are in reporting them. But there is no question that something is going on out there."

In voiceover, Tom Jarriel begins the segment with a litany of seemingly unrelated incidents across the nation, including acts of animal mutilation, vandalism, and graffiti. These incidents are all purported to be evidence of satanic activity. Jarriel explains that Satanists are very secretive but come from all walks of life. A series of pentagrams, skulls, and goat heads flash across the screen. As scenes from the film *Rosemary's Baby* play, Jarriel somberly intones, "The zeal of these fictional devil worshippers is strikingly similar to that of real-life Satanists."

Next, Christian comedian and evangelist Mike Warnke shows Jarriel a variety of objects which he claims are used during secret, satanic rituals. Items include swords, chalices, robes, and candles. Pointing to a human skull and holding up a bone, Warnke explains that these body parts are used in the practice of dark magic.

As Warnke comments on being lured into the cult at a young age, there is a hard cut to black and white crime scene photos of a dead fifteen-year-old boy. In voiceover, Jarriel explains that the boy "wanted to feel special," when he hanged himself to death. Satanic writing was allegedly found on the boy's body. This case, Jarriel says, brought two officers together. Officer Sandi Gallant, of the San Francisco Police Department, and Deputy Chief Dale Griffis, of the Tiffin, Ohio police department, are shown walking side by side down a hallway.

Sitting across from Jarriel, Dale Griffis ominously warns, "We have kids being killed. We have people missing in America. We have our own MIAs right here. We have cattle being killed. We have all types of perversion going on, and it's affecting America."

A map of the United States appears on the screen. One by one, states change color from grey to yellow, until the entire map is illuminated. "Nationwide, we found that minor cases of satanic activity light up the map. Not a single state is unaffected," says Jarriel. "But even more frightening is the number of reported murders and suicides with satanic clues." Dozens of red dots appear all over the map.

As a scary devil face appears on the screen, Jarriel outlines three types of satanic groups. The first, he calls self-styled Satanists. This group is composed of teens who dabble in the occult or experiment with satanism. The second is called religious satanism, representing those who publicly worship the devil, which Jarriel notes is a right protected by law. The third group is called satanic cults. Jarriel says these are "highly secretive groups committing criminal acts, including murder."

The segment cuts to Tom Jarriel standing inside a local shopping mall. He points to three stores located side by side: a bookstore, a movie store, and a music store. For the next several minutes, Jarriel points out various forms of media which contain satanic or occult ideas. Next, the segment discusses "backmasking," which is described as secret or hidden messages that can be deciphered when records are played in reverse. Alongside Jarriel, DJ Chris Edmonds plays "Stairway to Heaven" in reverse on camera, saying many people hear the phrase, "My sweet Satan."

In the next section, two twelve-year-old boys, with their faces obscured, act out satanic sacrifices using dolls and various props. A grandmother, some parents, and several young children go on to describe atrocities they have witnessed or heard about, including sexual abuse, grave desecration, the eating of flesh and drinking of blood, and the ritual murder of children.

Periodically, Jarriel chimes in to remind the audience that police have found no evidence of murders or ritual human sacrifices. However, he says, the claims made by the children in the story have been "verified" by authorities.

In the final moments of the segment, Barbara Walters speaks to Tom Jarriel about the "terrifying stuff" she just witnessed. None of the anchors question the veracity of any of the claims presented in the segment.

8. Location, Location, Location
Thursday, June 20, 1985
1:00pm

Three hours had passed since the first backhoe had broken ground along Meilke Road, and no human remains had been found. The sheriff's press conference had imparted a sense of imminent danger, raising the specter of murderous cult members behind every corner, but searchers had unearthed next to nothing.

At this stage, the lack of compelling results was frustrating, but deputies saw no reason to call off the search too early. Officials would not openly cast doubt on the veracity of their information until later, but as the day wore on, expectations became more measured. Deputy Trilby Cashin said "I believe the bodies are out here. We just don't have the right information to find them."[1]

At one point, Sheriff Telb himself acknowledged that the dig had been unproductive, pointing to one area where the backhoe had previously operated and saying they had uncovered nothing more than "a big pile of dirt and some weeds over there."[2] G. Michael Pratt, an archaeologist and professor from Heidelberg University in nearby Tiffin, was brought to the scene to consult on the dig. By noon, he told the press they had uncovered nothing more than an abandoned cellar.[3]

Around 1:00pm, they moved the digging equipment to a second location, about a quarter of a mile down the road from the initial search. There, investigators began to dig near an abandoned house. The structure was riddled with bullet holes, which investigators called a sign of possible nefarious activity. Residents countered that the bullet holes were most likely left by squirrel hunters who frequented the area.[4] Officers also found paper strewn about on the ground, covered in "cryptic" writing. Some suggested the strange symbols were satanic in nature.[5]

By mid-afternoon, investigators had uncovered an assortment of odds and ends from the dig sites. Officials would later attach significance to some of the recovered materials, but many observers considered the items involved to be little more than junk.

Officers found several animal bones. They also discovered what was characterized as an "inverted cross" with an American flag tied around its base. Sheriff Telb said this was a cult symbol.[6] At the second search location, rumors began to surface that deputies recovered an eight-inch dagger, which was later referred to as an athame, or a ceremonial knife.[7]

There was also a headless doll which had its feet nailed to a board. Around the doll's right wrist, someone had tied a small pentagram ornament.[8] Investigators also found wooden stakes arranged in a triangular configuration and the remains of a bonfire. Inside one of the abandoned buildings, numerous markings and symbols were written on the walls, some of which were said to be satanic.[9]

Headless doll, found near the site of the dig. Photo courtesy of Lucas County Sheriff's Dept.

How could these signs be interpreted? Of course, an archaeologist had already been summoned to assist with the dig along with experts from the Medical College of Ohio in Toledo, to help pinpoint how recently the alleged cult activity had taken place.[10] But none of those people had any experience with cult investigations. The sheriff needed an expert.

That's why, as the afternoon stretched into evening, Sheriff Telb commandeered a local hospital's medical helicopter and sent it to retrieve Dale Griffis.

Around 1984, satanic crime seminars began popping up at law enforcement conferences around the nation. Attendees often included active-duty law enforcement, corrections officers, probation officers, and juvenile court personnel. In these training sessions, presenters would often link symbols, images from popular culture, and unconventional behavior with violent criminality.[11]

Law enforcement expert and author Robert Hicks suggested the increase in police seminars on occult crime was significant for two reasons.[12] First, such seminars provided a mechanism for disseminating information about satanism quickly, to many people. Because officers attended training sessions to "avoid reinventing the wheel," this information spread quickly as people returned to their respective agencies.

Second, training seminars on occult crime were effective in shaping policies and practices. The people attending these workshops had real power: they could make arrests, launch investigations, and remove children from homes. If attendees came to believe satanic cults were active in their communities, it would undoubtedly shape their official actions. When public officials endorsed satanic threat allegations, it lent credibility to the notion among the public.

Many cult crime presenters began their sessions by acknowledging the lack of material evidence to corroborate their claims. Once this initial disclaimer was out of the way, most speakers went on to give detailed descriptions of the alleged cult's organization, motivations, and techniques.[13]

In May of 1989, "Police Satan hunters at a state-wide conference in New Hampshire said that there are over two million members of satanic cults in the United States, organized into 'criminal cartels.' According to these crime 'experts,' many unsolved kidnappings and serial murders in our country are committed by highly secret satanic cults."[14] Another cult crime trainer solemnly declared, "If even ten percent of this stuff is true, then we're in big trouble."[15]

Robert Hicks examined handouts and printed materials from over fifty cult crime seminars which took place between 1984 and 1990. Based on this research, he found that the satanic crime model presented remained virtually unchanged since its inception. The satanic crime model became the standard model for discussing occult crime and was widely shared among law enforcement agencies at the local, state, and federal level.

The model described four levels of satanic involvement.[16] The lowest level, called dabblers, referred to teens and young adults who listened to rock music with occult themes, showed interest in satanic imagery or ideas, or became involved in fantasy role-playing games. Occult dabblers were said to be at risk of suicide, narcotics, violent criminal activity, or animal cruelty.

The second level of satanic involvement, according to the model, was "self-styled satanism." This level of satanic crime was populated mostly by psychopathic or sociopathic criminals who engaged in dangerous and deviant behavior, often incorporating violence and drug use. Discussions of this level of satanism frequently included figures like Charles Manson and Henry Lee Lucas.

The third level of satanism was called "organized satanism." This category referred to people who were public Satanists as part of an organized movement, such as the Church of Satan or Temple of Set. These people were characterized in the literature as "unpredictable, intelligent, and curious." These people may not commit crimes, but they were to be considered dangerous because "their ideology might attract criminals."

Finally, the fourth level of the satanic crime model was "covert satanism." According to the model, this category of Satanist was characterized by multigenerational family involvement in a secretive, highly exclusive cult. These types of Satanists were said to be involved in various crimes including child abuse, human sacrifice, brainwashing, sexual violence, and international conspiracy. This level included "high level public officials, police, judges, and lawyers." When citing evidence for the existence of this group, presenters relied almost exclusively on cult survivor stories and ritual child abuse allegations, like those in the McMartin Preschool case.

Because this model lacked evidence suitable for prosecution, seminar presenters recommended investigating a wider sphere of noncriminal acts which were said to be "associated with criminal behavior." One early seminar on occultism suggested police officers should examine rock and roll lyrics, graffiti, suspected animal mutilations, and vandalism as potential evidence of satanic cult activity.[17]

Although these seminars were aimed at law enforcement officers, few of the presenters were police. At a seminal conference on satanic crime called "The Emergence of Ritualistic Crime in Today's Society," in Fort Collins, Colorado in 1986, only one speaker had a background in law enforcement. Presenters included Officer Sandi Gallant, of the San Francisco Police Department; television producer Ken Wooden, who produced the infamous *20/20* segment on devil worship; Christian evangelist Mike Warnke; Pat Pulling and Rosemary Loyacano, of Bothered

About Dungeons & Dragons (BADD); and Dr. Lawrence Pazder, author of the book *Michelle Remembers.*[18]

During this conference, Pazder advised law enforcement personnel to dig deeper in their communities, saying, "Your interview techniques must be reversed... You should develop resource teams. Include a knowledgeable-but-cool clergyman, an open-minded-but-stable psychologist, and a survivor who has lived through the experience and come out successfully on the other side."[19]

Thomas Wedge, a juvenile probation officer from Logan County, Ohio, became another well-known consultant on cult crime. His book, *The Satan Hunter*, presented a distinctly fundamentalist view of Satan and his powers. Wedge was the main lecturer at a three-day seminar for law enforcement at the University of Delaware, as well as numerous other events around the country.[20]

A resource guide distributed by the Baldwin Park Police Department of California included investigative tips for pursuing secret Satanists. The pamphlet contained unverified, third-hand accounts of satanic violence. One section read, "A young couple was asked by an American family to come and babysit. When the parents came home, they found the young couple, who belonged to a satanic cult, had roasted the baby on a gridiron. The horrified parents had entrusted their child to devil worshipers." No documentation was provided.[21]

At a 1985 FBI-sponsored conference on satanic ritual abuse in daycare centers, Officer Sandi Gallant provided handouts which listed more than four hundred "occult organizations" around the country. The document provided no information about the size, activities, or sophistication of these groups, and did not distinguish violent groups from countercultural religious movements.[22]

The same document offered a list of dates for supposed occult festivals and a list of "ritual indicators" which were said to serve as clues of satanic practices. Some of these indicators included the presence of robes and pentagrams, chanting, singing, crying, invoking Satan, nudity, and a camera at the scene. Officer Gallant's guide was distributed to law enforcement agencies across the country, from the Bronx, New York to Michigan to California.[23]

In the decade that followed, more Satan-hunting guidebooks and manuals would be written. Modern experts in evil might choose to consult Kahner's *Cults that Kill* (1988), Langone and Blood's *Satanism and Occult-*

Related Violence: What You Should Know (1990), Sakheim and Devine's *Out of Darkness: Exploring Satanism and Ritual Abuse* (1992), Ryder's *Breaking the Circle of Satanic Ritual Abuse* (1992), or even Noblitt and Perskin's *Cult and Ritual Abuse* (2000).[24]

When naming factors contributing to the large-scale witch hunts of the sixteenth and seventeenth centuries, author David Frankfurter credits two key historical developments. First, there was the exportation of the religious concept of evil, which factored greatly into the ideology of witch hunting. Second, there was the development of centralized and coordinated methods for identifying witches, which were duplicated in various communities. This included the creation of numerous guidebooks and manuals, such as the *Errores Gazariorum*, Johannes Nidler's *Formicarius*, and Henry Institoris' influential tract, *Malleus Maleficarum*.

These witch-finding manuals were widely distributed among community leaders and tended to explain, in alarmist and pornographic detail, the conspiratorial links between local witches and Satan himself. Once local witch-finders identified their suspects, the torture they administered usually matched the procedures they had learned from their chosen guidebook.[25]

9. Explainer of Evil, Discerner of Demons
Thursday, June 20, 1985
5:30pm

Shortly after 5:30pm, Dale W. Griffis arrived on the scene in a helicopter borrowed from Toledo's St. Vincent Medical Center. Purported to be an expert in mind control, non-traditional groups, and matters of the occult, Griffis had been flown in from his home in Tiffin, where he served as captain of the police force.[1]

This was not the self-proclaimed cult expert's first time in the spotlight. He had gained notoriety speaking to schools, churches, and civic groups about the dangers of witchcraft and satanism. A consultant on cases throughout the country, Griffis was often quoted in the media. In fact, just a few weeks before the incident in Spencer Township, he had appeared on that jarring episode of the national news program *20/20*, in a segment entitled "The Devil Worshippers."[2]

As Griffis disembarked from the chopper, deputies brought him up to speed. They showed him the various items they had recovered at the scene so far before escorting him to an area near an abandoned house. There, Griffis wasted no time flagging four locations which he suspected might be burial sites. He said one spot seemed particularly suspicious because it was covered with wire mesh, possibly to keep animals from digging up the remains. Investigators marked the specified locations to be excavated the following morning.[3]

Upon seeing the headless doll, wooden crucifix, and other assorted objects found by officers, Griffis confirmed they were all indicative of cult activity. Pointing to these items, Griffis later told reporters the investigation was uncovering "more and more credible evidence" of a satanic cult in Spencer Township.[4]

Even though there were no signs of murder, investigators kept speculation running high among the press by periodically sharing new pieces of information. The information was often vague or impossible to verify. One such example came from the cult expert's son, Dale Griffis Jr., who was also on the scene. At one point, he said the authorities had been told by five different sources that eyewitnesses had observed human sacrifices taking place in the area.[5]

Dale Griffis shows reporters a "horned devil" from his own collection. © Ron Kuner – USA TODAY NETWORK

Although he was brought in to offer technical assistance, Dale Griffis soon took on the role of media liaison. While journalists had the run of the place in the early hours of the investigation, officers later corralled the media into designated areas. The arrival of the nationally known occult specialist proved to be a shot in the arm for reporters in the flagging hours of the late afternoon.

Griffis took charge of the press.[6] In a pool of microphones and television cameras, the expert answered questions and regaled the press with his own stories of regional satanic worship. He declined to make any connection between his stories and the current Lucas County investigation, but the parallels were clear.[7]

Since Griffis had arrived, more alleged evidence had surfaced in a nearby abandoned house. Investigators found about fifty articles of children's clothing, a knife, and a syringe. Griffis found significance in the syringe, saying drugs were sometimes used during satanic rituals. After finding a tin can, a small bone, and some feathers, Griffis led the search of a second abandoned house nearby.[8]

Alongside his son, Griffis was photographed with a collection of items recovered from the dig. To keep reporters entertained, he recapped all that had been found. There was the headless doll which had been nailed to a board and adorned with a pentagram. Griffis suggested the doll may have been used in a dark ceremony. The doll also had a toy telephone receiver tied to its finger with a piece of string and a dirty rag.[9] When asked about the significance of the toy phone, Griffis admitted, "I'm trying to work that out."[10]

The two "oddly shaped" knives were said to serve a ceremonial purpose, along with the wooden cross. Investigators found assorted rags, body paint, and written correspondence.[11] They also found two pairs of glasses, a radio with a list of phone numbers inside it, an aluminum jug, and a birthday card featuring the cartoon image of a red devil.[12]

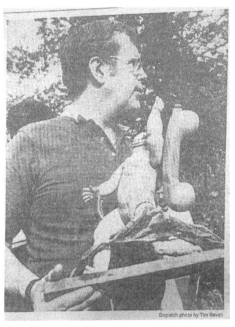

Dale Griffis speaks to reporters, holding headless doll.
© *The Toledo Blade*.

A sign on the premises had been defaced with "occult markings." Within one of the ramshackle houses, someone had painted a symbol depicting horns, eyes, and a goat's head, all in red paint. Investigators also said they found a book featuring instructions for how to dissect a human heart.[13] "The evidence just keeps piling up that something of an occult nature is happening here," Griffis told reporters.[14]

As Griffis described the findings, there were no shocked gasps or awestruck stares. Reporters listened intently and documented fully, but none of the presented evidence seemed conclusive. As the expert listed examples, ambivalent reporters occasionally called out questions like, "Just how occultish is this?"[15]

Griffis mollified some dissatisfied reporters by breaking from law enforcement protocol, leading a small group out of the designated press area to tour one of the cordoned-off dig sites. Journalists followed him through a wooded area, swatting at mosquitoes and examining themselves for ticks. In the process, some of the reporters unwittingly trampled parts of what Griffis had minutes earlier described as a possible crime scene.[16]

At one point, a group of reporters climbed a small bluff to observe a spot Griffis was describing, which he said was clearly indicative of cult activity. They had chosen the higher vantage point to avoid another trek through muddy terrain. Huffing and puffing at the crest of the bluff, reporters waited expectantly to see Griffis' presentation of the evidence.

"That pink string you see on that branch there is used by some cults to mark off an area," said Mr. Griffis, after several long minutes of buildup. One disappointed reporter referred to this display as a *Waiting for Godot* moment, referring to Samuel Beckett's famous play where the titular character never shows up.[17]

Photo of the infamous "red string" taken by investigators on the first day of the dig. Photo courtesy of Lucas County Sheriff's Dept.

Griffis eventually acknowledged that much of the evidence was in the eye of the beholder. A cross with a string attached, said to be used in a ritual, might have been one half of an old clothesline. Strands of cord which were said to be used by cult members during devil worship looked a lot like idle pieces of string tangled on a tree branch. This was no smoking gun.[18]

In the twilight hours of the first day of digging, without any hint of human remains, some authorities still insisted the evidence was mounting. At least one cult cop believed he could see the signs. More than two-hundred murderous cult members were sacrificing children in their neighborhood right under their noses, and if an expert had not come along to interpret the evidence, the residents of Spencer Township might have missed it altogether.

Dale Griffis speaks to reporters at the site of the dig. © Ron Kuner – USA TODAY NETWORK

When he arrived in Spencer Township, Dale Griffis had spent the entirety of his twenty-three years in law enforcement at the Tiffin Police Department. Even though he described himself as a small-town cop in his late forties, Griffis came to be nationally known as an expert in occult and cult-related crime.

"He is well thought of by the law enforcement community," said George Lewis, the chief of basic training for the Ohio Peace Officer Training Council. By 1984, Griffis was already lecturing around the country on the topics of mind control, cults, satanic worship, and the dangers posed by destructive religious groups. He had also been a certified law enforcement instructor for around twenty years, fourteen of which were spent as school commander for the Ohio Peace Officer Training Academy in London, Ohio.[19]

Griffis said he first became interested in the occult around 1967, when he saw Hare Krishna devotees standing in the airport and wondered what might drive a person to take on such a lifestyle. His first official occult related case did not come until later, sometime around 1976, shortly after he graduated from Heidelberg College.

According to Griffis, "one of the local police chiefs" in an unnamed Ohio town called him to consult on a case which "threw him for a loop."[20] A teenage boy had died by strangulation in the attic of his home. Griffis said the boy was nude and had symbols and messages written on his body, including "666," an inverted cross, and the words, "Lord Satan, I'm coming home."[21]

Investigators ruled the death accidental, saying the boy had hanged himself while attempting to perform an autoerotic act, but Griffis came to a different conclusion. "I'm convinced now that it was a self-sacrifice to Satan," he said, six years after the case.[22] Griffis seemed to be referencing the same case mentioned during his 1985 interview on *20/20,* which included a photograph of a boy in similar circumstances.[23]

After this incident, Griffis began collecting books on a variety of subjects, ranging from mind control to devil worship to werewolves. One reporter noted in 1984 that Griffis kept copies of *The Modern Witch's Spell Book* and *The Book of Ceremonial Magic* in his office, right next to *The Constitutional Rights of Prisoners* and *Techniques of Investigation.* Griffis also spent time visiting detectives in San Francisco and Los Angeles to learn more about cult-related cases.[24]

Griffis' appearance on *20/20* in May 1985 drew a lot of attention. One central Ohio newspaper advertised, "Viewers who saw Tiffin, Ohio Deputy Police Chief Dale Griffis on last week's *20/20* can attend his lecture at 7:30pm on Thursday. Talk entitled, 'A Discussion of Non-Traditional Groups' and destructive cults. Open to public."[25]

In 1986, due to increasing demand, Griffis retired from the Tiffin Police Force to establish his own cult-crime consulting business. He also wrote several pamphlets and guides.[26] In his consultations and seminars, Griffis emphasized the clear and present danger of satanic cults, particularly for teens and law enforcement officers. He somberly warned, "Fully one third of kids in satanic cults are willing to kill."[27]

Not all teens who used satanic symbols were involved in a cult. Griffis frequently reassured parents there was still hope for their children, even if they showed signs of occult involvement. When speaking with a group of teachers and counselors, Griffis commented on teens who dabbled, saying, "Don't get upset with them, try to find out why they're doing it."[28]

Griffis always remained tight-lipped about specific dates and locations of the cases he worked, making it impossible to corroborate his stories. Griffis openly acknowledged it was difficult to document his claims. Sometimes he omitted key details because the investigations were still active. Sometimes he withheld details so as not to stigmatize, embarrass, or draw unnecessary attention to the various municipalities where incidents occurred.[29]

"It causes sensationalism by the media, and citizen unrest," Griffis told one reporter. Most law enforcement officers were baffled when they encountered their first occult-related case and were quick to show skepticism. When they eventually decided it was time to call Griffis, most agencies wanted to keep it quiet, which became an often-cited reason for Griffis to avoid sharing dates and locations in his stories.[30]

Griffis said he had been called to advise officers who had discovered bloody animal bodies and satanic symbols inside a church in an unnamed Ohio town. Somewhere in Indiana, he said he worked on a case where a man was found shot to death, naked and surrounded by neatly arranged sticks and rock. Allegedly, police found red and black robes in the victim's home and his co-workers claimed he had a habit of drinking blood from a Thermos during his lunch break, which he apparently gathered from animal sacrifices.[31]

An unnamed community in Kansas had called Griffis when sixteen graves were dug up in a local cemetery. The perpetrators allegedly decapitated the exhumed bodies and placed their heads on spikes. In West Virginia, Griffis said a woman had roasted her baby in the oven to please Satan. Somewhere in eastern Ohio, someone had allegedly killed rabbits and placed their heads on stakes within a five-pointed star. In characteristic fashion, no documentation was provided for any of these stories.[32]

Griffis frequently shared "a story that circulated among police agencies," about two officers who were killed by devil worshipers. Apparently, these officers had stumbled upon a cult meeting in progress and were murdered when they "crossed the boundaries of a five-pointed star used for a ritual." Griffis acknowledged he could not verify the location or date of this incident but pointed instead to a telling passage from *Necronomicon*. The passage reads, "If thou happenest upon such a cult in the midst of their Rituals, do but hide well so that they do not see thee, else they will surely kill thee and make of thee a sacrifice to their Gods."[33]

Necronomicon, also known as the Book of the Dead, is a fictional book based on the works of H.P. Lovecraft. Still, Griffis contended that young and impressionable people might be tricked into believing the fictional elements were true. He also believed it was possible for people to be deceived by cunning cult leaders, which would ultimately lead to a psychological break.[34]

Griffis acknowledged that many reported cases of satanism turned out to be pranks, hoaxes, or criminals trying to confuse investigators to cover their tracks.[35] Non-traditional groups could act any number of ways. If investigators did not know how to interpret the signs, the murderous satanic cult might escape notice altogether.

⛥

In moments of great moral anxiety, people often look to authority figures for reassurance and guidance. The satanism scare of the 1980s, and other events like it, opened new roles for the discernment of evil which anyone in a recognizable authority role could often fill.[36]

Throughout history, ambiguous situations of misfortune have often produced the "exorcist" figure. This figure often rises to serve as the discerner of demons and provider of answers in times when people feel perplexed, frightened, or overwhelmed. Whether it be illness, infertility, catastrophe, or impurity, the situation does not necessarily mean there is a demonic presence. Often there are other explanations. It is up to the exorcist or the prophet or the ritual expert to identify and interpret the presence of evil amid misfortune.[37]

The exorcist figure, or demonologist or ritual expert, generally projects a sense of expertise when others are uncertain. They may propose innovative ways to expose or eliminate evil, and they can often situate real-world circumstances into a wider cosmic framework. All these actions require an audience. The role of a ritual expert is a theatrical one; by enacting their various processes, they project a sense of comprehensibility on that which has been considered incomprehensible.[38]

In conjuring up ideas of counter-realms of demons, or witches, or secret subversives, the expert becomes a heroic, solitary warrior against evil. By projecting order onto scenes of ambiguity, the ritual expert gains preternatural power.[39] The more important the expert becomes in discerning evil, the more indispensable they become.[40]

The presence of a witchfinder in a community often results in anxiety about the alleged presence of witches, but also about the potential for being named among the suspects. Naysayers risk being accused of participating in the hidden conspiracy. For this reason, the presence of a witchfinder has not historically been met with a wave of fanaticism or rejection, but rather increased deference to their wisdom and reliance on their clairvoyant powers to discern evil.[41] No one wants to publicly question a witchfinder.

Most experts in evil have developed their role out of some prior position of authority. Priests, police officers, judges, social workers, or civic leaders – these positions come with a built-in sense of credibility and authority. To every case, these experts bring the badges and idioms of their respective institutions, solidifying their own distinctive abilities to discern unseen evils.[42] When that kind of witchfinder speaks, people listen.

10. Closing Time
Thursday, June 20, 1985
6:00pm

"We didn't jump the gun – you guys jumped the gun. We just came out here for a nice little search. I can guarantee you, if there was a planned sacrifice for this weekend, we stopped it," said the sheriff to members of the press. "We hope our information was incorrect."[1]

At 6:00pm, Sheriff Telb held a press conference at the site of the dig. Speaking to a mob of reporters, many of whom had been present at the site all day, the sheriff announced that they would be pausing their search until the following morning. They still had several sites to explore, including those suspicious areas pointed out by Captain Dale Griffis.

Sheriff Telb and Dale Griffis speak to a reporter at the site of the dig. Photo courtesy of Lucas County Sheriff's Dept.

Even though they had not yet recovered any bodies, the sheriff defended the investigation. He told the press that the items recovered during the search were definitive proof of cult activity in Lucas County. He added, "We're still going to continue our investigation with the evidence we found. There may still be bodies out there."[2]

In private, authorities doubted they would find human remains at this location. They left the door open for such a possibility, especially considering the supposed insistence of their unnamed informants, but it now seemed unlikely. Uncomfortable with the amount of attention his investigation had attracted, Telb eventually conceded that he might have been the victim of a hoax.[3]

"We don't feel as confident about our sources as when we first started," he later told reporters. In retrospect, he also acknowledged that it may have been premature to announce such a large number of potential victims.[4]

"We could sit back and do nothing or do what we did today. Maybe we are going to determine that nothing happened. We have to be sure there are not any bodies out there," he said, vowing that the search would go on.[5] "It was really too early based on the information we had, but we couldn't wait until Monday and find that someone had been sacrificed."[6]

Telb remained unwilling to reveal any information about his sources. Despite persistent questioning from the press, he would only say that his information had come from three different people who may or may not have been involved in cult activity in the past. Telb went on to specify that the informants had not witnessed any actual human sacrifices.[7] In response to reports that a central informant was a woman, Telb said, "We are not going to put out whether they are male or female. I don't want anybody getting hurt."[8]

An unnamed sheriff's deputy later confirmed that one of the sources was female but gave no further information. When reporters asked Telb if an earlier agreement meant that the informants would never be publicly identified, Telb replied, "I imagine that was the way it was made."[9]

The sheriff insisted he was not embarrassed that the heavily publicized search had yielded no evidence of human sacrifice. If anything, the public should be relieved. While the search had drawn national media attention, Telb maintained that the overall result was good for the community.

"You have to have faith and confidence in your sources. We went for it, and it didn't cost us much at all. [There was] minimal overtime. Most of our people were on duty for their regular shift."[10]

Before leaving town for the evening, visiting consultant Dale Griffis praised investigators for taking the situation seriously. "Based on the information the sheriff and his officers had, they had no alternative to this course of action. You've got to give them credit, because this is such a highly speculative thing to begin with," he told reporters.[11]

The sheriff reiterated that his information had indicated the possibility of another looming sacrifice, on June 21, to coincide with the summer solstice. If they had not acted swiftly, another child may have been sacrificed by the bloodthirsty cult.[12]

"The publicity of the dig may have scared them and prevented other sacrifices anywhere. If we prevented any sacrifice, it will have been worth it," he said.[13]

The next morning, a headline in *The Toledo Blade* read, "Area witches express doubt of sacrifices by Satanic cult."[14] The few witches who were willing to speak to the press expressed incredulity at the idea of numerous victims of human sacrifice buried in Spencer Township. Because terms like "the occult" and "satanism" were commonly used alongside terms like "witchcraft," mostly by self-proclaimed experts, some members of the public had difficulty making any distinction between local groups and the alleged secret murder cult.

"It worries me," said a witch named Gia. "There are a lot of people, very spiritual people, who are liable to get hurt from adverse publicity connecting them with this type of thing."

Gia went on to explain that she and her friends did not harm others but practiced "earth magic." She explained, "Earth magic people feel there is a need to get back to nature, that people have misused the earth for so long." A male witch named Loki added, "We use herbs, for example, to call on the forces of earth and nature. It's a positive, spiritual thing."[15]

While they had heard rumors about the recent animal mutilation investigations in other communities around Ohio, Gia and Loki had heard nothing about human sacrifice. They insisted that rituals among local witches were peaceful and mostly symbolic and that only a "sick individual" would harm a living creature during such practices.

The rumors referred to a satanic group with hundreds or even thousands of members, but when it came to the number of practicing witches in the area, the answer was difficult to determine. Loki told reporters, "A lot of us value our privacy. You'd be surprised how we can seclude ourselves – even from our mates. It's a minority religion. Personally, I know maybe four dozen people."[16]

Lady Circe, a prominent witch and earth magic practitioner, was well-known and respected in the Toledo area. Living in Michigan at the time of the Spencer Township dig, Lady Circe described her former home of Toledo as a significant location for witchcraft, particularly in the 1960s and 1970s.

"It was not only a center of witchcraft, but the entire Ohio valley had one of the largest groups of psychics in the country," said Lady Circe.[17]

The same weekend as the dig, a gathering of local witches took place at a campground in Logan, Ohio. Eighty people attended the gathering, including families with children. Although it was the third annual event in the same location, attendees had hoped to gather privately without drawing a lot of attention.[18]

The term "witch" often has a wider usage, but those gathering in Logan were Wiccans who at the time believed they were the only group who could properly call themselves witches. Their protective instincts related to terminology was justifiable, especially considering how often they were confused with Satanists, devil-worshipers, or murderous cult members. One Wiccan woman told reporters that Satanists drew on Christian theology not Wiccan beliefs, adding, "They are your problem."[19]

Members at the gathering expressed skepticism at the allegations of ritual cult killings, but they also insisted, if such reports were true, people should not blame Wiccans or even practicing Satanists. Lady Samantha said, "I think we're talking about heavy drug users and negative magic." Another unnamed woman added, "Let's call it what it is. It's murder." Lady Feather agreed, calling allegations of ritual murder in Spencer Township, "Wretched! Horrible and disgusting!" Lady Brigid clarified, "The atmosphere that we have here is what we call perfect love and perfect trust."[20]

This was not the first time the group had been subjected to scrutiny. One man told reporters that he could not publicly express his religious beliefs for fear of losing his job, where he worked with members of the public. "Now that's persecution," he said.

Members of the group went on to say they would not be intimidated by the uproar taking place in Lucas County and other communities. Lady Samantha added, "If you're looking for a panic, you are not going to find it here. We've been through this before."[21]

When individuals build up tension from frustration, anger, and fear, they often release this tension in the form of angry attacks against others who they blame for these feelings. The psychological mechanism involved is called displacement or displaced anger. The creation of scapegoats is not only society's collective extension of this psychological process, but also a reflection of social conflicts within society.[22]

Rumors can function as "improvised news," to provide explanations for ambiguous sources of shared social concerns. Stories of secret subversives and covert evildoers help produce fantasy scapegoats who can be blamed for all kinds of misfortune. Author Jeffrey Victor described this phenomenon, writing, "The evil internal enemy in blood ritual subversion stories is usually some widely despised group. Such groups function as scapegoats for anxieties caused by widespread social stresses."[23]

Sometimes, the enemy is framed as an external threat. In this way of thinking, the enemy is "over there" somewhere, seeking to do harm to those of us who are "over here." In this case, the enemy is coming for us, or trying to invade our spaces. Whether real or imagined, the external enemy is often portrayed as evil and immoral. "They" are the reverse mirror image of "us," and onto them we project all those qualities we most detest and condemn.[24] For example, one might frame immigrants as an external enemy, claiming they are coming to steal jobs or to replace our values and beliefs with their own.

Sometimes, the threat is framed as an internal one. In this case, the enemy is not coming for us; they are already here. These people are often described as traitors, infiltrators, or deviants, who have ignored, subverted, or otherwise failed to live up to our collective shared values. The secret devil worshiper living on our block, the abuser working in our child's daycare, or the heretic who has infiltrated our church are all hypothetical examples of internal enemy figures.[25]

When people begin to name enemies within or surrounding their in-group, talk of conspiracy usually follows. If there are evildoers among us, working to achieve their own twisted goals, there must be some level of planning and coordination involved. This realization makes the underlying threat even more insidious, for the narrative no longer centers on a few bad apples or lone deviants; now the discussion centers on orchestrated, intentional collusion for the sake of doing harm.

As fears about satanic ritual abuse grew and spread, certain commonalities surfaced in the conspiracy stories. They all had something to do with abducted, abused, or sacrificed children. They all involved a secret group of individuals, bent on corruption and atrocities. The stories all included characterizations of conspirators featuring inclinations and habits which demonstrated they were not quite human. And these conspiracy stories were all presented with a sense of authority or authenticity.[26]

External enemies, or the Enemy Outside, would often be conspicuous or alien; theoretically, they would stand out as being part of some other out-group. The Enemy Within, however, could blend in and undermine the group while masquerading as a member of the team. Fears of the Enemy Within are quite common, for most suspicions in day-to-day life relate to friends, relatives, and work associates. Some scholars have pointed out that, prior to the Salem witch trials, there were pre existing feuds based on gossip and bad blood.[27]

But the Enemy Within and Enemy Outside are not the only tropes which surface in conspiracy stories. There is also the Enemy Below, or the alleged threat represented by those who come from lower classes, socio-economic conditions, or stations in life. The fears and suspicions in this trope center on the idea that those "below us" will rise up and threaten that which is "ours."

In the 1870s, as an economic depression ravaged the country, newspapers around the United States promoted a "Tramp Scare" by blaming homeless and transient individuals for societal problems. A report in New York's *World* offers a typical example, listing a series of "outrages by tramps," including several recent fires which were "presumably set by tramps." Prior to and during this time, influential people and authority figures also stoked fears about slave uprisings or the dangers inherent in granting freedom to former slaves.[28]

If the Enemy Below is to be feared, so then is the Enemy Above. In conspiracy stories, it is often posited if not assumed, that people in positions of power and authority are manipulating us, through lies and deception or nefarious machinations behind the scenes. Perhaps there are hidden puppeteers above us, pulling the strings and orchestrating specific outcomes without our knowledge. The face of the Enemy Above is generally associated with a large institution, such as hospitals, academia, government, powerful corporations, or secret societies, like the Illuminati.[29]

Satanic cult rumors contained elements of all these enemy types. There were Enemies Outside, invading predominantly Christian neighborhoods, importing strange teachings and new religious ideas. There were Enemies Within, infiltrating daycares, playgrounds, and local institutions with their nefarious practices. Many law enforcement personnel warned of the Enemy Below in the form of self-styled Satanists, who were often characterized as drug-using, under-achieving criminals.

In most satanic cult rumors, members of the cult were also said to have infiltrated the highest positions of power. In Lucas County, Sheriff Telb said cult members came from various socioeconomic backgrounds, with varying levels of resources.[30] Deputy Trilby Cashin asserted that devil worshipers included doctors, lawyers, and police officers, with people from "the highest class down to the scum."[31] In Union County, Sheriff Overly expressed a similar sentiment while investigating animal mutilations, and Christian speaker Mike Warnke claimed that police, coroners, and judicial court personnel were all involved in covering up satanic crime at the highest levels.[32]

But one might ask, if these various enemies were so active at every level of society, why had so few people noticed?

11. TGIF
Friday, June 21, 1985
8:00am – 5:55pm

When investigators returned to Spencer Township for a second day of digging, the proceedings were much quieter. They still had several sites to examine, including those pointed out by Captain Dale Griffis the day before, but they hoped to carry out the search with a smaller audience. Even the digging equipment shrank. Investigators brought in a smaller bulldozer for the next stage of the excavation because the backhoe they had used previously was too heavy.[1]

Still reeling from the intensity of the media attention from the day before, Sheriff Telb decided to bar press from the dig site. When a group of twenty reporters arrived to document the proceedings, they were surprised to find that the road had been blocked. They were asked to wait for updates approximately half a mile from the action. Other teams of reporters would come and go throughout the day. A few photographers tried their luck from the air, passing over the dig site in helicopters.[2]

Marvin Reams, public relations officer for the Lucas County Sheriff's Department, was stationed at the corner of Angola and Crissey Roads to block entry to the area. He did not explain why the changes had been made. As the second day of digging wore on, Reams did his best to answer questions and provide updates for the hungry crowd of journalists.[3]

"We would like to clear things up today, one way or the other," said Reams. Following hours of sifting through piles of dirt with rakes and shovels, everyone involved hoped to have some definite answers before sundown.[4] Reams also acknowledged that the information given to deputies may have been misleading, especially if the cult knew they were under surveillance. After the publicity of the search, they may have moved to another location.[5]

There was nothing left to do but wait. In the hours that passed, reporters carried out interviews with various residents, particularly those who had been impacted by the investigation. They exchanged information between themselves whenever something moderately interesting came to light, checking in frequently with law enforcement personnel to see if there were any updates.

Nothing happened. Officers found no new evidence of cult activity. There were no human remains, nor were there any signs of foul play. When all was said and done, officers had dug up numerous sites at three different locations over the course of their two-day investigation.[6]

As the second day came to an end, Sheriff James Telb called another press conference. Standing in a garbage-strewn wooded area, the sheriff told reporters they were calling off the search. It was not entirely clear whether this halt in digging was permanent or temporary.

"We have temporarily stopped our digging here. We may be out in a few days or never again," said Telb. Even though his information had allegedly come from several independent sources familiar with the cult, and even though Telb claimed the informants had provided solid leads in the past, he acknowledged he was beginning to question the credibility of his sources.[7]

Lt. Kirk Surprise acknowledged that their extensive excavations had not turned out as expected, but he expressed no doubt regarding the presence of a satanic cult in the area. "We'll regroup. We'll go back and try to gather more intelligence," he said.[8]

Both Surprise and department spokesperson Marvin Reams expressed their doubts that they would find the fifty to seventy-five bodies Sheriff Telb had said may be buried there.

"I would just assume this thing all will turn out to be a fairy tale."[9]

And just as quickly as it had begun, the search ended. There had been no explosive revelations, no conclusive evidence, no earth-shattering discoveries. Hopefully, the community would be able to put this unfortunate incident behind them and move forward with their reputations intact. Surely there would be no reason for officials to return to Spencer Township for more digging.

One could only hope.

Satanic cult rumors emphasized the secretive, hidden nature of the groups involved. They operated covertly, often in contested domains such as cemeteries, heavily wooded areas, abandoned houses, and underworld criminal rings. Sometimes, the cult members relied on a chameleon-like ability to disguise themselves within legitimate and presumably secure locations, such as churches or childcare centers. Because these alleged cults operated underground, it was impossible to spot their work until the damage had already been done. An absence of evidence served as further confirmation of the cult's secretive ways.[10]

But how did these groups remain a secret? How did they avoid detection, especially when carrying out such shocking crimes against numerous victims? Conspiracy believers had various elaborate explanations to account for this perpetual invisibility.[11]

Some believed children had shared eyewitness accounts of cult activity, but because the stories were so bizarre or fantastical, adults dismissed the stories as untrue. Some satanic cult experts even posited that perpetrators intentionally acted in unusual ways so victim accounts would be considered outlandish and implausible.

Others believed cults had escaped detection because victims or eyewitnesses had been intimidated and threatened into silence. Some conspiracy theories suggested cult members had infiltrated various institutions so high-ranking infiltrators could cover up cult activity, deflect or shut down investigations, and warn their fellow perpetrators about possible law enforcement action.

Some satanic cult experts complained that devil worshippers hid behind the United States Constitution. By invoking religious liberty, Satanists could thwart police investigations and commit various crimes behind closed doors. Because it was difficult for outsiders to break into the group without becoming implicated, the true nature of satanic cults remained a mystery. One officer said, "There's a real problem investigating these things. You can't get into it without being part of it. And you can't be part of it without doing things that are unspeakable."[12]

The devil worshipper cult rumor served as a perfect conspiracy story, incorporating fear of the occult and supernatural figures while blending in paranoia about the evil influence of higher institutions, such as the state or government officials.[13] Such conspiracy stories provided "ways of thinking about Otherness, of imagining an upside-down world that inverts our own, of encountering local malevolence suddenly in universal scope, and sensing the collapse of vital boundaries between 'us' and those monstrous 'others.'"[14]

12. In the Wake
June 22 - 25, 1985

In the days following the dig, Sheriff Telb vowed to continue his investigation. Although they had turned up no solid evidence of satanic killings over the two-day excavation, the sheriff still considered his unnamed sources to be "reasonably reliable." After reviewing information from his sources and reexamining the evidence, in addition to a few new leads generated by the publicity, Telb told the press he may resume digging in "the very near future."[1]

The media attention had been far more intense than anyone could have anticipated, but in the immediate aftermath of the incident, the sheriff maintained that he was not embarrassed. Law enforcement agencies had to act on the tips they received, he said, and perhaps their time in the national spotlight would yield some positive results. There was no way of knowing for sure, but Telb speculated that the publicity might have frightened the cult members away and stopped them from carrying out a human sacrifice.

"We'll stay out there and do what we have to do as long as we have to do it. The township trustees or anyone else aren't going to force us to curtail our investigation in any way."[2]

Telb had good reason to mention the township trustees specifically, because even as the dig was underway, some local officials took umbrage at the sheriff's actions. Elected leaders in Spencer Township had no advance warning about the investigation. Like everyone else, township trustees first heard about the supposed satanic cult when the allegations were broadcast on the news.

The chairman of the board of trustees for Spencer Township, D. Hilarion Smith, was not impressed with the sheriff's handling of the situation. Smith believed that Sheriff Telb had "bordered on being an irresponsible public official," when he had called a press conference and announced his search to the public before any evidence had been recovered. Smith worried that the investigation would tarnish the reputation of area residents.[3]

"The sheriff has done my township great damage. People chanting in the woods... this is crazy. This may be going on, but it is not going on in Spencer Township."[4]

72

Although the forty-five-year-old trustee had been out of town when the dig first started, D. Hilarion Smith had quickly heard the news. He had traveled to Ontario, Canada for the weekend, hoping to enjoy the annual Stratford Festival. Instead, Smith found himself racing back to Ohio when he saw international news reports talking about his hometown and the ghastly allegation that "children were killing children" in tribute to the Devil.[5]

As soon as Smith got home, he began doing damage control. He spoke to the press whenever he could, pushing back against the reports of cult activity. He also penned a letter to the sheriff. Smith wrote:

"Dear Mr. Telb: Enough is enough. You did what you thought and believed you had to do. You have had your public fun at our expense.

Trustee Smith's letter to Sheriff Telb, printed in © *The Toledo Blade*.

"The Township of Spencer will give you 24 to 48 hours to physically provide your first illegal 'human remains.' Otherwise, with all due respect to your office and by all that is holy, please cover up the holes you are in and pack up your equipment and round up your band of good Christian deputies and quietly steal away from Spencer Township."[6]

Smith told reporters that his letter never got a reply.

One of the trustee's chief concerns was the reputation of the area. For a small, tight knit community, a national media frenzy could potentially do permanent damage to residents' way of life. "All people are going to think is, 'You bloody devil worshipers.' That is what is coming across, even in Canada."[7]

Smith acknowledged that he had no legal authority to stop the sheriff from continuing his search, but he wanted them to limit their digging. He reiterated the contents of his letter to reporters, saying the sheriff "has twenty-four hours to find his first body, and if he doesn't, I want him to pack up his equipment and his men and get out."[8]

"He should have had better information before he went off and started digging," Smith added. "As far as I am concerned, he is standing in the hole he has dug."[9]

D. Hilarion Smith was not the only trustee who believed the community had been slandered. Rosella Pepper scoffed at the idea of occult involvement among her neighbors. "I think this is a bunch of baloney," she said.[10]

Pepper had hoped to purchase one of the dilapidated houses next to the dig site. The owner of the house protested that the intense media attention and malicious rumors might lower his property values. As a longtime resident who had seen no evidence of cult activity, Pepper said she saw no reason to abandon her plans. "I'd move right in. There's nothing out there... it's just a big joke."[11]

While Spencer Township officials attempted to navigate the aftermath of the dig, a resident in neighboring Springfield Township was weathering a storm of her own. Laretta Harris lived near the intersection of Crissey and Angola Roads, diagonally adjacent to the Litton residence, which had been raided by deputies on the first day of the investigation. During that morning's press conference, officers had shown a map of the area which incorrectly identified Harris' home as a "cult house."

Even though she had no knowledge of the alleged cult, Harris told reporters, "People have been driving by, yelling 'Murderer' and 'We'll get you!'" Harris had not been home when the raid occurred. "I was in Monroe, Michigan when all of this happened yesterday. I didn't even know a thing about it."[12]

Despite her innocence, Harris said the sheriff's press conference had painted a target on her home. She said there was a steady stream of journalists knocking on her door all day, asking her about her connection to the satanic cult.

"I called the sheriff's department, and all they could tell me was they made a mistake," said Harris. "Their big mistake is causing me a lot of anguish and a lot of fear."[13]

The Columbus Dispatch printed a photo of Laretta Harris, wiping tears from her eyes. "I believe in God," she said. "I don't believe in the devil. Why did they do this to me? I've come home to find my house is labeled as a cult house."[14]

By Monday morning, the coverage in the local newspaper had moved beyond mere reporting and into the realm of commentary. Chase Clements, political reporter for *The Toledo Blade*, summed up the entire incident as a valuable lesson for certain "Democratic officeholders" in Lucas County. Clements suggested that, while there was nothing inappropriate about the sheriff investigating possible criminal activity, "maybe it's not a good idea to go off talking about satanic cults until there is a little more hard evidence to back it up."[15]

Clements noted that it would have been possible to execute the search warrant without holding a press conference first. Routine searches like this one happened frequently. Sheriff Telb could have easily "poked around in Spencer Township without attracting the attention of *The National Enquirer*." Even if the sheriff had announced that they were looking for human remains, he could have done so without mentioning fifty to seventy-five victims. Clements did give the sheriff full marks for his sense of humor, acknowledging that the man had spent several hours in the middle of a media circus where he was forced to repeat the same speculations again and again as each new camera crew arrived on the scene.[16]

An editorial in the Tuesday edition of *The Blade* echoed these sentiments, indicating that the incident might have left the sheriff's department with "a fair amount of egg on its face." The column reiterated that it would have been possible to investigate the claims without drawing national media attention. "The bizarre nature of Lucas County Sheriff James Telb's investigation into the possibility of finding victims of Satan worshipers buried somewhere out in Spencer Township almost guaranteed a certain amount of sensationalism." And furthermore, the sheriff's comments on the matter, "while well-intentioned, only fueled speculation about sacrificial murder."[17]

The editorial was accompanied by a cartoon by Kirk Walter. Composed of two panels, the image shows a stern-looking detective dressed in a G-Man suit and hat as he squares off against a stereotypical representation of a housewife. In the first panel, the detective holds up a jar and says, "Out with it, Devil worshiper! I want to know what's in these jars we found in your basement! Eyes of newts? Bat wings? Lizard tails?" In the second panel, the puzzled housewife meekly responds, "Pickled beets."

"Ah-ha!" replies the cartoon detective. "Now we're getting somewhere!"[18]

Editorial cartoon by Kirk Walter, © *The Toledo Blade.*

13. Unforgetting the Forgotten

In 1980, Sister Margaret Ann Pahl was brutally murdered. Her body was discovered on Holy Saturday, one day before Easter, in the chapel sacristy at Mercy Hospital in Toledo, Ohio. The killer had attacked early in the morning as the nun went about her various duties in preparation for that day's services. After strangling the woman from behind with a piece of cloth, the perpetrator had stabbed her repeatedly in the chest, left side, and neck before leaving her body stripped and exposed on the cold chapel floor. The puncture wounds over her heart formed the shape of an upside down cross.[1]

The shocking nature of the crime left the community reeling. Who could have carried out such a vicious murder, in such a sacred space, against such an innocent victim? What was the significance of the cross-shaped arrangement of wounds? Was this killing somehow related to the occult? As rumors and speculation began to swirl, investigators had already identified their main, and only, suspect.

Father Gerald Robinson was a Jesuit priest who served as the chaplain at Mercy Hospital. He was the only other person who had access to the sacristy and several witnesses had seen him in the area shortly before the murder. The first officer who arrived on the scene later reported, "I asked everyone who did this, and they all said 'Robinson' or 'the priest.'"[2]

In the ensuing investigation, police received dozens of calls and letters, including one which claimed the culprit was a psychopathic devil worshiper who hated Catholics and nuns. All kinds of strange characters came out of the woodwork to offer tips and personal theories on the case. Through it all, the police maintained, "There was only one suspect – Father Robinson."[3]

Of course, the priest was questioned, but there was no physical evidence to lead to a conviction. For more than twenty years, the case went unsolved.

And then, Sister Mary Curtiss remembered.

"Sister Mary Curtiss" is a pseudonym given by journalist David Yonke in his definitive book about the case, *Sin, Shame, and Secrets: The*

Murder of a Nun, the Conviction of a Priest, and Cover-up in the Catholic Church. In legal proceedings, she was known as "Survivor Doe."

In 2003, Sister Curtiss went before a Catholic Center review board to seek restitution from the church for abuse she had experienced at the hands of Father Chet Warren, a priest who had been defrocked in 1996 because of rape and molestation allegations. Curtiss would later say she had been molested by Father Warren. Not only that, but she had been physically, psychologically, and sexually abused by a group of men and women. One of the perpetrators, she alleged, was Father Gerald Robinson.[4]

From there, the allegations grew darker. Curtiss claimed some priests, and several women dressed like nuns, were involved in "a satanic group that performed rituals in honor of Satan on a regular basis." She identified three priests, a well-known pediatrician, two female teachers, and her own father and grandmother as members of the satanic cult. Before the review board, Curtiss shared numerous graphic accounts of the abuse she had allegedly experienced at the hands of the devil worshipers.

When she was five years old, Curtiss claimed she had been taken into the basement of an abandoned house where her father and others wore black robes while her sister hacked the family dog to death with a meat cleaver. One of the priests had told her the dog had to be killed because Curtiss had "been bad." If she really loved the dog, the cult told her, then she should have the power to bring it back to life.[5]

Also at age five, Curtiss claimed she was taken to a cemetery late at night. Cult members placed her inside a coffin, releasing cockroaches on her body so the bugs could "mark her for Satan." At age six, the cult officially initiated her by ritualistically raping her while onlookers played drums. At age eleven, the cult forced her to eat an eyeball, a symbolic reminder that the cult was always watching her. During this incident, the cult also murdered a girl in front of her, who appeared to be about three years old.[6]

Because of these traumatic incidents, Sister Curtiss had been undergoing prolonged and intensive therapy, having been diagnosed with a dissociative disorder and PTSD. Curtiss petitioned the board to reimburse her for these expenses and pay for her future therapy.

The members of the review board were stunned. Most doubted the allegations were true, finding them too inconsistent or implausible to be believed. One member of the board named Dr. Cooley, who happened to be a licensed psychiatrist, believed they should report these claims to the authorities.[7]

Others in the group were skeptical. David Yonke writes about their reaction, saying, "Some argued that Sister Mary Curtiss could be telling the truth – as she sees it. But she could be a victim not of an adult perpetrator in real life, but of her own overactive imagination. A satanic cult in Toledo? Priests worshiping Satan? Human sacrifices? Maybe she watched too many horror movies or read too many Stephen King novels. She could have some kind of mental health instability that makes her unable to separate fact from fantasy, they contended."[8]

The board ultimately voted against calling the police.[9]

Disagreeing with the board, Dr. Cooley went to the police. When investigators heard Father Gerald Robinson's name being mentioned in relation to alleged sexual abuse, exploitation, and dark rituals, they decided they had enough to revisit a cold case from 1980.[10]

The investigation into the murder of Sister Margaret Ann Pahl was officially reopened.

Armed with new allegations from Sister Mary Curtiss, two detectives began reexamining the facts of the Pahl case, including any information they could find about their main suspect, Father Gerald Robinson. Because of the alleged ritual or occult elements of the murder, and because Sister Mary Curtiss had claimed Robinson was in a satanic cult, investigators consulted with occult experts.

Meanwhile, for Sister Mary Curtiss, new memories continued to surface.[11] Further memories, recovered through therapy, involved Curtiss being driven to an old, abandoned farmhouse where she was forced to kill a three-year-old girl with a machete. This was the same three-year-old girl who had been murdered by the cult in earlier versions of the story.[12]

By October of 2003, Curtiss' stories were far more graphic and disturbing than when she had first given testimony before the board. Many believed there was no question that the woman was convinced her stories were true. Investigators sought evidence to corroborate her allegations, but the existence of a secretive satanic cult was never proven.

In 2006, based on witness testimony and evidence recovered in the investigation, Gerald Robinson was convicted of the murder of Sister Margaret Ann Pahl. In 2014, the former priest died in prison.

The prosecutor acknowledged that some occult experts were convinced the murder had been a satanic ritual, but it could not be proven. The prosecutor believed there was a simpler explanation: Robinson had humiliated and killed the nun in a fit of rage.[13]

"Recovered-memory therapy" played a pivotal role in the conviction of Father Gerald Robinson, not because of the factual accuracy of Sister Mary Curtiss' claims, but because her fresh allegations prompted investigators to reexamine a suspect they'd had in mind from the beginning.

According to proponents of recovered-memory therapy, when an individual experiences extraordinary trauma, they might "split off" memories of the traumatic experience through the psychic mechanism of dissociation. These memories do not go away but are hidden behind an amnestic barrier. In essence, people "forget" what happened to them. When triggered, these hidden memories may reappear as fragmentary reliving of the trauma, emotional conditions, or somatic states.[14]

Recovered-memory practitioners try to recover hidden memories, sometimes called repressed memories, using a variety of methods. These methods include hypnosis, guided imagery, regression therapy, and other practices.

In 1980, a book entitled *Michelle Remembers* hit bookstores. Written by a Canadian psychiatrist named Lawrence Pazder and co-authored by his patient, the book allegedly detailed Pazder's efforts to help a woman reconstruct her childhood experiences as the victim of ritual abuse at the hands of a satanic cult.

Marketed as a factual account, *Michelle Remembers* served as a pioneering account of satanic cult abuse, effectively shaping the entire "occult survivor" genre that would follow. The book is framed as a series of recollections documented during months of intensive psychotherapy with Michelle in 1977 and 1978. In sessions with Pazder, Michelle recalled lurid and elaborate satanic rituals, which allegedly took place in the 1950s. The book is significant because it included all the elements which would later become hallmarks of cult survivor accounts: devil worship, ritual child abuse, blood sacrifices, mutilation of animals and babies, mock burials, and the desecration of religious artifacts.[15]

In the book, Michelle Smith (the pseudonym used by Pazder's patient, Michelle Proby) claimed she was abused as a child in Victoria, British Columbia. Michelle claimed to have witnessed the murder of adults and children. She was tortured, imprisoned, and locked naked in a cage. On one occasion, the cult sliced a fetus in half and rubbed it all over her. She had horns and a tail sewn into her flesh, which were later ripped out, and she was covered in tiny, red, biting insects. Ultimately, Satan himself appeared during one of the rituals. Fortunately, Mary and Jesus intervened, saving Michelle's life.[16]

As Michelle's psychiatrist, Pazder resorted to several unconventional methods to draw out horrific memories, ranging from hypnosis to physically cuddling with Michelle during sessions. In one session, he arranged for Michelle to be baptized by a Catholic priest. Prior to working with Michelle, Pazder had served as a physician in West Africa where he became very interested in the study of black magic rituals. He gathered an extensive collection of photos from various ceremonies he had witnessed, which he referenced frequently.[17]

Also, during their therapeutic relationship, Pazder left his spouse and married Michelle, who had also left her husband.[18]

Dr. Pazder and Michelle were frequently featured on television programs, where their claims were mostly presented uncritically, in full, gruesome detail. Few outlets questioned the stories or sought corroboration. When asked why he had not gone to the police about Michelle's alleged abuse, Pazder insisted the cult had orchestrated an elaborate cover-up to remain hidden, causing car accidents and destroying records to cover their tracks. Besides, he added, "It is not our desire to go and cause a witch hunt."[19]

After *The National Enquirer* covered their story, the pair gained an even wider audience. They also gained significant wealth from the exposure, collecting an unheard of $100,000 advance on hardcover sales and a $242,000 advance on paperback sales.[20] As their influence grew and spread, so did the stories.

In 1980, *Michelle Remembers* told the story of one woman's ritual abuse; by 1982, the FBI was receiving similar reports from women all over the country. After that, the stories started coming from children.[21] As new stories emerged, "satanic ritual abuse" came to be a central focus of evangelical Christian leaders, law enforcement agencies, child-welfare advocates, social workers, and mental health clinicians, all of whom suddenly served as professionals in the identification and expulsion of evil.[22] In the late 1980s, one survey identified over two-hundred fifty mental health practitioners who claimed to specialize in satanic ritual abuse. All of them reported full caseloads.[23]

In 1984, the First International Conference on Multiple Personality/Dissociative States was organized in Chicago for mental health clinicians. At the second annual conference in 1985, clinicians said twenty-five percent of their clients were reporting abuse at the hands of devil worshipers. When the conference was held again in 1986, nine different papers were presented about satanic cult abuse, all of them treating satanic cult abuse as literally true without offering a single alternative model. By 1989, a full twenty percent of all content at the conference centered on satanic abuse, along with a full-day post-conference workshop dedicated to the topic.[24]

By this time, some patients who had "recovered" memories of satanic abuse had moved on from the initial validation of their therapist to the public validation offered by religious leaders who found their stories helpful for evangelistic purposes. Many therapists and survivors joined a growing network of "cult experts" who advised parents, police officers, and mental health professionals based on their experience.[25]

Popular books about recovered memories often included checklists of possible symptoms for readers to self-evaluate whether they might be harboring repressed memories of past abuse. The list of symptoms was quite broad. An interest in religion, a preference for baggy clothes, promiscuity, celibacy, workaholism, breast lumps, trouble sleeping, fear of closets, fear of coffins, alertness, vagueness, and gambling were among the dozens of possible signs of satanic ritual abuse.[26]

As a growing number of people came to believe that they had been victims of a satanic cult during their childhood, these beliefs were often treated as "eyewitness testimony." Corroborating or refuting such testimony became a formidable task. At best, anyone questioning the notion of a vast satanic conspiracy could be accused of further traumatizing the victim; at worst, they could be accused of being part of the conspiracy themselves.[27]

The infamous McMartin Preschool case was not heavily publicized until February of 1984, but the first allegations surfaced in 1983. The mother of a two-year-old boy made a series of allegations to officials in Los Angeles and Manhattan Beach, California. Not only did she claim that her son had been abused by staff at the preschool, but she also said he had been victimized by strangers following her on the highway and male models she saw in advertisements. She said the perpetrators wore masks and capes, taped her child's mouth shut, jabbed him with needles and scissors, and made him drink blood. The woman was later diagnosed with paranoid schizophrenia.[28]

Following the initial allegations, investigators sent a form letter to over two hundred parents in the community, telling them their children may have been abused. In the following months, hundreds of children were interviewed by Kee MacFarlane and her associates from Children's Institute International. The interviewing techniques were designed to uncover or "draw out" memories of abuse from the young people. It was thought that the children were either repressing memories of abuse or keeping the stories secret because they had been threatened.

Child allegations of cult abuse from this time were replete with opportunities to be contaminated by stories from adults. In some thirty-five studied cases, investigators admitted to meeting with satanic conspiracy theorists, or even using written materials provided by them, while checking into claims of abuse. In 1985, during the height of the McMartin case, Ken Wooden mailed out questionnaires to over three thousand district attorneys, listing suggested questions for children in cases of suspected abuse. Some law enforcement officials even used *Michelle Remembers* as an investigative guide.[29]

By the end of the process, approximately three-hundred sixty children were said to have been ritualistically abused. Transcripts and video recordings of the interactions show the interviewers' techniques to be leading, coercive, and adult directed. Often, bizarre and horrific details were introduced to the suggestible and eager-to-please children by the interviewers themselves.

Repressed or recovered memories are extremely difficult to assess and are still considered a mystery to most experts. Recovery of traumatic memories may be possible according to some, but such memories are not likely to return in unadulterated form, untainted by images and fantasies acquired later in life.[30] People commonly repress thoughts, desires, or urges, not usually memories of past suffering. Some studies show that a small percentage of victims may forget past physical or sexual abuse, but even for those cases, recovered-memory techniques have not been proven to be reliable or accurate.

In 1993, when stories of satanic abuse were surfacing with great regularity, the American Psychiatric Association said, "It is not known how to distinguish, with complete accuracy, memories based on true events from those derived from other sources." In 1994, the American Medical Association said it "considers recovered memories of childhood sexual abuse to be of uncertain authenticity, which should be subject to external verification."[31]

Kenneth Lanning, a former FBI agent who gained notoriety for training officers how to investigate recovered memories of ritual abuse, said, "Some of what victims allege may be true and accurate, some may be misperceived or distorted, some may be screened or symbolic, and some may be 'contaminated' or false. The problem for law enforcement is to determine which is which."[32]

Satanic material is often introduced through leading questions, subtle suggestions, and even cross-contamination from stories about past cases. In one series of ritual abuse cases in Utah, each case surfaced shortly after the same therapist arrived in the community. Leading questions and coercive techniques were also enough to create doubts for the jury in the McMartin Preschool case.[33]

Satanic cult survivors were not all saying the same thing, but they were all being heard in the same way. *Michelle Remembers* did not teach clinicians to listen to and believe their clients, but rather to believe their silence was evidence of repressed trauma and brainwashing.[34]

Starting in 1990, the claims in *Michelle Remembers* began to unravel in earnest. Investigators could find no evidence to verify any of Michelle's memories. Reporters tracked down Michelle's two sisters and father, who had not been mentioned in the book. They all denied her claims of childhood abuse.[35]

In a bombshell article which debunked the claims in his book once and for all, Lawrence Pazder gave away the game. He told reporters, "It is a real experience. If you talk to Michelle today, she will say, 'That's what I remember.' We still leave the question open. For her, it was very real. Every case I hear, I have skepticism. You have to complete a long course of therapy before you can come to conclusions. We are all eager to prove or disprove what happened, but in the end it doesn't matter."[36]

14. Branded and Besmirched
July 2, 1985

When the sheriff returned to Spencer Township to continue his search for victims of a satanic cult, he chose to skip the press conference.

On Tuesday, July 2, 1985, nearly two weeks after the digging first began, Sheriff Telb gathered a team of officers and revisited the garbage-strewn wooded area at the end of Bemis Lane. Although the search was focused on the same area, the third day of digging was a much quieter affair. Some would even call it stealthy. Township officials weren't even aware of the search until later in the day, when efforts were wrapping up.

Searchers brought three police dogs to scour the area, including a bloodhound. No bodies were discovered. After eight hours of searching, Chief Deputy Tom Wilson told reporters he no longer expected to find any bodies at that location. The search was called off indefinitely.

Wilson said officers had returned to the site to reassure themselves after their confidential informants had reaffirmed that they had been digging in the correct location. Lt. Kirk Surprise justified their continued investigation, saying, "If in fact these things are going on and we just cast the allegations aside, we're not doing our job."[1]

Sheriff Telb reiterated that his information had come from confidential sources, which he still declined to identify. Telb maintained that the first excavation on June 20 and 21 had been necessary due to the upcoming summer solstice, when more sacrifices were anticipated. He also said that new information had come to light, which prompted their return to the area.[2]

When he learned that Sheriff Telb had returned to Spencer Township for more digging, Trustee D. Hilarion Smith was furious. "I notified the sheriff [after the first dig was called off on June 21] that he had twenty-four to forty-eight hours to find the first body, otherwise we were going to court to stop him. For the second time, he didn't consult us, and for the second time, he found nothing."[3]

The moment he heard digging had resumed, Smith took time off from his job as a mechanical designer to meet with reporters. Described by the press as a "slightly regal man of rare proportion," Smith pulled no punches in his criticism of Sheriff Telb and his investigators. "Society cannot put up with this kind of conduct from people who carry guns.

Maybe the sheriff thought he could get away with that kind of conduct, but he belled the wrong cat. You just don't do that in Spencer."[4]

The angry trustee continued, "So far, the sheriff's taken the view that 'I'm the sheriff, I've got the gun and I can bring the bulldozer and dig holes in your township whenever I want.' Since he has not found what he wanted, as far as I'm concerned, he's dug his own grave. And I'm going to bury him."[5]

Officer Marvin Reams, who had been shielding Sheriff Telb from reporters since the first dig, found little reason to be concerned over the trustee's comments. "He thinks this is a game, but he's protecting the interest of his constituents. We understand that. He fails to realize we were doing a police investigation and he has no jurisdiction over that. He's way out of line. He's playing a game. He thinks the sheriff is playing a game, but we know for a fact that he's playing a game."[6]

Lucas County Prosecutor Anthony Pizza would later meet with D. Hilarion Smith about the investigation, saying that Spencer Township officials had no legal recourse against the sheriff. "There's no legal action there. The trustees all agree with me that the sheriff has full authority to investigate crimes."[7]

After three days of unsuccessful digging, the raiding of one house in neighboring Springfield Township, and the public identification of another house as a cult house, Smith believed he and residents were owed a personal apology. The day after he restarted the dig, Sheriff Telb sent two deputies and a former township police chief to Trustee Smith's home, hoping they could appease township officials while acting as proxies. When he saw that the sheriff had declined to come in person, Smith was outraged.

"There are three things you don't do to me," said Smith. "You don't bribe me, you don't intimidate me, and you don't send fools to talk with me. The sheriff's very foolish not to see me. He could have avoided any contention with the township if he would have offered to see me… Now it's too late."[8]

Trustee Wilma G. Thomas was also frustrated by the sheriff's actions. She told reporters, "It's embarrassing to the trustees as a whole not to be notified of the situation. We hope that the sheriff will get with us and try to iron this thing out." Thomas also cast doubt on the veracity of the sheriff's claims. "Personally, I think it's ridiculous. I really don't think there's anything back there. I've lived out here for forty years, and I've never seen or heard anything like this."[9]

Thomas continued, "If something happens in the woods, we usually hear about it – unless they were quiet chanters." Spencer Township Clerk Evva Copeland agreed, saying, "Our population is only 1,742. You can't know everybody, but we never heard of any such thing as sacrifices being done here."[10]

Township officials were not the only ones who wanted the sheriff to answer for his actions. Alvin and Patricia Litton, whose home had been raided by deputies, maintained they had never heard of Leroy Freeman or his alleged cult. In the days following the investigation, the Littons said they and their five children had been subjected to unrelenting public scrutiny and ridicule.

"It really gets to me," said Patricia Litton. "People come by and yell, 'child killer,' 'murderer,' things like that. Come bedtime, it's really hard to get these kids to sleep. They're really scared."[11]

Laretta Harris was also scared. She told reporters that she had faced significant hardship since her home had been incorrectly identified as a cult house during the sheriff's press conference. Her home contained five Bibles and assorted religious knickknacks and she insisted she had never been involved with a cult. "The sheriff apologized to me and said the picture wasn't even supposed to be shown to the press. You know what I told him? That he and his deputies are all a bunch of idiots."[12]

In the 1980s, Jim Peters was the music director at Zion Christian Life Center in St. Paul, Minnesota. By then, he had already gained a bit of notoriety within Christian circles for conducting seminars that warned parents and youth about the dangers of rock and roll music. Alongside his brothers, Dan and Steve, Jim Peters spoke at numerous churches and showcased a documentary film called *Truth About Rock*. The Peters brothers also instigated a record-burning campaign in 1978.[13]

It's unclear if Jim Peters was the first person to publicize rumors about a hidden meaning behind the Procter & Gamble logo, but his allegations were certainly among the earliest. In a 1980 article for *The Minneapolis Tribune*, Peters claimed to have found evidence that the corporate logo had ties to ancient occult practices. Allegedly, Peters had found a copy of the logo in a book called *Amulets and Superstition* by British Egyptologist E.A. Wallis Budge.[14]

Procter & Gamble was a well-known consumer goods corporation, specializing in a variety of beauty, grooming, health, and home care products. Since their founding in 1837, P&G had diversified their portfolio, acquiring and managing such popular consumer brands as Ivory soap, Pampers diapers, Pepto-Bismol, Folgers coffee, Iams, Pantene, Old Spice, and others.

After his initial allegations in *The Minneapolis Tribune,* Peters openly warned churchgoers to avoid Procter & Gamble products. Paul Martin, director of a Minnesota Youth for Christ high school club, recalls, "These three brothers from the Zion Christian Life Center – Dan, Steve, and Jim Peters – came to speak to my boys to tell them to burn their rock music albums. They showed a slide of the Procter & Gamble symbol and said it was the same as the Church of Satan in Minnesota." Martin was skeptical though. He added, "I felt like rock music was doing more damage on kids than a product symbol."[15]

There were also fleeting allegations that the moon and stars in the P&G logo were definitive proof that the Cincinnati-based company had been taken over by devotees of the "Moonie" cult, Reverend Sun Myung Moon's Unification Church.[16]

When word of these rumors reached Procter & Gamble, the company largely ignored the allegations. A member of the company's public relations team responded to the 1980 *Tribune* article, saying, "This is the kind of rumor we can't do anything about. People will believe what they want to."[17]

And people did.

In January 1982, newspapers across the Midwest began running cheeky headlines like, "Soap Baron Battles Devilish Rumors," as claims about the P&G logo began to resurface.

The new rumors took a particular interest in the moon man's beard. Each curl in the mascot's hair and beard vaguely resembled the number six. In some sections of the image, these curls were grouped in threes. This pattern, along with a purported design within the thirteen stars, was said to represent the number 666, or the biblical Mark of the Beast.[18]

In the spring of 1982, someone mailed thousands of mimeographed letters to residents throughout California, alleging that the P&G logo was a symbol of devil worship. As a result of those anonymous mailings, P&G's Ohio headquarters became inundated with over 15,000 concerned phone calls and angry letters throughout June and July of 1982.[19]

Procter & Gamble executives were perplexed by the allegations. They publicly denied the rumors and did everything they could to reassure concerned customers that their beloved household brands had no connection to Satan. They reiterated that P&G had been using the same logo for one hundred years and that the symbols therein contained no secret meanings. Having responded to the public, the company decided to give it a little time. The gossip had died down once before; surely it would die down again. How long could the rumors possibly persist?

Early in 1985, mysterious leaflets began appearing all over the New York metropolitan area. No author was named, but each copy was boldly addressed "To All Christians."

According to the leaflets, a high-ranking executive from P&G had appeared on a national television program to discuss Satanism. Some versions of the flier said it happened on *The Phil Donahue Show* (also known as *Donahue*). Others claimed it happened on *60 Minutes* or *The Merv Griffin Show*. During this alleged television appearance, the company man had also openly boasted about sharing profits with the Church of Satan.[20]

Having been vexed by the same problem for more than four years, Procter & Gamble decided to take a more direct approach. Their strategic, multipronged assault on misinformation began on April 17, 1985, when the company held a press conference. A senior vice president named W. Wallace Abbott spoke about the rumors, saying, "They simply are not true. We haven't the vaguest idea how it started, all we know is people are believing it. Do you know how hard it is to fight a rumor?" Abbott also denied serving the Church of Satan, adding, "We didn't know what that was until we started getting these calls. We're still not sure what it is."[21]

The company also prepared and distributed tens of thousands of anti-rumor kits, which included a history of the company logo and supportive letters from *The Phil Donahue Show*. Producers of the show, who had received over one hundred phone calls because of the anonymous leaflets, wrote, "It never happened! Anyone who claims to have seen such a broadcast is lying! Anyone repeating the rumor is bearing false witness!"[22]

Procter & Gamble also set up a toll-free phone line to address the rumors, which connected directly to the company's Cincinnati headquarters. The company received over 9,600 calls in two months. Thanks to the recently distributed flyers, around sixty percent of these calls came from New York, New Jersey, and Pennsylvania.[23]

Because the messaging had targeted Christians, P&G also reached out to prominent religious leaders. They asked notable figures such as Jerry Falwell and Billy Graham to speak out against the rumors, along with various cardinals and archbishops throughout the area. Monseigneur Franklyn M. Casale of the Archdiocese of Newark sent out a firm letter to the churches under his jurisdiction, warning them that "a false rumor is being circulated by some groups in our parishes."[24]

Procter & Gamble also announced they would be taking legal action against individuals or organizations who played a role in spreading the rumors. They hired two private investigation firms to root out the sources of misinformation. At the time of the press conference, five lawsuits had already been filed against seven individuals.[25]

While the earliest rumors had been treated as inconsequential, the lasting impact became impossible to ignore. By 1985, Procter & Gamble estimated they had spent over $100,000 to combat misinformation. Given the widespread call for consumer boycott, the company almost certainly suffered a loss in sales. A company spokesperson at the time said, "It's impossible to determine a specific figure, but we must be losing money. We get hundreds of calls from people who say they will not buy our products."[26]

Despite significant ramifications for the company, some treated the situation as a joke. A Chicago based advertising magazine held a contest, asking readers to design a new logo for P&G. Many of the reader submissions took on a playful or mocking tone, including one design which added devil horns to the existing logo and another which featured two angels carrying the company name. Some of these tongue-in-cheek images were reprinted nationally in *The Wall Street Journal*.[27]

As the company invested time and resources to combat the rumors, some wondered if it might be easier for Procter & Gamble to simply jettison the old logo and create something new. Why not start over?

"It's on buildings, it's on stationery, it identifies Procter & Gamble. It doesn't stand for anything but our company," said Senior Vice President Abbott. "We will not change it."[28]

The company did keep their logo, but by the end of 1985, P&G had removed the symbol from all consumer-facing product packaging. Surely, the rumors were gone for good this time. Surely.

The Brooklyn Bottling Company was on the verge of bankruptcy in 1987. In hopes of generating more sales, they began producing a new line of sodas. Because these sodas were inexpensive to produce, they could be sold at a lower price. They began marketing and selling these cheaper sodas in various lower-income communities throughout the area.

In 1990, the company introduced Tropical Fantasy, a new flavor which quickly became popular. Shortly thereafter, mysterious fliers began to circulate throughout predominantly Black communities.

"ATTENTION!!! ATTENTION!!! ATTENTION!!!" read the flier. "BLACKS AND MINORITY GROUPS. DID YOU SEE (T.V. SHOW) 20/20? Top Pop & Tropical Fantasy 50 cent sodas are being manufactured by the Ku Klux Klan. Sodas contain stimulants to sterilize the Black man, and who knows what else!!! They are only put in stores in Harlem and minority areas. You won't find them downtown. Look around. YOU HAVE BEEN WARNED. PLEASE SAVE THE CHILDREN."[29]

The company tried to combat the rumors with information campaigns and "truth kits," and they even got an endorsement from the mayor, but the damage was done. By 1991, sales had dropped by 70 percent.

In 1991, Reverend Jay Hurley switched to Cottonelle toilet paper. The pastor of Greenbriar Baptist Church in Boonsboro, Maryland had previously stocked his bathroom with rolls of P&G's White Cloud, but those days were behind him. Hurley told *The Washington Post*, "I didn't buy Folgers coffee either; I'm going to replace that brand with Nestle's."[30]

Hurley was one of thousands of Americans who continued boycotting Procter & Gamble products well into the 1990s, fully convinced that the company was in league with the Devil.

In mid-to-late 1991, anonymous fliers began circulating around rural Maryland. The latest version of the flier was headlined, "The Phil Donahue Show," in large, bold font. In this version of the story, the president of Procter & Gamble had appeared on *Donahue* on March 1, 1991. On the program, the company man allegedly announced that he was "coming out of the closet" about his ongoing support of the Church of Satan. Misspelling the name of the corporation, the flier went on to claim, "He stated that a large portion of the profits from Proctor & Gamble products goes to the support of the church."

When Phil Donahue asked if such an alliance would hurt their sales, the president of P&G made his most villainous assertion yet: he looked smugly into the camera and boasted, "There are not enough Christians in the U.S. to make a difference."[31]

When a friend gave him the flier, Reverend Hurley wasted no time passing it along. He distributed copies throughout his congregation and posted one on the church bulletin board.

"Before the service, I read it to my congregation. I made copies of it and asked them to take the copy with them to the store. I asked them not to buy these products," said Hurley.[32] The rumors were also passed on to neighboring congregations.

Much of the information on the flier could have been easily debunked with an even cursory glance at the facts. For example, the flier listed forty-nine P&G products and encouraged Christians to go to the store and check for themselves by finding the hidden 666 within the bearded face of the company logo. This would have been impossible at the time, as the logo had been removed from all products in 1985.

Similarly, the allegations about *Donahue* could have been easily debunked. The flier had given a specific date when the president of P&G allegedly took to the airwaves in celebration of the Dark Lord. On the date mentioned, March 1, 1991, no such episode aired. In some areas of the country, viewers that day saw an episode entitled, "Families of Hostages: Lebanon, Iraq, and Vietnam." In other areas of the country, viewers saw an episode entitled, "How to Cheat on Your Spouse and Not Get Caught."[33]

Much like the rumors in 1985, the latest round of fliers triggered an influx of phone calls to *Donahue*. There were so many calls to the program's New York headquarters, they set up a voicemail recording that said, "If you are calling about Procter & Gamble, press 6 now... The president of

Procter & Gamble has never ever appeared on the 'Donahue' show. If your family and friends say they've seen it, they are quite mistaken."[34]

Even though the claims in the flier were demonstrably false, there is no indication that anyone had bothered checking the veracity of the information before passing it on. Speaking with *The Washington Post*, Reverend Jay Hurley encouraged others to boycott while acknowledging his own uncertainty about the claims. He said, "If it is true, I hope the boycott grows. It's time to take a stand. The Bible speaks against Devil worship."[35]

Procter & Gamble again found themselves investing time and resources to combat the rumors. Throughout 1990 and 1991, the company received between 50 and 350 calls every day. Company representatives issued a public statement calling the rumors "poppycock," and Reverend Jerry Falwell told the press, "The people who have spent much of the past six years attacking Procter & Gamble for its corporate logo could make better use of their time fighting real and serious problems in our society."[36]

The company would eventually redesign the logo, straightening the mascot's beard to eliminate the problematic curls. Even then, the company denied that this change was a concession to their opponents. The eventual redesign was intended to give the logo a "friendlier, modern, global look."[37]

By 1995, Procter & Gamble had found a degree of success in identifying the culprits behind the rumors and holding them accountable. Some of the rumors were traced back to the Peters brothers from Zion Christian Life Center in Minnesota. A television weatherman from Atlanta had also spread the rumors during speaking engagements before local community groups.[38]

Even a competing company had gotten involved. Two door-to-door salesmen from Amway spread rumors to their clients, and one Amway distributor even confessed to using their automated phone system to send out a message telling thousands of customers that Procter & Gamble supported satanic cults. That distributor later sent out a second message retracting the statement, but the damage was done. P&G filed more than a dozen libel lawsuits, and ultimately won $19.25 million from Amway in a civil suit.[39]

In 2013, Procter & Gamble introduced a simplified logo, featuring the company's initials within a blue circle. Along one edge of the circle is a simple crescent shape, a subtle reference to the moon and stars design of the original trademark. By then, the story had persisted for so long, the

Church of Satan had published a statement on their website, specifying that rumors were false.[40]

In 1978, two years before the earliest rumors about Procter & Gamble, a letter arrived at the McDonald's corporate headquarters in Illinois. In the letter, an Ohio woman wanted to know if it was true that McDonald's founder Ray Kroc donated twenty percent of the fast-food chain's profits to the Church of Satan. Officials laughed it off, thinking it was a joke.

Then more letters came.

By October 1978, the questions and complaints became impossible to ignore.[41] Puzzled by the persistence of this misinformation, McDonald's sifted through piles of correspondence, piecing together a rough timeline of the spread of the rumor. The trail led them to Akron, Ohio.

A pastor in the Kenmore neighborhood of Akron, Reverend John Macfarland, told the McDonald's communication team that a former parishioner had told him a shocking story which he immediately printed in his church newsletter.

The pastor wrote, "It was brought to my attention a few days ago that the president of McDonald's Inc., a multimillion-dollar enterprise, recently appeared on *The Phil Donahue Show*, a nationwide syndicated TV program." Disclosing that Mr. Kroc had proudly pledged to share his profits with the Church of Satan, the pastor continued, "Every time you and I have eaten at McDonald's, we have unknowingly been financially supporting the worship of Satan and the promotion of his cause. Just the thought of it makes me feel sick inside. I don't think I can ever eat at another McDonald's under those conditions."[42]

It turns out, Mr. Kroc had appeared on *Donahue*. The episode first aired in May of 1977 and was repeated in June of 1978, but there was no mention of Satan or devil worship. After the church newsletter in Akron, the rumor spread rapidly from church to church.

McDonald's considered an advertising campaign to combat the rumors, but ultimately decided on a quieter approach. Company executives visited church groups throughout the country, distributing sworn statements from television producers attesting that Ray Kroc had never gone on television to talk about Satan. A few years later, the rumors would shift to Procter & Gamble. After that, similar stories began to surface about the women's fashion company Liz Claiborne.

When he realized the information was false, Reverend Macfarland of Akron was deeply embarrassed. He issued an apology and printed a full retraction in the next edition of his church newsletter. By then, the fire had spread. When asked about the parishioner who shared the initial story with him, Macfarland said, "She evidently wanted to hear it so bad, she just heard what she wanted."[43]

15. Burying the Hatchet
July 10, 1985

On the same day D. Hilarion Smith had arranged to meet with Lucas County Prosecutor Anthony Pizza to explore his legal options, Sheriff James Telb was summoned to a regularly scheduled trustee meeting to account for his actions. Three weeks had passed since the media spectacle first began and many people in Spencer Township were still waiting for answers. In stark contrast to the highly publicized dig, only a few local reporters attended the meeting.

As the meeting began, Township Hall overflowed with residents who had come to hear the sheriff defend his investigation. Despite the oppressive heat, approximately fifty people crammed into the small room. Others stood outside the building, listening from beyond the door or through the open windows. Most were there only to hear the sheriff. There was a mass exodus from the building as soon as his comments concluded.[1]

Sheriff Telb was not apologetic about his investigation, but he was not unsympathetic. He said he would continue digging in Spencer Township if he found cause to do so, but he promised to keep future phases of the investigation quiet. He blamed the media for disrupting the lives of township residents. Telb assured those present that, if he came back to dig again, he would not tell anyone.

When the dig began, Telb went on record saying, "There is no question about the cult operating here." On the night of the trustee meeting, the sheriff took on a more tentative tone. "If in fact there is a cult – and I say if – it involves a lot of people," he said. "We've always said if our information is correct – if, if, if."[2]

As his brief comments concluded, most people were satisfied with the sheriff's assurances. Some questioned why the sheriff started digging before he had any evidence of human remains. Walter Miller, who had owned property in the area for over twenty years, said, "I'm curious about why your department didn't ask informants where the bodies were."[3]

Sheriff Telb replied, "We did not dig the whole township up. We dug in three separate spots." He also said deputy sheriffs had used infrared photography, police dogs, and archaeological consultants to help pinpoint where to dig. Sheriff Telb did not believe his informants were lying or wrong, but he acknowledged that their information was "just maybe not totally, fully accurate."[4]

Explaining why he had not given advance notice to township officials, Telb cited two reasons: secrecy and urgency. Telb said he had only been able to share information with a select team of officers. He also repeated his belief that it was necessary for the search to happen before June 21, because the summer solstice was an important observance for devil worshipers. "If there was a cult out here and if they had been planning a sacrifice on the summer solstice, we scared them off."[5]

In the days following the media frenzy, some had characterized the sheriff as defensive. During the trustee meeting, Telb expressed confidence in his decision to proceed with the investigation. "Some critics say, 'You've got egg on your face.' Whatever. We'll take egg on our face before blood on our hands," said Telb.[6]

Chairman D. Hilarion Smith had been a vocal opponent of the investigation since the beginning, but he accepted the sheriff's explanation of events. If the sheriff believed people had been killed, the man was just doing his duty. "What we disagreed with is the manner in which he performed his duties," said Smith. He concluded by expressing confidence that this public meeting had successfully brought the dispute to an end.[7]

Part Two:

Digging Deeper

16. From the Case Files of Lt. Kirk Surprise

The following information comes directly from the official case report, obtained from the records department of the Lucas County Sheriff's Office. The contents of the case report have been summarized in narrative form. Section headings have been added by the author for the benefit of the reader.[1]

June 8, 1985

To: Chief Deputy Tom Wilson

From: Lieutenant Kirk Surprise
    Corporal Ronald Collins
    Deputy Sheriff Trilby Cashin

Subject: Investigation into Local Cult Activities

The Initial Phone Call
April 17, 1985
Approx. 1100 hrs.

Lt. Surprise received a telephone call from a woman who wished to initiate an investigation into the activities of a local cult, which she believed had connections to missing children.

Before telling her story, the woman said she felt it was necessary to establish her credibility because the events in question were somewhat unbelievable. She disclosed that she was a member of the local school board. The woman went on to share her true name, address, and telephone number, but because of the sensitive nature of the situation, she insisted that officers refer to her by a pseudonym. Throughout the investigation, this contact is referred to solely as "Mrs. Jones."

Mrs. Jones said she had initially called the Children's Services Board regarding the matter, but they had referred her to the Homicide Squad of the Toledo Police Department. When it was determined that the locations involved fell under the jurisdiction of the Sheriff's Department, Mrs. Jones called Lt. Surprise.

The caller went on to explain that she had a friend who had recently joined her church. This friend wanted to report some activities involving a coven of witches and the sacrifice of children to Satan. Mrs. Jones said her friend had been a member of the cult before leaving the group and rejoining the Christian church. The friend had shown Mrs. Jones a site where satanic rituals had occurred, a site where victims of human sacrifice were buried, and at least two homes where cult members lived.

Surprise arranged a time to meet with Mrs. Jones and her friend.

First Meeting with the Confidential Informant
April 17, 1985
Approx. 1430 hrs.

Surprise arrived at Mrs. Jones' residence, accompanied by Sgt. George Damasco. Mrs. Jones introduced her friend as "Sandy," stating that the informant did not want her real name to be used in reports or taped conversations because she feared retaliation from other cult members. In the report, Surprise made a note that both he and his sergeant knew Sandy's true identity. The conversation was recorded and transcribed.

Mrs. Jones explained that she had recently seen a television special about ritual abuse and satanic worship. The day after the special aired, Mrs. Jones mentioned it to Sandy, asking her if she could imagine such ritual abuse taking place. Sandy replied that yes, she could imagine such a thing, because she had been involved in a satanic group herself.

Mrs. Jones went on to explain that Sandy had left the cult and joined the Christian church because the satanic rituals she had witnessed were too "horrible." During Mrs. Jones' introduction, the officers noted that Sandy was shaking and visibly nervous.

When prompted to share her story, Sandy said she was aware of many activities being carried out by a satanic cult in Lucas County. She said the cult often brought children from other places to use in their rituals. Sometimes they used local children. When asked if she knew of any child victims from the Toledo area, Sandy said she knew of one for certain, but there were probably more.

Sandy could not provide the name of the local child she mentioned because names were never used during the satanic rituals. She described the girl as pretty and young, probably five or six years old, with blonde hair. When asked for clarification, Sandy said this child had been sacrificed during a ritual sometime in the late 1970s at a house on State Route 295 in Spencer Township.

The informant indicated she had personally witnessed the sacrifice. Sandy said the girl was in a trance when cult members brought her into a ritual space and killed her. When asked to explain in further detail, Sandy said the girl died of suffocation while a member of the cult sexually assaulted her. She said the perpetrator was a large Black man named Alex. Sandy also said she personally witnessed the girl being buried and could show officers where to find the grave.

The officers asked Sandy when she last visited the house on State Route 295, where the alleged murder had happened. She said she had been there three weeks prior, sometime in late March. She had gone to the house with her husband to visit a woman. Surprise noted in the report that further questioning "at this point revealed that the lady was called Circe and that she is the real owner of the property on 295." Although Sandy claimed Circe had gone to Mexico and had not yet returned, Surprise wrote that Circe was known to be back in Toledo at the time of the interview.

Sandy proceeded to give descriptions of two other locations on Schwamberger Road where cult meetings allegedly took place. She also shared more about Circe. Sandy believed Circe was the true owner of the cult house on State Route 295, not the current occupants. Circe used to be a registered nurse in a Toledo hospital, according to Sandy, and while the woman did spend some time at the cult house in Spencer Township, she mostly stayed at a house she owned in Toledo.

Sandy talked about a man she knew who was heavily into satanism. She described him as a large, Black man who went by the name of Willie. Willie lived at the end of Meilke Road, near Bemis Lane. His house appeared to be abandoned, but Sandy said it wasn't. Willie spent a lot of time with Alex, the man who had killed the young girl during a ritual.

Sandy said Alex was the leader of the group and that he was instrumental in "breaking in" new girls who were brought into the cult. Those joining the cult had to be initiated by presenting themselves to Alex sexually. During these initiation rituals, Alex would usually be seated in a chair, completely naked except for various pieces of elaborate and symbolic jewelry which depicted naked men and women intertwined.

When asked how many people would usually attend cult gatherings, Sandy said it would depend on the type of meeting being held. She had seen as many as one thousand attendees in the past, but that event took place in a secret underground temple. The hidden temple could be accessed by passing through Circe's store front in Toledo, which disguised the entrance. During the day, items were bought and sold in the shop, but cult members could go through the store, down into a "huge subterranean temple." Sandy said people came from all over the country to visit the temple.

Surprise asked what sort of activities could be expected "at her level" of the cult. Sandy indicated she was at the third level. She did not know what was required of fourth level members, other than finding people to be used as sacrifices. To join the cult, Sandy said one must believe in Satan and "really want to do whatever they're commanded to do, no matter what was required."

Sandy said the typical sacrificial altar was small and portable so it could be easily stored when not in use. The altar would usually contain an inverted cross with Jesus hanging upside down. There would also be a sword stuck into the Jesus figure, or into the cross. The altar table would be prepared with candles, a bowl of blood, and whatever instrument was needed for the specific ritual being performed, most commonly a sword or knife. Sandy also indicated that higher-ranking members of the cult had portable altars in their homes.

At this point, officers asked Sandy how many children had been killed. She said she had personally witnessed two burials at the end of Meilke Road. Sgt. Damasco and Lt. Surprise suggested Sandy take a ride with them in their car to point out the cult houses on State Route 295 and the burial sites. Mrs. Jones and Sandy agreed to come along.

As they were leaving Mrs. Jones' house, they asked Sandy when the next cult meeting was scheduled to take place. She said the next meeting would be on Saturday, April 20, at one of the houses on State Route 295. She was not sure what type of meeting it was going to be, but she knew a gathering was scheduled.

In the car, Surprise took out a photo of Charity Freeman, a child who had been missing from Lucas County since 1982. He showed Sandy the photo and asked if she had ever seen the girl before. Surprise noted in the report that Sandy seemed "hesitant" before answering, "I've never seen this picture."

Surprise wrote, "It should be noted that this officer was watching Sandy's reactions in the rear-view mirror, and it was obvious to this officer that Sandy did, in fact, know who the girl in the picture was; if not by name, at least by sight."

Surprise then showed Sandy a picture of Leroy Freeman, Charity's grandfather who was wanted for stealing the child from their home. Sandy reacted to this second photo the same way as the first, indicating she had never seen it before. Both Damasco and Surprise later agreed that the woman was lying.

In the case report, Surprise typed the next paragraph in capital letters, apparently for emphasis: "IT MUST BE NOTED AT THIS POINT, THAT THE HOME ON STATE ROUTE 295 IN SPENCER TOWNSHIP, POINTED OUT BY SANDY AS THE LOCATION OF THE LAST SACRIFICE SHE PERSONALLY WITNESSED, IS THE EXACT SAME HOUSE THAT CHARITY FREEMAN WAS REPORTED MISSING FROM BY HER MOTHER, KAREN FREEMAN, IN 1982, ALLEGEDLY STOLEN FROM KAREN FREEMAN BY LEROY FREEMAN, KAREN'S FATHER. AS OF THE DATE OF THIS INTERVIEW, THE MAILBOX FOR THIS HOUSE BEARS THE NAME OF 'CAMPOS.'"

After Sandy pointed out the other cult houses on Schwamberger Road, they proceeded to the end of Meilke Road, turning south off Angola. They came to a dirt lane extending from the intersection of Meilke Road and Bemis Lane. There they saw a circular turnaround along the edge of a large ditch. Sandy pointed to the spots where she claimed to have witnessed the burial of two little girls. Sandy said many other bodies were buried further back from the road, in what appeared to be an old, disused farmer's field. She also referred to an old house which was now nothing more than a foundation.

When asked about grave markers, Sandy stated that each victim's grave was marked by a stake at the time of the burial. Each stake was marked with a goat's head, representing Satan. Sandy did not know what happened to the stakes after the burial was completed. She said she had marked the graves of the two little girls herself, using chunks of broken cinder blocks. The report noted that no cinder blocks could be seen in the area.

Sandy, Mrs. Jones, and the two officers spent thirty minutes at the site, trying to find the exact location of the graves. Sandy said she could not find them because the area had become overgrown. She insisted she was in the right general location because she remembered standing alongside the fence and looking toward the dirt lane.

After half an hour of searching, Sandy became very concerned about being seen. Her main concern was "Weird Willie," who she said lived in the area. This was the same Willie she had mentioned earlier in the interview, in connection with the satanic cult. Sandy told officers that the area at the end of Bemis Lane was basically Willie's backyard and that he roamed the property carrying a shotgun. She claimed the man would not hesitate to kill them.

All parties returned to Mrs. Jones' house. Surprise told Sandy they would work to verify some of the things she had shared, then reconnect with her for further information. The interview ended at 1600 hrs.

Preliminary Reconnaissance
April 18, 1985
Approx. 1000 hrs.

Surprise contacted Deputy Sheriff Trilby Cashin from the Lucas County Sheriff's Department Photo/Crime Lab, asking her to collect the necessary equipment to take surveillance photos of the areas mentioned by the confidential informant one day prior. Together, they drove to Schwamberger Road.

The two officers pretended to be a photographer and a model, with Cashin posing while Surprise took photos. Under this guise, they took photos of the various locations where Sandy said cult activities had taken place.

The final stop was the burial site on Meilke Road. Once again, the officers posed as a photographer and model, believing the ruse would give them cover to get out of the car and walk to the sites Sandy had identified. While photographing the area, Surprise found a small child's saddle shoe lying in some brush, which he confiscated.

As they walked further into the field, Cashin found what appeared to be torn pieces of cloth, which were black and flimsy in texture. These fragments, which were also confiscated, were discovered under fern bushes.

After capturing their desired photos, the two officers began walking back to their car. They saw a blue Chevrolet Chevette approaching the area from Angola Road. In the report, Surprise noted what happened next.

"This vehicle, rather than swing west onto Bemis Lane, simply stopped on Meilke at the approach to the dirt lane and observed us. At this point, this officer took several photographs of Dep. Cashin in the lane area and slowly proceeded back to my vehicle. I sat in my vehicle and observed the blue Chevette back into Bemis Lane, as if turning around to return to Angola Road. Rather than returning to Angola Road, it again stopped, and the occupant just watched us."

When Cashin reached the vehicle, the blue Chevette drove off. The officers could tell the driver was a white female. As the car drove away, north on Meilke, Cashin was able to capture a photograph.

Briefing the Chief Deputy
April 18, 1985
Approx. 1430 hrs.

Officers Surprise and Cashin returned to the Sheriff's Department and briefed Chief Deputy Tom Wilson on the status of the investigation. Chief Wilson indicated that, based on what he was hearing, it was time to bring the county prosecutor up to speed. They contacted the prosecutor's office and scheduled a meeting for the following morning.

Developing and Analyzing Photographs
April 18, 1985
Approx. 1500 hrs.

Surprise and Cashin proceeded to the Photo/Crime Lab, along with Corporal Ronald Collins, to develop the photographs taken earlier in the day. Due to the "unusual appearance" of the blue Chevette they had seen on a "normally desolate road," they also developed the photo Cashin had taken of the vehicle. After enlarging the photo several times, they were able to obtain the license plate number and identify the driver.

Neither the person nor vehicle had any known connection to the investigation.

Briefing the Prosecutor's Office
April 19, 1985
Approx. 0900 hrs.

A briefing was held in the Chief's conference room to share information about the investigation with the prosecutor's office. Present at the meeting were Chief Deputy Tom Wilson, Lt. Kirk Surprise, Deputy Trilby Cashin, and Corporal Ronald Collins of the Lucas County Sheriff's Department, along with Chief Assistant Prosecutor Curt Posner and Assistant Prosecuting Attorney George Runner. Later, Chief Deputy Kenneth Perry would join the meeting, along with Public Information Officer Marvin Reams. Bud Weaver, a detective from the Oregon Police Department, also joined the meeting to provide technical consultation related to the photographic evidence.

The group discussed the facts of the case and explored future investigative options. They decided to carry out some preliminary digging at the burial site later that afternoon. Collins and Detective Daryll Symington were sent to the County Recorder to determine the ownership of the various properties involved. Dr. G. Michael Pratt, an archaeologist from a nearby university who was conducting some excavations nearby, agreed to accompany officers to the site to render any expert assistance possible.

Preliminary Digging
April 19, 1985
Approx. 1330 hrs.

Surprise and Cashin met with the two men from the prosecutor's office and the archaeologist at the Sheriff's Department substation at King and Angola Roads. After gathering some necessary equipment, they drove to the burial site at 1400 hrs. Pratt, the archeologist, indicated that, if there were graves present, it might be possible to see the various layers of moved earth by digging some test holes at the suspected site.

The area believed to be a grave site was limited to one hundred square yards alongside the fence at the south end of the dirt lane. They dug approximately three test holes, but the results were inconclusive. Pratt suggested a bulldozer could be used to layer the area since the overgrowth made hand digging impossible. The preliminary digging ended at approximately 1530 hrs.

When Surprise and Cashin returned to the Sheriff's Department to update Chief Wilson, they learned that Marvin Reams had arranged a meeting with Chief Deputy Dale Griffis of the Tiffin Police Department. Griffis had agreed to come to Lucas County to share information regarding cult activity as he was "considered an expert in the area." The meeting was scheduled for the following evening, the soonest Griffis was available.

Greeting the Occult Expert
April 20, 1985
Approx. 1700 hrs.

Surprise and Cashin met with Marvin Reams and Dale Griffis in the lobby of the Holiday Inn. After some preliminary conversation, it was determined that a complete briefing would be needed to discuss surveillance techniques for the upcoming observation of the suspected cult house on State Route 295. According to the confidential informant's tip, a cult meeting would take place that evening. At the full briefing, Griffis would provide background information about the occult. The briefing was scheduled for approximately one hour later at the Sheriff's Department.

Briefing with the Occult Expert
April 20, 1985
Approx. 1800 hrs.

A team assembled at the Lucas County Sheriff's Department to prepare for that evening's surveillance. Dale Griffis joined Lt. Surprise, Deputy Cashin, and Corporal Collins, along with Marvin Reams, who was serving as liaison officer. Detective Bud Weaver from the Oregon Police Department was also present, along with four Lucas County Sheriff's Deputies who would be providing backup during the operation.

The team sketched out their plan and assigned roles. Surprise, Cashin, and Collins would enter on foot, hiding in a wooded area just east of the target house. From this secluded vantage point, they would watch and listen for any cult activity. One deputy would be in a marked police vehicle, parked just north of the target house. Another deputy would be in a marked vehicle covering the entrance to Meilke Road at Angola. Two deputies would be circling the area in an unmarked vehicle, beginning just south of the target house. Griffis, Reams, and Weaver would also be circling the area in an unmarked vehicle.

During this meeting, Dale Griffis also provided a "briefing on white and black witchcraft, depicting the signs and symbols associated with both."

Surveillance at the Suspected Cult House
April 20, 1985
Approx. 2200 hrs.

The onsite team of three arrived at their position in the wooded area east of the house. After giving radio confirmation to their backup units, the team noticed that several cars appeared to be driving up and down State Route 295. Based on the briefing with Griffis and prior information provided by their confidential informant, these passing vehicles were believed to be "sentries" keeping watch for the cult.

The case report noted that lights were turned on in the target house until after 2300 hours, "when they suddenly went off." The report also noted that the house directly north of the target house had a light in their yard, which turned off and on several times before remaining off.

Almost immediately after the lights went out, a vehicle exited the driveway of the target house and turned north. At this point, passing vehicles continued to drive by the wooded area where the team was hiding, "slowing down more and more with each pass." Because they could see these passing cars, the team moved throughout the woods to stay out of sight. They changed positions four times.

At 2358 hours, all three team members heard a dog bark two or three times in a row, followed by a bark that abruptly ended in a yelp.

At 2400 hours, Surprise and Collins "distinctly heard a female scream for a period of three to five seconds." Cashin could not positively state she had heard a scream.

Just after midnight, "a chorus of male voices could be heard chanting" for approximately thirty seconds. The voices were saying, "MORE, MORE, MORE." This chanting was immediately followed by organ music. After this, the area fell silent again. All these sounds came from the heavily wooded area behind the target house.

Because they could still see vehicles on the road, "the team decided to abandon its position after being convinced of being detected by the sentries." They attempted to call for a car to pick them up, but this attempt failed. After switching to another channel, the team was able to make contact and arrange a pickup.

Debriefing After Surveillance
April 21, 1985
Approx. 0130 hrs.

The entire team gathered at the Sheriff's Department substation for debriefing. The three officers who had been hiding in the woods soon learned that one of the cars driving slowly past the woods had not been occupied by sentries for the cult after all. When the team was first dispatched on foot, Dale Griffis and Marvin Reams had not heard the predetermined code spoken over the radio for confirmation. Out of concern, they proceeded to drive slowly up and down the road, searching for the team in the woods. At least one of the suspicious vehicles spotted by the surveillance team had been driven by their own colleagues.

Upon learning that Griffis and Reams had not heard the radio code, and because there had been trouble with the radios when the team attempted to arrange an extraction, Surprise checked the equipment. He found the radios in perfect working order. Surprise seemed puzzled by this development, writing, "There is no explanation for that fact."

One of the deputies stationed in a marked police car believed they may have also heard a female screaming, but deputies stationed in the other vehicles had heard nothing.

The on-site team proceeded to tell Griffis about the chanting they had heard. He said he believed some sort of ritual had taken place, although he was unwilling to say for certain if it had been a human sacrifice. Because the on-site team had been approximately three hundred yards away from the target area, they could hear the sounds coming from the woods, but could not get visual confirmation of what had transpired.

Based on the calendar the cultists seemed to be using, Griffis told the team he believed they were dealing with a non-traditional cult. He said the upcoming date of April 24 would likely be a significant night for cult members as they prepared for an upcoming holiday. April 30 would be "WALPERSNACHT," or the night of fire, when satanic cults traditionally commemorated the burning of witches in Salem, Massachusetts. On that night, cult members would be very afraid, and at sunrise they would "cleanse their souls in the dew of the dawn."

Griffis suggested further observation on the nights he mentioned, offering to loan the department specialized equipment for night surveillance. The debriefing concluded around 0230 hours.

Further Preparations
April 22, 1985
Approx. 1000 hrs.

Contact was made with Mrs. Jones, asking for her help in scheduling another interview with Sandy "to further explore the situation with the cult and to try to identify some members." A meeting was scheduled for later that day.

Around 1030 hours, Surprise and Cashin met with Detective Weaver to discuss the possibility of aerial photography over the sites on State Route 295 and Meilke Road. Weaver suggested the use of both color and infrared photography. The detective also said he was friends with a pilot named Dr. Culver and that he would arrange for the doctor to fly them over the area in his airplane.

17. Confessions on Cassette Tape: April 22

Meeting with the Confidential Informant – Recorded Interview
April 22, 1985
Approx. 1745 hrs.

At an unnamed neutral location in western Lucas County, Lt. Surprise and Deputy Cashin met with Mrs. Jones and Sandy for the second time. The interview was recorded on cassette tape and later transcribed in full.

Sandy said she had been involved in the occult since 1965, having been introduced by her father-in-law while living in Laredo, Texas. In 1969, she relocated to Perrysburg Township, Ohio, where she became involved with the cult in Lucas County. There was a group of approximately thirty members in Perrysburg Heights which functioned as a satellite group of the main cult in Toledo.

Sandy said cult meetings could have up to one or two hundred attendees, especially on important dates. When asked why the group in Lucas County was larger than the one in Perrysburg Township, Sandy said this group was higher in rank within the cult's organizational structure.

The cult was based out of a house in Toledo. According to Sandy, one of the leaders was a large Black man named Alex. There was also a white man, but she could not remember his name. Sandy could also not remember the name of the cult. At one point, she referred to people in the Detroit chapter as "just Satan worshipers, same as us."

Whenever officers prompted her to give the name of the cult, Sandy said she could not recall. In response to one question, she said, "The black sssss." Surprise offered, "Something black?" Sandy replied, "Like Sundays, or black…" Later, Sandy would say it was "just a group" without a real name.

She said the cult did not always meet in the Toledo house. The group had previously operated from a house next to a funeral home near Parkview Hospital. Sandy said the cult would play "games" in the basement of the funeral parlor. These "games" were mostly "blood draining."

The following exchange is taken directly from the interview transcript.

111

LT SURPRISE: Blood draining, what do you mean? I... you'll have to explain.

SANDY: It's... they have blood that they use in a lot of things. They have what you call blood draining when you bring somebody in for a... to be a... depends on what they are bringing them into. Then you have to take this blood and wash them down in it and they stand on this... it looks like a star; it's got many points in it, in a circle, and they stand in there. And then they wash them down in the blood.

LT SURPRISE: Okay. You refer to that as blood draining, or are we talking about draining something to get the blood?

SANDY: No. We call it blood draining.

LT SURPRISE: Okay.

DEP CASHIN: Where did the blood come from? Is it in bottles and you pour it on them?

SANDY: No. They're drained from, most of the time, from a goat.

MRS JONES: Is it there?

SANDY: The goat? To cut its throat.

LT SURPRISE: Okay, so that's done fresh on the spot and then, say you are entering in at a certain level, then you would be bathed in this goat's blood. And that takes you into whatever level you are talking about.

SANDY: Right, or part of it.

The case report names the only funeral home in the area Sandy referenced. After the cult stopped meeting in the funeral home and adjacent house, Sandy said they began meeting in a home owned by Circe. She said Circe was a former registered nurse who had worked in a Toledo-area hospital. Circe had a spider tattooed next to her left eye and typically wore a lot of jewelry associated with Satan. Sandy drew pictures of the jewelry for the officers.

Sandy went on to describe a special belt worn only by people in the upper levels of the organization. She said women in the cult would wear the belt while men of similar rank would wear a medallion bearing the same symbol. In Toledo, only Circe wore the belt. A Black man named Pearl would sometimes come from Detroit to join in meetings, and a white woman named Diane would come from Findlay, Ohio wearing a belt of her own.

Sandy also described various robes worn by cult members at different levels. These robes were said to be like what a priest might wear, "not heavy, yet not lightweight." Cult members wore different colored robes to identify their status within the group. Only the men wore hoods, while women wore their hair pulled back. Sandy also mentioned that there was an option between wearing slippers or going barefoot, but if one goes barefoot, they must first darken their feet using a round, charcoal-type substance which had a star imprinted inside a circle on one side.

Next, Sandy talked about recruiting new members. Prospective members would be taken to the cult house in Toledo. A contact person from the cult would explain the necessary classes to attend before being permitted to join. While new initiates attended classes, the other cult members would be watching closely and completing background checks to learn everything about each new member, including information about their families.

When asked what would happen if a new member had a relative who served in law enforcement, Sandy said this would not disqualify a person from joining the cult because that information could be used against the person later. When asked if the cult performed criminal background checks on members, Sandy answered in the affirmative.

Sandy also said some members of the cult were police officers, which might be how the cult would have access to police records. When asked if these police officers were selling access to records to the cult for money, Sandy said she had seen police officers at actual cult meetings, including human sacrifices.

Further questioning revealed that one of the officers involved in the cult was a Black man named Marcus. Marcus was not his real name, but his cult name, and he was a deputy who patrolled Lucas County. Sandy gave a physical description of the man but indicated she had not seen him in several years. This officer had visited Sandy's house in Spencer Township, when she previously lived on Crissey Road. When she saw the cult-involved deputy, Sandy said, "He just sits there and stares at me, and I stare at him."

There was also another officer in the cult, a white man whose cult name was Raymond. Sandy believed he served with the Toledo Police Department. Raymond was a stocky man with brown hair who identified himself as a detective.

Returning to the topic of cult recruitment, Sandy said new members were mostly young runaways. These members largely came from a specific housing project in Spencer Township. Sandy said the cult also took in runaways from Florida. She named two individuals who had joined the cult after moving from Florida, saying they had joined the group over twenty years ago but remained active members in Detroit. Sandy indicated these two individuals would be in their early thirties at the time of the interview, meaning they would have joined the cult as children.

Regarding the classes for new cult members, Sandy said the first step was to learn "The Handbook of Witchcraft," which teaches how to cook and how to cast spells, along with the basic beliefs of Satan worshipers. Anyone joining the group had to denounce their existence in the world, giving their life over to Satan. The cult would tell them exactly what to believe. Sandy referred to the process as a "mind wash." While new recruits attended classes, the cult would continue investigating their background and family members.

Sandy said the cult supplemented their brainwashing efforts by serving food which contained drugs and blood. Once victims were in a drug-induced state, "the satanic beliefs are constantly pounded into one's mind, taking it over for the cult." These drugs were made specially by cult members and were not available in any drugstore.

Sandy said cult classes happened for a period of three weeks, for three hours per class. When asked if this combination of threes held any significance, Sandy said the cult did use numbers, the same way they used cult signatures. These signatures would enable cult members to communicate effectively, because the unique signatures would indicate who sent each message who should be contacted. Sandy said her cult name was "Dana," and her husband's cult name was "Bachuka," which meant "spirit."

At this point, the officers questioned Sandy about her husband's involvement in the cult. Sandy said Bachuka was a very dangerous man and that she would "be dead, buried, and forgotten," if her husband ever learned she had spoken to the police. Bachuka was a High Guard for the cult. When asked what this meant, Sandy explained that during rituals, there were three lines of defense to ward off "breakers," or anyone who tried to "break in" on their rituals.

The first line of defense would be a cult member simply telling a breaker to leave because they were trespassing on private property. The second line of defense would include an attempt to scare the breaker away from the area, including tactics such as shooting in the general direction of the breaker with no intention of hitting them. Bachuka was the third and final line of defense. If a breaker made it that far, Bachuka would kill the outsider without hesitation.

When asked who might be considered a breaker, Sandy pointed at the officers and replied, "YOU."

During rituals, Sandy said the entire area would be full of sentries to keep breakers away. Surprise asked if the sentries would have been able to see the officers who had carried out surveillance on April 20th. Sandy asked about their location in the woods. Surprise declined to give Sandy any information, "other than to inform her that the activities we had heard had occurred back in the woods, behind the house and barn on 295." The transcript indicates that officers later told Sandy what they had seen and heard in the woods that evening.

Sandy expressed surprise that the officers had been in the target area. Based on the information the officers gave, Sandy said the incident on April 20th had either been a human sacrifice or the initiation of new girls into the cult.

In the case report, Surprise wrote a note in all caps, "WHEN LATER REVEALED THAT THESE OFFICERS HEARD A CHANT OF 'MORE,' SANDY FELT THAT THAT WAS THE MALE MEMBERS ENCOURAGING CONTINUED SEXUAL ACTIVITY WITH THE NEW MEMBER. AGAIN, THESE OFFICERS DID NOT TELL SANDY, OR INSINUATE, WHAT WAS HEARD UNTIL AFTER THE SESSION WAS COMPLETED."

Sandy then returned to the topic of initiation. As summarized by Surprise in the report, she said the purpose of the classes was to "acclimate a new member to Satan and, at the same time, determine what type of position, or work, a new member would be most proficient at." After completing the classes, new members would need to attend a special meeting before being accepted into the group. At that meeting, new members would give themselves to Satan.

During the initiation meeting, each new member would enter and find a statue of Satan. This statue was said to be roughly the size of a human. The new initiate would kiss the statue on the buttocks, then move to the next station, which featured a round, oval-shaped mirror. When a prospective member looked into this mirror, the other members of the cult could determine whether they were worthy of joining.

According to Sandy, if the person's reflection in the mirror showed darkening around the eyes and hollowed cheeks resembling Satan, they would be accepted into the cult. If the person's reflection looked disfigured, they would be removed from the meeting immediately. If the cult decided it was appropriate, these rejected members might be given the job of a worker, such as making candles or grinding marijuana to be put in jars to be added to the food later.

When the officers asked what would happen next if a member was found to be acceptable to join the cult, Sandy said they would be required to remove their clothing and enter the meeting space. The new member would eat drugged food, then be subjected to "having a lot of sex" with the other members. When questioned further on this, Sandy said she first had to submit to the "High Warlock" and then to the "Warlock" directly beneath him in the cult's structure.

The officers pressed Sandy to identify the High Warlock, but she could not remember his name. Officers stated the Black man named Alex was the lower-level Warlock. When pressed to identify the High Warlock, Sandy could say only that he was a white man. The following exchange comes directly from the interview transcript:

LT SURPRISE: Have I showed you a picture of him before?

SANDY: No.

LT SURPRISE: Okay.

MRS JONES: Did anybody show you a picture of him before?

DEP CASHIN: Or a picture that looks like him?

MRS JONES: Yeah, something like him.

LT SURPRISE: Is it the picture that we had out there the other day? That is him?

SANDY: Something like him.

LT SURPRISE: You're telling me that's him, right?

SANDY: That could be.

MRS JONES: Describe him.

SANDY: Describe him? The man I know?

MRS JONES: Yeah.

SANDY: Alright. He's white, he's got a lazy eye, what we call a lazy eye, you know. He does a lot of running. What we call running.

LT SURPRISE: What is that?

SANDY: Well, he might run somewhere to pick up a sacrifice and bring it back.

LT SURPRISE: Take the sacrifice... what would the sacrifice be?

SANDY: A little girl.

At this point, the report noted that the photograph referenced in this interaction is the photograph of Leroy Freeman which officers had shown to Sandy at their first meeting.

When the officers asked where the little girls used in sacrifices came from, Sandy said most of the victims were stolen. When asked if cult members ever donated their own children, Sandy said that sometimes they did. Surprise asked if the High Warlock was required to donate his own child to the cult to keep his position. Sandy replied by relating a Bible story, saying, "God told a man to give his son to Him... he did it. He took him to the mountain, and he was going to kill his son."

Sandy implied this same level of reverence was due to Satan. Interpreting this to be an affirmation regarding a relationship between the High Warlock and a child being sacrificed, the officers questioned Sandy further. The case report duplicated the following interchange, taken from the transcript of the recorded interview:

> LT SURPRISE: Okay, so it's not so much he has to do that to maintain his position, but once he gets there, he considers it an obligation.
>
> SANDY: Or an honor. Yeah...
>
> DEP CASHIN: It's an honor?
>
> LT SURPRISE: Okay. Did this man do that with...
>
> SANDY: With the little girl he brought in?
>
> LT SURPRISE: Yeah. Was it his own?
>
> SANDY: No. It was not his own.
>
> LT SURPRISE: Do you know if he has ever given his own?
>
> SANDY: I've heard that.
>
> LT SURPRISE: His daughter or granddaughter?
>
> SANDY: It was his granddaughter, I think. Pretty sure.
>
> LT SURPRISE: What did she look like?
>
> SANDY: She had blonde hair.
>
> LT SURPRISE: About how old?

SANDY: About 4 or 5.

LT SURPRISE: Is that one you personally witnessed?

SANDY: Uh-huh.

LT SURPRISE: And you heard that that was his granddaughter? Did you hear that later?

SANDY: Well, I heard it was related to him. That's what I heard.

LT SURPRISE: Okay, you heard that it was related to him. Okay, go ahead. Let me ask you this, is it the girl I showed you in the pictures?

SANDY: I don't want to say it is because like I said, everything looks different at night, in candlelight.

DEP CASHIN: How about your own suspic-... what do you call it... what do you think?

SANDY: Well, when I first looked at it, it could have been.

DEP CASHIN: Uh-huh.

LT SURPRISE: I was watching you in the rear-view mirror, I knew it registered with you; but I knew you didn't... wouldn't want to say. As far as you're concerned...

SANDY: Could have been.

LT SURPRISE: Could have been. Okay, how long ago was this?

SANDY: Umm... must have been about three years ago.

LT SURPRISE: Alright, do you remember what time of year?

SANDY: I'm not real sure.

LT SURPRISE: What particular holiday was being celebrated? Or festival day, whatever occasion that they do this on?

SANDY: It had to be... it was warmer out, not too cold, like in October.

LT SURPRISE: In October?

SANDY: Uh-huh.

LT SURPRISE: Okay, what holiday?

SANDY: Had to be in October.

LT SURPRISE: What holiday is that?

SANDY: It was around the twentieth of October.

LT SURPRISE: Okay, is there a name for that?

SANDY: Black... black day.

LT SURPRISE: Okay, it's a black day because there's a sacrifice involved?

SANDY: Uh-huh.

The case report notes that the above-mentioned interchange would place the human sacrifice on October 20, 1982. Sandy said the cult uses a variety of factors to determine which days to hold a sacrifice, based on times when Satan will be the strongest. She said the twentieth of the month is a significant date for the cult and sacrifices generally occur every three months, with several special sacrifices spread throughout the year.

At this point, Sandy began describing sacrificial rituals in depth. The conversation jumped around quite a bit, shifting from topic to topic.

Surprise summarized the ritual in what he believed to be chronological order.

Upon arriving at the site of a sacrificial ritual, cult members were given a drink which contained drugs and blood. Higher-level members had their own special goblets, which Surprise surmised would get more "sophisticated and ornate as one gets higher in organizational levels." Sandy said she had a silver cup which depicted Jesus upside down on a cross. This cup also had her cult signature and name on the back. Sandy claimed it was possible to discern a person's rank in the cult based on the cup they carried.

Because she had become inactive in the cult, Sandy no longer had the cup in her possession. She said the group's chalices were stored in the house on State Route 295. After taking the first drink from their chalice, cult members would eat food, "just as if one was at a normal social gathering."

After eating and drinking, the next step would be for members to prepare themselves. This would normally be done in a room where one could be alone. This was meant to be a time of mental preparation for what would follow.

Once a certain length of time had passed, which varied based on the ritual, sentries would be posted, and members of the cult would move to the sacrificial area. Members would then engage in sexual activity. The reporting officers noted that this sexual contact was "indiscriminate of partners and/or sexes." Cult members also used drugs.

At some point during the revelry, a goat would be brought into the ritual. The goat would have jewelry around its neck. If the goat was meant to be sacrificed alongside a human, it would also be draped in black cloth. The goat's horns would be wrapped in black cloth with gold, thimble-like cups on the tip of each horn. Cult members would have also painted black circles under the goat's eyes. They would then chant over the goat.

Sandy said the cult members would engage in sex games with the goat. This would continue until all cult members were fully satisfied. In the case report, Surprise ominously noted, "At this point, a member of the group would realize that 'game time' is over and would know to bring the sacrifice victim into the ritual."

Sandy indicated that the goat's horns would factor into the proceedings. The following portion of the interview transcript appears in the case report:

SANDY: Like, if you had a child there, for instance, and you were going to sacrifice her, maybe she was a small child... ah, you know... horns would be used. Maybe to hurt her, like... uh, the piercing of the horn is what they call it, it's the horns...

DEP CASHIN: Where would they pierce?

SANDY: Well, mostly... the vagina, yes.

DEP CASHIN: The vagina.

LT SURPRISE: So, what size child are we talking about here? I mean, there's...

SANDY: Well, I've seen it done to that little girl.

LT SURPRISE: The five-year-old or whatever?

SANDY: Yeah. But that's not how she died!

Sandy marked a hand-drawing of the property, indicating various points where guards would be stationed and the different sites where rituals would take place. The informant claimed most of the surrounding land was cult-owned and that many people in the area were either cult members or involved in covering up cult activities. She said area residents formed a protective layer of sentries to guard against intruders. In the event of an intrusion, cult members could quickly disassemble their altars and dispose of any visual evidence in the blink of an eye.

Late in the conversation, as Surprise stepped away to respond to an interruption, Deputy Cashin implored Sandy to try to remember the name of the Lucas County officer who she believed to be part of the cult.

"If you can think of the deputy's name it would be really important to us," she said. "The reason being is there's only four of us involved but we definitely want to make sure he's not part of this investigation."

As the interview ended, Sandy answered questions about the names and descriptions of cult members. She reiterates that some of the Satan worshippers were doctors, lawyers, and prominent businessmen. They were everywhere.

18. From the Case Files of Lt. Kirk Surprise, Continued

Reconnecting with the Cult Expert
April 23, 1985
Approx. 0900 hrs.

Surprise contacted Dale Griffis to speak about the potential for upcoming cult activity in the coming days. Griffis predicted the activity would be limited to organizational meetings in preparation for the cult holiday on April 30. He renewed his offer to lend the officers specialized nighttime surveillance equipment for use in future operations. Arrangements were made to pick up the equipment the next morning in Tiffin, Ohio.

Arranging Aerial Surveillance
April 23, 1985
Approx. 1030 hrs.

Detective Weaver, of the Oregon Police Department, said he had contacted Dr. Robert Culver, who had agreed to make his airplane available for deputies with minimal notice. To protect the integrity of the investigation, Weaver had told Dr. Culver that the police were investigating a stolen property ring, not a satanic cult.

Canceling the Airplane
April 23, 1985
Approx. 1330 hrs.

Corporal Ron Collins informed Surprise that he had received a tip through informants indicating that Dr. Culver was a member of the cult himself. According to the tip, Dr. Culver had been a Satan worshiper for over twenty years.

Surprise promptly contacted Weaver and asked him to cancel the arrangements to use Dr. Culver's aircraft.

Instead, he contacted St. Vincent's Medical Center Life Flight, arranging for the helicopter to fly him and Deputy Cashin over the various areas where cult activity was suspected. The Life Flight personnel were told that a criminal investigation was underway which required aerial photography, with no further details.

Aerial Photography
April 23, 1985
Approx. 1500 hrs.

Approximately forty-five minutes after calling in Life Flight, Surprise, Collins, and Cashin were picked up by helicopter and flown over the indicated areas on State Route 295 and Meilke Road. Collins took infrared photos of both areas while Cashin took color photos. The flight concluded about thirty minutes later. At 1930 hours, Cashin returned to the Photo/Crime Lab and developed the photos that had been taken while airborne.

Second Night of Surveillance
April 24, 1985
Approx. 1900 hrs.

Using the specialized nighttime surveillance equipment on loan from Dale Griffis, officers conducted moving surveillance of the house on State Route 295 and two houses on Schwamberger Road. Their strategy was to move from site to site, stopping periodically to observe at each location.

From their vantage point on a road southwest of the house, the team of Surprise, Cashin, and Collins spotted some activity at a house on State Route 295. Looking through a break in the trees, the officers could see a bonfire.

At one suspected cult house, they could see some sort of house or structure in the woods, obscured heavily by trees and shrubbery. Surprise wrote, "On at least one occasion during the evening, all three officers observed four or five people carrying lit torches at the front of this house."

Later, they observed a vehicle driving at a high rate of speed in the general vicinity of the house. The officers did not believe they had been detected by anyone during their surveillance. At approximately 0130 hours, they ended their observation.

Reporting to the Cult Expert
April 25, 1985
Approx. 1000 hrs.

Surprise called Griffis to tell him what had been observed the evening prior. Griffis indicated that the type and amount of activity they had observed was consistent with a preparatory meeting for the upcoming satanic holiday on April 30. He told Surprise to keep the nighttime surveillance equipment for further use.

Third Night of Surveillance
April 30, 1985
Approx. 1900 hrs.

Surprise, Collins, and Cashin again carried out moving surveillance of the various target locations. At approximately 2300 hours, they met with another patrolling deputy who informed the team that Lady Circe had a new house on Clover Lane, just north of the Michigan line. This new home was said to sit far back from the road but could be easily identified by its distinctive domed roof.

Because there was no visible activity at any of the target locations, the team traveled to Clover Lane at approximately 2320 hours, trying to locate Circe's home. When they arrived at what they believed to be the correct house, they found the area dark with no signs of activity. However, the report noted that the house across the street appeared to be active. Officers saw a bonfire in the backyard, near a wooded area, with an "unknown number of people surrounding the bonfire."

Later, the team saw two vehicles leaving the property. They followed one of them and obtained a license plate number. The second vehicle turned from Clover Lane into a housing development, where they lost it.

The team continued moving surveillance for several more hours, alternating between the sites in Spencer Township and just past the Michigan line on Clover Lane. Finding no activity, they discontinued their surveillance at 0400 hours.

Reconnecting with the Cult Expert
May 2, 1985
Approx. 1230 hrs.

Surprise and Cashin drove to Tiffin, Ohio to return the borrowed surveillance equipment. While there, they spoke with Griffis about the events of the past two weeks. They also gave him a partial transcript of the interview with Sandy, which had occurred on April 22. After viewing aerial photographs taken of the suspected cult locations, Griffis pointed to two areas which he believed depicted the number 6. He said these symbols may exist on the ground in those wooded areas.

Griffis also expressed a deep interest in the yard behind "Weird Willie's" house at the end of Bemis Lane. He asked why certain areas were fenced in while others were not, suggesting that such an area could be a burial site. He pointed out two shaded areas on an infrared photograph which might also be graves. Griffis said the team's observations during their surveillance operations were consistent with traditional cult activity days, but he still believed the cult in Lucas County to be non-traditional.

Attempt to Contact Confidential Informant
May 6, 1985
Approx. 1100 hrs.

Officers attempted to contact Sandy through Mrs. Jones, hoping to arrange another interview. Mrs. Jones replied that Sandy was unavailable because she could only talk with officers when her husband was away.

Initial Report from the Cult Expert
May 8, 1985
Approx. 1300 hrs.

Dale Griffis completed an initial report from his observations on the evening of April 20. Surprise received this report through the mail. The following quotations from Chief Griffis were included in the official case report, with the exact spelling and grammar duplicated here:

"Based on observations and data of confidential informant, plus that seen in evening, one certainly would conclude some form of questionable behaviour is being done. The extent will give away to fact which is being collected. I feel the early arrival of persons gives credit to the fact they fell very secure in their setting and possibly been there for some time.

"To the amount of problem or total extent of activities the evening brought out the need for more intelligence and investigation. Should the CI continue to bring forth data it should be examined and verified for source. Confidential facts should be kept that way for as soon as any digging or overt act is spotted the people will go very far underground. Also the fact that enforcement personnel being part of the group has not been ruled out.

"Measures for up coming meetings should be well thought out. If sacrifices are human and being seen ready to happen, exigent means of going in to area are going to have to be well planned out. A copy of laws are attached for review and should be discussed with proper authority. If you do not act the public will hold you responsible for the death."

19. Confessions on Cassette Tape: May 17

Meeting with the Confidential Informant – Recorded Interview
May 17, 1985
Approx. 1505 hrs.

Approximately one month after his last recorded interview with the informant, Lt. Surprise convened another meeting at a neutral, unnamed location. Corporal Ron Collins and Deputy Trilby Cashin were also present, along with Sandy and her friend Mrs. Jones. Most of the interview was recorded on cassette tape and fully transcribed.

After recapping their prior conversations, Surprise immediately asked Sandy to provide names of the doctors and police officers involved in the cult. Both officers listed several individuals and asked if they were cult members. Sandy confirmed some names and denied others.

Surprise confirmed that Sandy was at "level three" of the cult when she left the group. Sandy said she had been very close to attaining level four status, having rapidly risen through the ranks because of her proficiency in carrying out assignments from the cult leaders. She claimed she had progressed from the second level to the third in a matter of weeks. If she had stayed active, she believed she would have reached a much higher ranking.

To assuage Sandy's fears and encourage her to share more openly, the officers made Sandy a promise. In an apparent offer of full immunity, Surprise gave a "personal guarantee" that Sandy would not be prosecuted for anything she said during the interview. The following exchange appears in the transcript:

LT SURPRISE: Let me tell you this right now, here on tape in front of all these people, that regardless of what we find out about this, there's going to be no way in the world that you're going to be prosecuted for anything you tell me. And that's a fact. Right here in front of Cpl. Collins, Officer Cashin, Mrs. Jones, and of course, yourself. I mean that, and it's right here on the tape.

DEP CASHIN: But there are things... please. Without this... we've got to know because you're the one that wants this out. And now that you know you won't be prosecuted, we've got to know.

Surprise and Cashin would reference this promise again at different points in the interview, particularly when Sandy expressed hesitation or uncertainty. As Surprise told Sandy, it was time to get down to business.

Surprise revealed that he, Cashin, and Collins had been hiding in the woods on the night of April 20th, saying they believed they had observed evidence of cult activity. "I told you about that," said Surprise. "That got to be a little spooky after a while."

He asked Sandy if her husband was present at the suspected cult ceremony that evening. Sandy said he was not present because he was working at the time. She also denied being present at the ritual herself. Despite her absence, Sandy named several individuals who she believed to be present.

Cashin reminded Sandy, "You said between the last taping and this taping, you'd be able to find out what happened the twentieth. Were you able to?"

Sandy replied, "No, I haven't been anywhere... I haven't had a car." Upon hearing that Sandy had not been present on April 20th, Surprise asked her to describe what happened anyway, based on her "knowledge of the cult."

The following exchange appears in the transcript:

LT SURPRISE: Here I want you to be very honest with me, and keep in mind the guarantee I gave you. Have you seen more than two sacrifices?

SANDY: Yes.

LT SURPRISE: How many altogether have you seen? Round numbers.

SANDY: (silence)

LT SURPRISE: Ten, twenty, thirty, forty...

SANDY: Over that.

LT SURPRISE: Over that. Since you've been in Lucas County?

SANDY: Yeah. Since I've been involved, yeah.

MRS JONES: Human?

SANDY: Some. Some.

LT SURPRISE: Okay, how many human sacrifices have you seen?

SANDY: Well, there's been... since I've been here in this county?

LT SURPRISE: Right.

SANDY: Probably about forty.

Sandy went on to say that most of the human sacrifices she had witnessed were little children. The victims had mostly been girls, but there were some boys as well. When Surprise asked the age of the oldest victim, Sandy first said it was a teenager. When Surprise pressed for details, Sandy replied, "The oldest one I've ever seen sacrificed was a grown woman."

Sandy said she thought the woman's name had been Judy and that she had been killed by the cult because she was "too loud." Later, Sandy reiterated that she could not remember this woman's name. She said this woman had been killed sometime in 1970, 1973, or perhaps in 1974 or 1975. Hearing this timeframe, Surprise asked about a previous homicide case he was familiar with, which he thought had happened in 1975. Sandy said she could not remember.

According to the story, "Judy" had been executed for speaking about the cult. Investigators began referring to this alleged murder as a "trial" administered by the cult. Surprise asked, "Who would have been the prosecutor?" Sandy answered, "Satan." Surprise replied that Satan would be the final judge, not the prosecutor. Sandy agreed.

The last human sacrifice Sandy had witnessed took place sometime around 1982. In that case, a little blonde girl had been killed by a cult member who she referred to as Dead-Eye. Based on previous testimony,

Surprise then attempted to calculate how many total sacrifices had occurred during Sandy's time with the cult.

> LT SURPRISE: So, there's been maybe forty, and I think you told me before, five, six a year. Something... about five, was it?

> SANDY: Yeah.

> LT SURPRISE: Five sacrifices a year.

> SANDY: About the average.

> LT SURPRISE: About average. Almost certain dates of the twentieth?

> SANDY: Yeah. Uh-huh.

> LT SURPRISE: So that would run... were you pretty consistent prior to '82? I mean, you wouldn't miss a sacrifice, so you can take us back at least eight years prior to '82?

> SANDY: Yeah.

> LT SURPRISE: So, somewhere in '74?

> SANDY: Yeah

This interchange served as the basis for the Sheriff's Department's eventual estimate of fifty to seventy-five victims.

Surprise pointed out that Sandy had been involved in the cult for five years before she witnessed her first sacrifice. Sandy said she had missed the sacrifices during those years because she was busy serving as a "runner." A runner was a person who procured and transported sacrifice victims and other needed materials, such as drugs.

As a runner for the cult, Sandy said she had brought in six children from Mexico, four from Laredo, Texas, and two from San Antonio. Regarding how she had crossed the border between Mexico and the United States, Surprise referenced an earlier explanation given by Sandy, which does not appear in the transcript. Apparently, Sandy had earlier claimed that she used a birth certificate from one of her biological children to serve as documentation for children she had kidnapped. Sandy later said a group in Detroit supplied her with stolen children.

At first, Sandy could not remember any of the names of children she had taken. After Surprise pressed for specific information to secure her immunity deal, she said she could recall a little boy from San Antonio. The boy was Mexican and about three years old, with curly hair. She believed his name was Manuel. When Surprise asked how she got the child, Sandy said, "He was standing at a store, in front of a little store. His house was, like, right next to the store and he was just playing. And we came up in front of the store, and we just took him."

Sandy said another cult runner named Maria had been with her. The boy climbed into their car willingly but started crying when they closed the door. They had calmed him down by buying something for him at a local store. When Surprise asked if they had drugged the boy to keep him calm, Sandy replied that they had slipped something into his drink. When Surprise suggested the cult must have been watching the boy for several days before they stole him, Sandy agreed.

Sandy also remembered a young girl they kidnapped from a housing project in Texas. In that case, the child was outside playing in front of a house when they drove by and stole her. Later in the interview, "running" for the cult would be expanded to include human trafficking, drug trafficking, and the exchange of large sums of money. Sandy said her cult runner accomplices were in their late teens or early twenties. Surprise noted that these cult members would be in their thirties at the time of the interview.

Sandy alleged that cult members hid children in cult-owned houses in Spencer Township or in a trailer court in Perrysburg Heights. The children were drugged and always kept out of sight. Sandy added, "They are never let outside to play."

At the end of this exchange, investigators arrived at the conclusion that the house on the southeast corner of Angola and Crissey Roads was involved in cult activities. There was also discussion of various weapons and cult materials which might be in the house, as well as underground tunnels leading away from the house, which Sandy believed might have been under construction at the time of the interview.

Following a series of questions, Surprise came to believe that Leroy Freeman was being hidden in the house. He also came to believe that Leroy Freeman had changed his personal appearance through corrective surgery, weight gain, and change in hair color.

At different points in the interview, Sandy became emotional. The transcript notes several times when she began crying and, at one point, Deputy Cashin was said to be kneeling next to Sandy, speaking softly with her arm around the woman. Mrs. Jones also reassured Sandy numerous times, encouraging her not to be afraid because there was "no spiritual power that can hurt you."

To wrap up the interview, Surprise asked Sandy to answer a litany of questions giving only yes or no answers. During this line of questioning, Sandy said yes to the existence of the satanic cult, the October 1982 killing of Charity Freeman at the hands of cult leader Leroy Freeman, her subsequent burial in "Weird Willie's" backyard at the end of Bemis Lane, and Freeman's efforts to change his appearance and hide from authorities.

After these questions, Surprise ordered everyone out of the room except for himself and Sandy. He explained that he did not want the woman to be "badgered from all sides" as he asked his final questions. Surprise had already taken Sandy's earlier comments as confirmation that Leroy Freeman was involved in the cult, so he next tried to get Sandy to identify another woman by name, who Surprise believed to be the "true mother" of the missing child. Growing increasingly emotional, Sandy repeatedly denied knowing the woman Surprise had asked about.

Noting that they were running out of tape, Surprise ended the interview. The conversation lasted three hours.

20. Confessions on Cassette Tape: June 3

Meeting with the Confidential Informant – Recorded Interview
June 3, 1985
Approx. 1800 hrs.

The final recorded interview with Sandy took place at an unnamed neutral location. This time, the meeting was attended by Lt. Surprise, Deputy Cashin, Mrs. Jones, and Sandy.

Cashin took the lead, asking Sandy to use a red marker to circle and initial burial sites on aerial photos of the area. They discussed the locations of various cult materials, such as altars and ceremonial chalices. Cashin also asked about "sacred children" who might have been buried in alternate locations. According to the theory, child victims who were related to high-ranking cult members might have been buried in special plots.

Cashin asked if the cult members, including Willie or Leroy, had any videos or photos of victims or cult rituals. Eventually, Sandy said there may have been pictures. Later Sandy said she had seen photos but did not know what happened to them.

Surprise reiterated that photographic or video evidence would be important because many people would find the claims unbelievable. He suggested that a picture of everyone dressed in their cult robes would be helpful.

Cashin added, "We've already added credibility to everything you've said."

Sandy replied, "It's hard to believe, I know that. Believe me, it goes on."

"It is hard to believe," echoed Cashin. When Surprise said no one was going to believe it, Sandy somberly added, "That's the saddest part about it, is that it happens."

They asked Sandy to draw a picture of Leroy Freeman's "cult signature," or the symbol which was used on his special chalice for identification purposes. Sandy complied, indicating the symbol would appear on the back of his robe as well.

This mention of Leroy Freeman prompted a short exchange between Mrs. Jones and Surprise, about the house on Crissey Road where they suspected the man was hiding. Mrs. Jones had noticed some work

135

taking place behind the house. Surprise mentioned he had also seen lumber out back, saying, "They're doing something. I don't know."

Sandy then discussed the cellar area of the house on Crissey Road. Although occupants were still in the process of digging the cellar, she said it was possible to hide items or a person in this underground space. When Surprise asked if they were building tunnels, Sandy said they could be. Cashin immediately asked her to mark the end of the tunnels on a photograph so officers could be stationed there to intercept escaping cult members during the raid.

Several times during the interview, Surprise referenced a diary which had been provided by Sandy. This diary had not been mentioned in any prior recordings, transcripts, or case reports, but Sandy had apparently arranged to bring the book at the officers' request. They commented on symbols drawn in the book and referred to some entries which evidently contained information about past cult activities in the late 1960s and 1970s.

The cult diary was written in reverse. Sandy told Surprise, "The book starts from the back to the front. I never go from the front to the back of the book. I don't like to use the front of the book first." When Surprise pointed out that several pages were missing, Sandy said she did not know what happened to them.

Surprise also referenced a second book, which had come up missing. This book was said to contain extensive information about cult activities, including "every name, every date." The officers asked what happened to this book, which would serve as vital evidence for numerous crimes committed by the cult. First, Sandy said her husband got rid of the book because they did not need it anymore. When Mrs. Jones later asked, "Did he burn it?" Sandy replied, "He said burned it."

Roughly an hour and a half after they had started, Surprise ended the interview by saying he would take some time to "get his ducks in a row." In this recording, Sandy got the final word.

"I don't know what's going to happen," she said.

21. The Affidavit for the Search Warrant

Nearly two full months after first contact with his confidential informant, Lt. Kirk Surprise presented an affidavit before a Lucas County Common Pleas Judge to establish grounds for the issuance of a search warrant.[1]

The first two pages are composed largely of Surprise's own handwriting. Filling in the various sections of a standardized form, the lieutenant identified the property to be searched, listed evidence they expected to find, and provided a narrative summary of the case up to that point.

In blue pen, Surprise wrote the following:

"On Sept. 5, 1982, one Charity Freeman (D.O.B. Jan 29, 1975) was reported missing by her mother to the Lucas County Sheriff's Dept. On December 9, 1983, a grand jury indicted Leroy Freeman on one count of child-stealing (2905.04) in connection with the disappearance of Charity Freeman – his granddaughter. Leroy Freeman has never been brought to justice and the Common Pleas Court issued a warrant for his arrest on 12-23-83. Affiant has verified that a federal fugitive warrant is also outstanding against Freeman.

"Affiant states that on May 17 and again on June 3, 1985, a confidential informant – who fears for her safety – told affiant that said Leroy Freeman was being hidden in a house at the southeast corner of Angola and Crissey Roads in Springfield Township, Lucas County. CI told affiant she knows Freeman and provided a physical description of him. On June 4, [illegible] conducting surveillance of the premises [illegible] observed a man matching the description in the yard of 915 S. Crissey, thus corroborating CI's information on Freeman's whereabouts.

"CI also stated to affiant that Freeman carries a weapon on his person at all times (on his left hip). This weapon is believed to be a stun gun. CI also stated that Freeman has 5 or 6 shotguns (or automatic rifles) concealed throughout the house on Crissey Road. CI told affiant she was last inside this house in April 1985.

"CI has also detailed to affiant accounts of certain satanic cult activities being held in western Lucas County. CI told affiant that said Freeman is a leader of the said cult and has described the use of controlled substances – including marijuana – in the cult rituals. CI told affiant that Freeman always keeps the drugs at the Crissey Road house for distribution to other cult members. CI has seen the controlled substances in small amounts in the house.

"Affiant further states that CI has witnessed cult activities, including the killing of Charity Freeman. The homicide occurred on or about October 20, 1982. Prior to and during the alleged suffocation killing, the members of the cult wore ceremonial robes and drank from chalices and chanted. (Affiant has nighttime surveillance at a location on State Route 295 that CI said was the site of a cult meeting on April 20, and did personally hear chanting of several persons saying, "More, more, more.") Affiant states that CI said Leroy keeps his robe and chalice and cult diary with him at all times. CI also told affiant that inside the Crissey Road house, there are 'pictures' of the cult altar, members of the cult in robes. These were seen by the CI in her last visit [illegible]."

In the accompanying four-page typed affidavit, Surprise put forth a series of observations about his confidential informant, seeking to establish her credibility. Surprise wrote that the confidential informant had no known criminal history and no known history of mental health issues, although she had admitted to participating in several felonies during taped conversations. Similarly, she had implicated her own spouse in the crimes of the cult.

Surprise wrote that the informant told him there was satanic cult activity on the evening of April 20, 1985. Citing their surveillance operation in the woods, Surprise said he "confirmed the activity as stated by the confidential informant." Dale Griffis further confirmed the cult activity through personal observation. In the affidavit, Griffis is identified as "a recognized expert in cults and cult activities in the United States."

The affidavit goes on to mention the surveillance operations on April 24 and 30, saying that both yielded eyewitness evidence of cult activities that were "consistent with those activities a satanic cult would be expected to engage in."

Surprise then made a list of allegations, asking the court to consider all to be credible and reliable facts. The list reads as follows:

1. The CI was a member of a satanic cult in Lucas County, Ohio, since 1969.
2. This cult engaged in human sacrifices on specific dates throughout the calendar year.
3. The CI had personally witnessed over forty human sacrifices in Lucas County.
4. The last human sacrifice witnessed by the CI occurred on October 20, 1982.
5. The victim of the sacrifice on said date was the missing child, Charity Freeman.
6. Leroy Freeman, the publicly recognized grandfather of the victim, was wanted by federal authorities for child-stealing.
7. Leroy Freeman, publicly believed to be the grandfather of Charity Freeman, was truly the father of Charity Freeman, having impregnated his own daughter, Charity's mother.
8. The CI could describe in detail the death of Charity Freeman, which transpired on October 20, 1982.
9. Leroy Freeman fled the state of Ohio with Charity Freeman in September of 1982, but it was only a ruse to deceive authorities in their initial search for the missing girl.
10. Leroy Freeman had fled to New Mexico in late 1982, but had secretly returned to Lucas County shortly after, where he had been hiding from authorities ever since.
11. Leroy Freeman had undergone surgical procedures to alter his appearance.
12. The CI had seen Leroy Freeman, with his new physical appearance, as recently as June 1985.
13. Leroy Freeman was the "High Warlock" of the satanic cult, and he personally orchestrated the ritual sacrifice of Charity Freeman.
14. The CI was able to mark the burial sites for sacrificial victims totaling between forty and seventy people, all within five hundred yards of the location where Judy Petrie was found dead in 1974.

15. The CI was able to mark aerial photographs, showing the burial location of the cult's "sacred children," including stolen or runaway children. The CI had witnessed two such child burials.
16. The national, regional leader of the cult was a woman named Circe. Circe had ordered the execution of Judy Petrie during a cult trial, which had been carried out by cult members.
17. The CI said potential victims were being stored in a trailer in Perrysburg Township which had been set up specifically to "stash" victims once they had been sedated with drugs.
18. The CI said victims were typically white females between the ages of three and thirteen, but the cult sometimes used infants. Cult rituals included sexual abuse.
19. Drugs and satanic paraphernalia were kept at a site on State Route 295, the location of some rituals.
20. The house currently occupied by Leroy Freeman contained not only drugs, but weapons, including a stun gun, and satanic materials associated with his position in the cult.
21. Another residence named in the affidavit contained a cult diary detailing specific activities of the cult. This diary was last seen by the CI during a visit in June of 1985.
22. Based on expert observations, Dale Griffis said another human sacrifice would occur on June 22, 1985, at the house named, adjacent properties, or at the home of "Circe" on Clover Lane.

Based on all of this "credible and reliable information," the affiant concluded by asking the court to issue search warrants for the locations involved, for simultaneous execution by the Lucas County Sheriff's Department and other parties. The final line of the document reminds the court of the urgency of the matter, referencing the looming sacrifice allegedly set to take place during the summer solstice.

AFFIDAVIT FOR SEARCH WARRANT

THE STATE OF OHIO)
LUCAS COUNTY) SS.

Before me, _____, Judge of the
Common Pleas Court of Lucas County, Ohio, the undersigned,
Lt. Kirk R. Surprise, Lucas Co. Sheriff's Dept.
being duly sworn, deposes and says that he/~~she~~ has reason to
believe that ~~on the person of/in the vehicle~~/on the premises
known as: *915 South Crissey Rd (see photo attached)*

in *Springfield Twp*, Lucas County, Ohio, occupied by

████████████████

and frequented by persons *including Leroy Freeman*

there is now being concealed certain property, namely:
persons

① *Leroy Freeman*
② *one shotgun*
③ *5-6 shotguns or automatic rifles*
④ *marijuana and other controlled substances*
⑤ *cult paraphernalia including chalices, ceremonial robes, photographs of cult activities and diaries*

which is/are in violation of (state the grounds for seizure of
the property and also state substantially the offense in relation
to said property) ① ② *§ 2905.04 (A) Child stealing*
③ *§ 2923.13 (A) (1) no person shall knowingly have a*
④ *2925.11 — Drug Abuse firearm while a fugitive from justice*
⑤ *§ 2903.02 murder (...) during a cult ritual*
the facts tending to establish the foregoing grounds for issuance
of a search warrant are as follows:

*On Sept 5, 1982 one Charity Freeman (d.o.b Jan 29, 1975) was
reported missing by her mother to the Lucas Co. Sheriff's Dept. On
December 9, 1983 the grand jury indicted Leroy Freeman on one count
of child stealing (2905.04) in connection with the disappearance
of Charity Freeman - his granddaughter. (Exhibit A) Leroy Freeman has
never been brought to justice and the Common Pleas Court
issued a warrant for his arrest on 12-9-83. (Exhibit B)
affiant has verified that a federal fugitive warrant is also outstanding against
Freeman.*

*¶ affiant states that on May 17 and again on June 3, 1985
a confidential informant — who fears for her safety — told affiant
that said Leroy Freeman was being hidden in a house at the
south east corner of Angola and Crissey Roads in Springfield
Township, Lucas County. CI told affiant she knows Freeman
and provided a physical description of him. On June 4
I/S Trilby Lashin, while conducting surveillance of the premises described above*

First page of the original affidavit for the search warrant. Courtesy of Lucas County Sheriff's Dept.

22. An Interview with Trilby Cashin

"Thank you for doing this because there is no doubt in my mind that this was happening in our area," wrote Trilby Cashin in January 2022, responding to the author's request for an interview about the cult investigation of 1985.

Nearly four decades after the digging ceased, Cashin considers the investigation to be one of the most influential events in her life. She still has hundreds of documents related to the case including reports and transcripts, newspaper articles, and court records. She has also investigated other cases with purported ties to cult activity, collecting many pages of her own research. Even now, she thinks about the case every day.

When this whole thing began, Cashin worked in the photo lab.

"I was in the basement. My job was crime scene investigation, but back then, I also had to develop crime scene rolls of film. I'd do a hundred rolls of film a day and print them out. And when I was done with my work, I'd help Kirk work on the witchcraft stuff."

Prior to 1985, Cashin does not remember having any knowledge of occult-related matters. If the allegations had not surfaced in her community, she may have never taken an interest in the topic. She only became involved when Kirk Surprise came to her.

Trilby Cashin searches for evidence at the dig site. Photo courtesy of Lucas County Sheriff's Dept.

"He was the lieutenant of the detective bureau. Instead of handing this case off to one of his detectives, he came downstairs and said, 'Why don't we work this one together?' And I said, 'Sure.' At that time, I didn't get to work on a lot of detective cases. I was busy printing homicides all day long, from Toledo. So, we started working it. We got more into it. We either got more lies or more truth, but we had to do something. We had to either discredit them or dig."

In retrospect, Cashin believes Surprise had his reasons for approaching her.

"I think the original reason he came to me was his detectives would have just laughed at it and closed the case, or said it was nothing. He knew I would care."

Not only did Cashin lend a sympathetic ear, but she was also an ideal partner for keeping the investigation quiet. Her workspace in the basement photo lab provided an ideal location for stealthy investigative work. Cashin pointed out, "I had privacy in the basement where nobody could get in the lab. It had a special key, and no officers could go down there to look at my stuff. We were able to work quietly and privately without other people knowing."

Given the shocking and unusual nature of the case, as well as the potential for cult members to infiltrate their ranks, Surprise and Cashin had to play their cards close to the vest. "I think that's another reason Kirk chose the lab in the basement. He didn't want anybody to know what we were doing because he didn't want officers to go out there and run their mouths. Maybe people [in the cult] would start packing stuff up or moving or burning stuff. We kept it quiet at the sheriff's department until we were ready to roll."

After Surprise and Sgt. George Damasco handled the initial contact with the informant, Cashin joined the team. In addition to helping with photographic documentation, Cashin also participated in interviews, transcribed the recordings, and took part in field surveillance efforts. Her first contact with the informant came when Surprise arranged a visit.

"The snitch had a religious friend, and she told her religious friend that she needed to get in touch with us. The friend was the one who contacted us."

Cashin had never met the informant or her religious friend before the investigation. The informant's identity was never revealed to the public, but Cashin described the woman as being in her late forties or fifties and from a lower socioeconomic status which some might derisively called "white trash."

"She was scared to death of her husband. He was supposedly level four in the cult. He wore the priest or goat costume or whatever they wore. She was scared to death of him."

Although the official case report and interview transcripts make little mention of this, Cashin remembers the informant worrying about the safety of her own child in proximity to the secret cult. "The snitch had a twelve-year-old daughter. I said, 'Why are you coming to me now?' And she said, 'Because I think they're going to sacrifice her.' And that's how all of this got started."

Investigators took the claims of cult activity seriously from the start, but Cashin acknowledges that she sometimes doubted the sincerity of her informant. Besides the three recorded interviews, there were numerous other occasions when the informant failed to follow through on promised evidence, neglected to show up to meetings, or became unreachable by phone. In one instance, she promised to meet Deputy Cashin at a secure location to hand over a murder weapon used by the cult.

"She was going to bring me the gun. I was sitting on the corner in a plain-clothes car, waiting for her to drop the gun off in the woods. She never came. She always had excuses for why she couldn't bring me that gun. All I wanted was something that could get us a search warrant so we could start looking for stuff."

Despite the lack of physical evidence, and despite the inconsistency of their primary informant, there were real incidents which appeared to lend credence to some of the allegations. First, there was the disappearance of Charity Freeman from the area, which could have been connected to cult activity. Then there was the unsolved murder.

Cashin recalled, "We had a girl who was murdered on the east side of Toledo. Our informants told us that the group killed her because she ran her mouth. We found her bones out there. That was a thing that got us going. We could never prove it, obviously, but she was discovered during our investigation... She was right where we were digging... Within feet of where we were digging."

Cashin was referring to Judith Ann Petrie, whose body had been discovered in Spencer Township more than a decade before the cult investigation began. The twenty-year-old babysitter from Oregon, Ohio had last been seen leaving a home in east Toledo on June 16, 1974. In mid-

October that same year, a teenage boy discovered her skeleton in a weed-covered lot near Angola and Meilke Roads, at the end of Bemis Lane. The coroner said her skull had long slit marks, most likely caused by a machete or large field knife.[1] Judith Petrie was later identified by her dental records.[2]

Authorities said the area at the end of Bemis Lane was frequently used as a dumping site because of its remote location. The same was true for other sections of Spencer Township. In August 1974, a woman named Linda Wolfe was found shot to death approximately a mile and a half from Petrie's body.[3]

When Cashin and Surprise interviewed the confidential informant on May 17, 1985, she had mentioned someone named Judy who had been executed by the cult sometime between 1970 and 1974. The informant also claimed that cult victims were buried in the same area where Petrie's skeleton had been discovered. This seemed to confirm that their informant was telling the truth.

After Surprise tapped her to be a part of the investigation, Cashin remembers being swept up in a whirlwind of activity. For a period of several months, her entire life was consumed by the cult investigation. Cashin stayed incredibly busy attending meetings, following up on leads, taking and processing photographs, and transcribing interviews late into the night. Eventually, her involvement in the case would morph into an unhealthy obsession.

In the beginning, she took a lot of photos. Cashin accompanied Surprise to various locations the informant had pointed out, including several suspected "cult houses" and the suspected burial location at the end of Bemis Lane. She sometimes posed as a model while Surprise took photos over her shoulder or behind her. Ultimately, they took to the air.

"We went over in a helicopter, with infrared film. It was the medical helicopter from St. Vincent's, and we went all the way out to the airport. We took three or four rolls of infrared film and touched back down in fifteen minutes back at St. Vincent's. It was really neat. We found some hot spots, but no judge would sign a search warrant."

Cashin also took photos at Wilkins Methodist Church. A few days before the excavation, someone broke into and vandalized the church.

Although there was no definitive evidence, investigators suspected the church incident may have been connected to cult activity.

Of her time inside the church, Cashin said, "I remember a cross turned upside down. I can't remember much more, but they did a lot of damage inside that church. It could have just been juveniles. They didn't leave a note that said, 'This is because of what you're doing.'"

Cashin's role was not limited to photography. She also became intimately involved in every aspect of the case. She attended every interview with the confidential informant, often contributing questions or observations and even coordinating contact through the religious friend, Mrs. Jones. She attended every briefing and meeting about the case, including meetings with representatives from the prosecutor's office. And when the department planned a series of surveillance operations to watch for cult activities, Cashin went along.

She still has vivid memories of the night she hid in the woods with Surprise, watching and listening to a suspected cult house. "We would lay in the woods at night and listen to chanting in the woods, but the sheriff wouldn't let us go in unless we could hear somebody screaming for their life. We couldn't go in, but we would listen with bionic ears. Dale Griffis had bionic ears, and he brought them so we could listen to chanting in the woods at night."

Cashin also remembers a startling incident during their night of surveillance in the woods. "It was really kind of a three-ring circus, because there was me and Kirk, laying in a ditch. We got bionic ears and we were both listening. We heard chanting. Can't hear what they were saying. Then, all of the sudden, there's a guy standing there, staring at us. He just appeared from nowhere, and we were in the middle of the woods. Kirk said, 'Get outta here!' and put a gun to his head. And this guy just turned around and disappeared. He wasn't even in sight. We don't know what happened to him."

The case report gives a detailed account of that night in the woods, but there is no record of this encounter. Surprise, who authored the report, did not mention seeing anyone in the woods, speaking to anyone, or drawing his weapon. Still, Cashin remembers the man vividly. She described him as blonde-haired and blue-eyed, and said he simply stared at the officers in silence. That is when Cashin decided to end their surveillance. "I said, 'I've had enough of this, Kirk. I'm going home. This was crazy.'"

146

Cashin never confirmed the identity of the mysterious stranger. "We don't know where he came from or if he was part of the cult. We were told, when they have a meeting, they have what's called sentries. I think that's what this guy was. Walking around the four corners, to make sure nobody is coming in."

Their night in the woods may have chilled them to the core, but they were not able to gather verifiable evidence of cult activity. "The sheriff did give us permission to go in if we saw or heard blood curdling screams, or even animals being killed. But we didn't. Just chanting. We couldn't do it without lying, and neither one of us was going to lie."

As they got deeper into the investigation, Cashin began seeing signs of cult activity all around her. Based on the testimony of their informant, most of the neighbors in the "Angola-Crissey area" were implicated. "We thought a lot of them were involved. According to the snitch, they were all aware of the rituals and the killing. We could just never prove it."

In addition to Sandy's testimony, Cashin began seeking other clues. When a friend of hers who worked in the county jail mentioned she had purchased a blanket from Circe's occult shop on Parkwood Avenue, Cashin suspected there might be evidence of foul play. At the time of purchase, Cashin's friend claimed Circe had told her the blanket had been used in cult rituals. After confirming that her friend had purchased the blanket directly from Circe, Cashin borrowed the blanket and sent it to be tested in a lab.

"I wanted to see if there was any trace evidence of blood or hair. I did scan it for blood. There was no blood, but Circe told her that it was an altar blanket used in sacrifices. I believe my friend. I believe Circe probably said that. But Toledo police analyzed it and said there was nothing there."

Cashin also showed the blanket to the confidential informant during one of their visits. She asked Sandy to identify the blanket and connect it to human sacrifice. Eventually, the informant agreed that she had seen the blanket hanging on a wall in Circe's home. The informant's religious friend, Mrs. Jones, is quoted in the transcripts speculating that the cult must have sold the blanket to hide the evidence of their misdeeds.

The staff of the Toledo crime lab were not the only ones to consult on the case. Over the course of their investigation, Cashin remembers interacting with various agencies. She remembers detectives from Florida spending one week with her, seeking information about possible child trafficking and other crimes related to a Cuban crime organization. She also visited Adrian, Michigan, where she interviewed a nine-year-old girl who police suspected may have been kidnapped by a cult. Kirk Surprise interviewed the girl's young brother.

"The little girl had been turned over to them, but I couldn't get anything out of her."

Cashin also remembers collaborating with the FBI. She believes the federal agents were waiting in the background, in case the situation developed into something bigger. "If we had found one bone, they would've shipped us out and taken over the scene."

Cashin also remembers Surprise visiting with a second informant. He met a young girl in a local motel to hear about her experience with the local cult. The girl claimed she had experienced satanic ritual abuse by the drummer of the band Aerosmith. Surprise recorded the interview and took extensive notes, but Cashin said the information could not be used because the girl attempted to solicit sex from Surprise as the interview came to an end. This made the information unusable for their case.

"I don't think we were going to take down the drummer from Aerosmith!" Cashin said.

When it comes to occult-expert Dale Griffis, Cashin does not remember their interactions fondly. She does not question his knowledge of cults and mind-control, but at times she questioned the man's sincerity. "That was my first contact with him. Tiffin, Ohio, where he was from, had a lot of supposed satanic stuff going on. He was very well-versed in it. But me and him had a problem. I just always got the impression that he was up here to play, and I didn't want to play. I had a job to do."

Being a younger woman, Cashin sometimes had the impression that Griffis was being flirtatious. "I didn't care for him. I don't know how well-versed he was. He had all these certificates, but so did I. When we started our case, I don't know how Kirk found out about Dale Griffis, or how they got connected, but that's when I met Dale. Then for three or four months, he was at our department all the time.

"I don't know if Kirk called him or if he called Kirk. I just know one day he showed up. Either that, or an article was put in the paper and Dale jumped in."

Griffis may have been unconventional, but he was not the most unusual consultant on the case. Cashin and Surprise also brought in some psychics to offer insights. Cashin remembers when Surprise brought in a husband-and-wife team from Toledo. The pair visited Spencer Township, offering their services as mediums. When the psychics offered no usable information, apart from their impressions of negative energy in the area, Cashin and Surprise were unimpressed.

"I believe in psychics. I absolutely believe," said Cashin. "But this wasn't one."

Cashin acknowledges that no bodies were found during the Spencer Township dig, but she is still convinced that there was plenty of evidence of cult activity.

"I think we found something like fifty pairs of little kids' shoes buried. Just the right-hand shoes. No left, just the right. Anything on the right hand of God, they would bury. And in an abandoned house, we found boxes of diapers. Brand new diapers. Like, Pampers, in that abandoned house. Something was going on out there. We didn't get it, but I still think we were on the right track."

Cashin vividly remembers finding these items, but in the case report and in the press coverage of the dig there is no mention of children's shoes or diapers being found. Weeks before the dig, Surprise noted in his report that he and Cashin found a single child's shoe near the digging location. This single shoe was taken into evidence. On March 22, 1989, Cashin told a reporter from *The Detroit News* that they had discovered seventy-two women's and children's shoes, all from the right foot. She theorized that bodies had been buried wearing the left shoe.

"We found gravestones. We found dolls with heads attached. We found diapers. We found little kids' clothes. Pentagrams. We found everything but bodies."

Cashin does not regret the investigation, but she wishes it had drawn less media attention. "Back in the eighties and nineties, kids were dabbling. They were killing animals. And the media craze in the eighties and nineties was all over the country. When Lucas County said they were going to dig up fifty bodies, I think that's where the craze came in."

Although she has the utmost respect for Sheriff James Telb, she thinks it may have been unwise to alert the media so early in the investigation. "The sheriff made a big mistake. He let the news media in, and he had a big chalkboard up where a house was listed as a cult house. The sheriff's department lost a lot of money on that one, because it was not a cult house."

Cashin pointed to a stack of court filings, representing the lawsuits which were filed against the sheriff's department because of the information shared in the press. Because she was never called to testify, she believes the sheriff settled each case out of court. Cashin also revealed that she could have been personally sued if things had gone differently.

The search warrant was granted, in part, because of eyewitness testimony which placed the fugitive Leroy Freeman at the home on Crissey Road. Cashin now admits that she was the eyewitness who made that claim. While watching the suspected cult house, she saw a man who she believed to be Leroy Freeman. She then called Surprise. Paired with the informant's testimony, this supposed sighting became instrumental in securing the search warrant. Officers later learned that Cashin had seen Patricia Litton's father and mistaken him for Freeman.

"If I had made that up, I would've been sued personally. But I didn't. The victim of the house proved they had nothing to do with any of this."

Cashin credits Telb for his fine work as sheriff, and she still believes they were justified in investigating the situation. "He put his faith in me and Kirk one hundred percent and I will always adore Telb for that. Telb always trusted me. He was a good sheriff, and I liked him."

She added, "I think he really thought we were going to find something. We did. We found a lot, but we didn't find bodies. People laughed at me. They made a joke out of us. But the things we found out there don't make sense if something wasn't going on. Especially if they had people kidnapping little kids from another state. Little ones, coming up here to be sacrificed. You've got to move on something like that. And I think that's how Telb looked at it. He was willing to look like a fool because of what we were told. I think he would do the same thing again."

Now, Cashin is not sure if child sacrifice ever happened in Lucas County. She has no doubts that it happened in other places, but she cannot prove it happened at the end of Bemis Lane. "I have mixed feelings on whether they brought it to this area, but I don't have any mixed feelings on these offshoot satanic groups that are snatching kids, which we can't ever find. Either they're in human trafficking or they've been sacrificed. I think a lot of these missing people, even the little ones, are being taken for human trafficking and human smuggling. Now they're making them work for them, or snatching them for sexual reasons, more so than witchcraft."

Much like cult expert Dale Griffis, Cashin emphasized the non-traditional nature of the group she was investigating. "I don't think it was, per se, the Anton LaVey satanic group. If you read the work of Anton LaVey, they may sacrifice animals, but my impression was that they did not sacrifice children... These were offshoots of real satanic believers. [Traditional Satanists] may sacrifice a goat, but I don't think they would sacrifice a child. I know they say they do, but unless I saw it with my own eyes, I would believe it would be a goat or a dog. You know, just an offering to Satan."

In retrospect, how does Cashin feel about the reliability of her confidential informant?

"Do I know whether she was telling the truth? I don't know. Do I think it happens? Yes. I think it can. And in fact, I think it was happening. With everything we knew then, I do think this stuff was going on."

Cashin's involvement with the case ended when her pastor called the sheriff on her behalf. The case was taking a tremendous personal toll. "My pastor ended up calling the sheriff, saying, 'You've gotta pull her out.' My pastor had me admitted to the anorexia ward right after they pulled me from the case. I was just dropping weight. I was obsessed with it. And my pastor said, 'You're playing with fire. You can get dragged into this stuff.' I ended up taking a month off and did some time in the psychiatric ward."

After months of sleepless nights and endless hours sifting through horrific stories of cult abuse, Trilby Cashin decided it was time to put her own health and safety first. Her obsession with the case had taken a toll on others as well.

"This case definitely caused my divorce. My husband became my ex-husband after the witchcraft. He was of the feeling that I was wasting my time. That I was wasting his time, and that I should be at home, taking care of my daughter. That this was more important to me. And he was right. It was. I was typing day and night, transcribing day and night. I was obsessed with catching these people, and it didn't work."

After Cashin was pulled from the case, the investigation fizzled out and ended. She later retired from the department after twenty-one years of service. In her time on the force, Cashin had to photograph a lot of violent scenes. One day, after a particularly gruesome death involving a young pregnant woman, Cashin decided it was time to leave. Prioritizing her own mental health and well-being, she walked off the job and never looked back.

"I think we hit on something, but we were the first ones to take the big step. We were going to find this. We never did. But not for one minute did I not think it was happening."

Trilby Cashin, holding a hand-written sign featuring the case number and address of the Litton residence on the day of the raid. Photo courtesy of Lucas County Sheriff's Dept.

Part Three:

Postmortem

23. Tying Up Loose Ends

On Friday, October 21, 1988, detectives visited an apartment in Huntington Beach, California. When they knocked, thirteen-year-old Charity Freeman opened the door.

Police said she was healthy, "in good physical shape," and was "not being held captive." She had not been tortured. She had not been sacrificed.[1] The manager of the apartment complex said the tenants kept their rent fully paid, but the home was sparsely furnished and "uninhabitable" due to the strong stench of uncleaned cat litter.[2] There were no signs of occult activity.

Charity was living with her grandfather, Leroy Freeman. Freeman had raised the girl for seven years before losing custody to the mother, Karen Creswell, Leroy's daughter. After an argument about how the girl was being raised, Freeman absconded with the child during his first court-ordered visitation.[3] After that, the pair lived a nomadic existence throughout the Southwest, living in Texas, New Mexico, and Arizona. At times, they were joined by the girl's aunt, Julie Freeman.

Charity was the result of an unwanted teenage pregnancy, Freeman later told *The Toledo Blade*. He explained that he and Charity developed a close bond during the seven years he cared for her. When Creswell married in 1982 and wanted the child back, Freeman said, "I took her. I told her we were going on a trip."[4]

On the flight from Orange County back to Toledo, Charity recalled her grandfather telling her they were going to see Mickey Mouse. She thought they were going to a movie, but they ended up at Disney World in Florida. Charity told investigators she had used the names Juanita and Susan as well as two or three other aliases, during their nomadic years.

Lucas County Sheriff's Detective Pam Crum said Charity appeared to be a "street-wise child" who was excited by the fugitive life. The girl tried to protect her grandfather from the authorities, who she considered "mean."[5]

"She said, 'You guys missed me every time,'" Crum related.

Authorities were able track Charity to the West Coast after a car purchased in Toledo by Julie Freeman was repossessed in Huntington Beach. When officers arrived at the apartment, both the grandfather and aunt tried to flee.

Karen Creswell's attorney said, "Thank goodness this may finally be coming to an end. It has been a long, long ordeal."[6] In a news conference, Charity's mother called the six-year absence of her daughter a "nightmare" that she would prefer to forget.

"The way I feel right now, I don't think any human being should have to go through what I've gone through, and I don't think anyone should have the right to do what he did to me."[7]

Speaking with reporters, Freeman admitted he took the child, but denied allegations of satanism and abuse. "I know that what I did was something out of necessity of the moment. I had no choice. I loved her, and I felt a responsibility for her." Of Karen Creswell, he said, "I think she'll be a good mother. I'd like to talk to her, but I don't know if I ever will."[8]

Freeman was later extradited to Ohio where he pleaded guilty to child stealing.[9]

News reports mentioned vandalism at Wilkins United Methodist Church in the days leading up to the Spencer Township dig, which some interpreted to be satanic activity. According to the police report, the incident occurred sometime on June 16 but was not reported until June 18, two days before the dig commenced.[10]

Pastor Franklin J. Frazier called the Sheriff's Department when he discovered someone had entered the church. He had been gone from the church for about a week at the time of the incident. Two men who had been seen running near the church approached Pastor Frazier to ask for gas money. When the pastor accompanied both men to the church, he "found the church a mess."

The perpetrator had entered the church through an unlocked side door. There were an unspecified number of broken lightbulbs and a "baby doll" was found at the altar. There were also three "markings" around the area. Newspaper reports later indicated these marks were made on the altar and stained-glass windows using soap. There is no indication whether these markings were letters, numbers, symbols, or drawings.[11] Some newspaper reports claimed a Bible had been burned, but there is no mention of Bibles or fire damage in the official police report.

In a 2021 email, the pastor of Wilkins United Methodist Church said no current members remember the incident and the church has no records detailing the vandalism. Investigators never identified the perpetrator, and no arrests were made.

In the weeks following the raid on their home, Alvin and Patricia Litton sued Sheriff James Telb for $1.52 million. Filing a lawsuit in the Lucas County Common Pleas Court, the Littons alleged that they and their five children had suffered severe emotional distress, false imprisonment, invasion of privacy, defamation, and trespass.[12]

Alvin Litton told reporters, "People still go by, staring, hollering, 'Murderer!' and 'Hey, Leroy!' We were completely innocent, but in the eyes of the public, I'm still guilty."[13]

The Littons contended that Telb and his deputies had failed to carry out a proper investigation before executing their search warrant. Leroy Freeman had moved away more than a year before the Litton family bought the property. Alvin added, "Telb said he'd investigated this for three months. Hell, he didn't even know who lived here. We bought the house and had it eighteen months. All they had to do was check the records."[14]

Sheriff Telb did not have any regrets. He acknowledged that he was a brand-new sheriff at the time but insisted his inexperience had not been a factor. "I'd do the same thing again," he said.

"I felt that we did what we had to do, based on the information available at the time. The focus of the investigation was all around Charity Freeman, who had been abducted by her grandfather. That's where the cult connection was… Given the set of facts and details and allegations and bits and pieces of information from years ago, yes, we would have to do the same thing again."[15]

Telb also responded to the allegation that his staff had failed to check property records. "Freeman never owned the house, for one. We did do checking, and it didn't make any difference who was the owner at the time. The information was Leroy Freeman was staying at the house."[16]

Laretta H. and Edward R. Never also sued the sheriff for defamation, in the amount of $975,000 because their house was falsely identified as a "cult house" during a press conference. In interviews following the incident, Laretta Harris Never discussed the emotional stress she had experienced, including constant hounding from reporters and suspicion or ridicule from neighbors.[17]

Telb said most residents believed he had acted correctly. "I've spent time in the community and the citizens of the county felt we did what we had to do. If it was their child missing, they would certainly want us to go looking for their child. The citizens were supportive."[18]

Telb was up for reelection in 1988, but he did not believe the Spencer Township incident would hurt his political chances. He insisted that politics did not factor into the investigation. His prediction proved to be accurate. James Telb remained Lucas County Sheriff until 2012.

In 1986, Telb suggested the investigation had also served a larger purpose in raising the public consciousness about satanic cults. "It did bring about an awareness by police around the country about the possibility of these things going on in their community. Before last June, it was new to us and new to a lot of people in the enforcement business. We did an awful lot of research prior to actually going onto the sites. It wasn't like we went off half-cocked and started digging holes in the ground."[19]

Regarding whether the rumors had ultimately been true, Telb never gave a firm answer. Reflecting on his confidential informants, Telb told reporters, "They said, 'You just missed it by five feet, you should have gone a little bit deeper.' We felt when we left there, there weren't any bodies there. Our sources of information pointed out spots to us, but they could have been one street off." Later, he added, "Was there a cult in Lucas County? At the time, I did truly believe that. I don't have any more evidence than you have about that now."[20]

English rock musician Billy Idol released "Rebel Yell" on October 24, 1983, as the title track on his album of the same name. When the single was reissued in 1985, it reached the top of the charts. The chorus, which is repeated many times throughout the song, goes as follows:

In the midnight hour, she cried more, more, more
With a rebel yell she cried more, more, more
In the midnight hour babe more, more, more
With a rebel yell more, more, more
More, more, more!

On the evening of April 20, 1985, investigators hid in the woods, watching a suspected cult house for signs of activity. Although they saw no people, the officers reported hearing something that sounded like organ music, along with a chorus of voices chanting, "More, more, more."

According to at least one media report, Kirk Surprise and Trilby Cashin claimed to have audio recordings of satanic rituals in progress. There is no mention of these alleged recordings in the case report or affidavit for the search warrant. In July 2023, a single cassette tape was recovered from the surviving case materials.

Cassette tape labeled "Satanic Recording." Photo by Jack Legg.

Dated July 3, 1985, the recording is only twenty seconds in length. On the tape, a young female voice can be heard shouting, "Satan rules! And he will rule the world always! Hail Satan!"

In the background, a man screams, "Satan!" The unidentified female begs Satan to visit her house, providing an address for a trailer park in Perrysburg, Ohio. Both voices begin screaming wildly as the recording ends.

The origin of the tape remains unknown.

In the weeks following the Spencer Township dig, Trustee D. Hilarion Smith openly shared his displeasure with the Lucas County Sheriff's Department. For Smith and other township residents, the most enduring questions were: who were the sheriff's confidential sources, and why was their information so wrong? When Telb refused to identify his sources, Smith spent two weeks investigating the matter himself.[21]

Smith first identified one of the sheriff's possible informants when Herman T. Haynes arrived at his front door. Haynes, commonly known as Teddy, was a Bible-quoting Baptist minister at the Indiana Avenue Baptist Church in Toledo. He had also served as police chief for Spencer Township from 1965 until 1973, before the township decided to dissolve the police force. Teddy Haynes had known Sheriff Telb for years, having enrolled in several law enforcement courses taught by Telb before he was elected.

The day after he restarted the dig, Sheriff Telb sent Haynes, his longtime friend, along with two deputies, to appease township officials while acting as proxies. Smith was outraged, telling reporters, "You don't bribe me, you don't intimidate me, and you don't send fools to talk with me." During this conversation, when Haynes was supposed to apologize on behalf of the sheriff, Trustee Smith said the minister outed himself as one of the sheriff's sources.[22]

Smith told reporters, "He informed me that there were devil worshipers all over the area and that the sheriff had asked him to talk to me and try to cool me down. I think he betrayed himself by coming to talk to me, because that's when it finally dawned on me: You're the one feeding the sheriff all this rubbish." When he realized Haynes was probably involved, that was when the incensed trustee knew they were "on a ship of fools."

Teddy Haynes denied he was a source of the cult rumors, as did Public Relations Officer Marvin Reams. When reporters questioned Pastor Haynes about his involvement in the case, he answered ambiguously and became evasive. At one point, Haynes acknowledged that he had known about the dig in advance because a portion of the search had happened on a parcel of land owned by Haynes himself.

The minister told reporters, "There's a lot of peculiar things happening around here. There are some people who just doesn't believe in

God. I just can't see these people who go around and worship the Devil, believe in the Devil, and say they are the Devil. I can't believe in that."

In an apparent admission that he had called the police about an alleged cult, Haynes continued, "That's why I agree with the sheriff. I say dig it up. I called them and told them, 'If you think there's anything on my property, go ahead and dig. Help yourself.'"[23]

Haynes' marshy property hosted a dilapidated shack and trash-filled trailer home. This property became the second site searched by investigators after the initial dig yielded no results. It was there that investigators found most of the items which occult expert Dale Griffis would later identify as evidence of cult activity. The headless doll with a pentagram tied to its wrist, the "ceremonial knives," a syringe, children's clothing, and other items all came from the buildings owned by Minister Herman T. Haynes.[24]

Officer Marvin Reams maintained that the items discovered on Haynes' property might be indicative of illicit cult activities. "Why would there be so much small children's and women's clothing in the area? That's what made us suspicious."[25]

When pressed for details, Sheriff Telb refused to identify his sources. He also declined to confirm if his friend Teddy Haynes was involved in the case. Telb told reporters that five different people had confirmed the existence of the Satanic cult. The case report, interview transcripts, and affidavit for the search warrant all mention a single informant: an unidentified woman, known only as Sandy.

Trustee D. Hilarion Smith was not the only person who remained unimpressed by the items recovered during the dig. Lucas County Deputy James Meredith had no suspicions about the items whatsoever.

Fifty-four-years-old at the time of the dig, Meredith was a lifelong resident of the area. He lived about a quarter of a mile from the first digging location. Both Spencer and Springfield Township were part of his patrol district. Meredith was well-known in the community and there was very little that happened in the area without his knowledge.

Meredith said the so-called satanic artifacts were nothing more than remnants of the life of a man named Louis Williams. Williams was a drifter who took up residence in the shack on Teddy Haynes' property. Deputy Meredith told reporters he had personally driven Williams to a local psychiatric institution several times only to have Williams return to the shack or the heavily damaged cinder block house nearby. These were the exact locations where investigators searched extensively for signs of cult activity.

Meredith was unsure of Williams' current whereabouts, but he told reporters about the mentally ill man's tendency to frighten others. "He'd scare people, tell them he was working for the FBI and CIA. He'd nail up old dog heads, put up 'keep out' signs with skulls and crossbones, stuff like that. Sometimes lovers would go back there, and he'd scare them, tell them he'd get in touch with Allah or whatever. They'd leave."[26]

Even though James Meredith was a lifelong resident of the area, and even though he actively patrolled the townships involved as a Lucas County Sheriff's Deputy, Meredith told reporters that no one from the department ever consulted him. At one point during the excavation, Meredith approached Sheriff Telb to tell him he had helped bury about one hundred dead hogs in the woods, so investigators would not be alarmed if they discovered animal remains. This was his only interaction with the case.[27]

Decades later, transcripts from interviews with the confidential informant reveal the true reason James Meredith was never consulted: investigators suspected he might be a cult member who had infiltrated their ranks. Sandy spoke of a nefarious Black police officer who patrolled the area. During their May 17 interview, Lt. Kirk Surprise provided James Meredith's full name to the informant, asking if he was involved in the satanic conspiracy. Sandy said she knew James and he was not a cult member.

As the investigation began to wind down, reporters asked James Meredith what he thought about the notion of devil worshipers in his community. He answered, "It's hard for me to believe they're in this area. Not here. The sheriff knows what he's doing, but I think he's got the wrong area."[28]

Author Bill Ellis posited another explanation for much of the alleged "cult activity" in Spencer Township: legend-tripping. Legend-tripping refers to the practice, typically by adolescents, of visiting supposedly haunted or marginal locations to act out or retell local superstitions as a rite of passage.[29]

Young people in a certain community might park their cars on the railroad tracks at midnight to see if the fabled ghosts will push their vehicle out of harm's way. Teens may gather in an abandoned house to hold a séance and play with a Ouija board. They may assemble in the old mausoleum to tell scary stories. Any of these ceremonial visits might be accompanied by other activities, such as drinking, smoking, or general partying. This type of legend-tripping behavior is common among adolescents, but for adults in the community, signs of such activity may be misinterpreted.

Claims of satanic cult activity are often supported by "evidence" like symbols or satanic imagery in the form of graffiti, desecration or vandalism of churches and graveyards, animal mutilations, stone circles in a field, decorated rooms in abandoned houses, and in some cases, even sightings of robed figures in fields and wooded areas. Any of these elements could be indicative of teen legend-tripping.[30]

About the Spencer Township dig, Bill Ellis wrote, "The truth is rather less sensational. Sorting out the site's history and the 'clues' followed by authorities, we can see that the deputies probably excavated a legend-trip site frequented by local teens for partying and imaginative scares. Nevertheless, Lucas County police were tied up for several days during the excavation, and two innocent families were publicly harassed as 'child-killers' after their homes were described in local papers as cult houses."[31]

In the 1980s, there were various local legends in the Toledo area which may have lent themselves to legend-tripping. One such story which circulated among high school students was that of the "Candlemen." These mysterious figures were said to hold strange rituals in Michigan, just north of Toledo. Teens believed the group performed human sacrifices once per year and, if you were caught spying on their rituals, the Candlemen would chase you down, strip you naked, stab you repeatedly, and hang you from a tree. This legend was active in northwestern Ohio before the Spencer Township investigation began.[32]

Even today, legend-tripping is a popular practice among young people. A quick search on any social media platform will yield dozens of photos and videos of young people visiting spooky, creepy, or notorious locations which feature prominently in local lore. In one recent Ohio-based example, YouTuber Lauren Elizabeth visited an infamous stretch of backcountry road where devil worshipers were said to be active.

Chronicling the trip on video, she referenced the work of Dale Griffis and recounted several local legends.[33]

     Confirmation bias refers to the tendency to interpret new evidence as confirmation of one's existing belief or theories. Rather than examining evidence to construct a theory regarding claims of satanic practices, some sincere investigators managed to force evidence into a pre-existing theory.

     During the Union County animal mutilation investigation, investigators betrayed their own biases when speaking with reporters. Faye Reese of the county Humane Society worked with Deputy John Lala in the animal probe. Reese was the first person to suggest satanic cults might be the culprit. After the theory had been publicized, Lala began to work backward, combing through past reports in search of incidents which could be included in the probe.[34]

     "When Reese and Lala began searching for Satanists inside the county, they found so many Reese said she now wonders what she overlooked in the past," wrote one reporter. Reese added, "The problem is that I think we've had this all along. I have a large box of pictures (of mutilated animals) at home that's unreal. These things have popped up through the years, but you think you just have some wacko out there."

     Deputy Lala agreed, saying, "I know we've overlooked things. We didn't have the knowledge of it (occult worship), and probably the majority of people in the United States don't have the knowledge of it."

     Commissioner Ernest Bumgarner went so far as to say, if it had not been for the sheriff's investigation, "I would have had no idea there was anything like that going on, especially in a small community like ours."[35]

     Investigators concluded that a cult was murdering animals, then combed through past cases to select evidence which fit their theory. When an investigator begins with the conclusion in mind, can they really claim they are following the evidence?

     In 1977, in Shelby County, Ohio, there were a flurry of reports of alleged satanism. Several witnesses came forward to say they had witnessed a mob of men dressed in white robes and hoods, marching through the county with lighted candles. Many residents suspected the witnesses had stumbled upon a rally of the Ku Klux Klan. Instead, investigators became convinced that underground devil worshipers were to blame. When no perpetrators could be identified, police told reporters, "Unfortunately, the

Satanists went even deeper underground before enough evidence could be gathered to justify arrests."[36]

Apparently, for some authorities, it was easier to believe in a secretive satanic cult than the KKK.

One of the reasons people find satanic cult stories so alluring is the potential to provide a tidy explanation for misfortune and ambiguity. Although the rumors could be quite shocking, there was a certain comfort in finding an invisible bogeyman to blame for all society's ills.

Maybe there is a satanic cult afoot, or maybe there are conditions of strife and domestic turbulence within our families, communities, and systems which might drive a man to abduct his own grandchild.

Perhaps the dilapidated house on the corner has been taken over by bloodthirsty devil worshipers, or perhaps that assortment of unfamiliar rubbish is evidence of poverty, homelessness, and untreated mental illness in the lives of the neighbors we've ignored.

Maybe there is a secret society of evil actors working to destroy everything we know and love, or maybe that secret society is a hate group, populated by friends and colleagues, who burn crosses on front lawns under the anonymity of a white hood.

Perhaps the evil cult is recruiting, stealing, and sacrificing our children, or perhaps we are still wrestling with our deep-seated fear that the young people in our lives might grow away from us.

No, the devil worshipers are better. Compared to these very real problems, the idea of a bloodthirsty cult is somehow easier to bear.

24. In the Lineage of Lady Circe

When BonaDea Lyonesse first entered the shop on Floyd Street, sometime in 1969 or 1970, she hoped she might catch a glimpse of the famed Lady Circe. As a "mousy college kid, afraid of everything," she visited the boutique with some friends to peruse the merchandise, explore new ideas, and perhaps even meet the Witch Queen of Toledo.

At first, BonaDea did not see the well-known proprietor. In a 2021 interview, she reflected on what happened next.

"There was this little hallway off to one side, so I thought, 'Maybe Circe is down the hallway. Maybe there are more rooms down there.' I slowly walked up to the hallway. I looked, and there was a figure at the end of the hall. All in black. And I jumped!"

BonaDea heard laughter.

"She was standing behind me. She had a full-length mirror at the end of the hall. What I saw was my own reflection, silhouetted against the sunlight coming in the door."

Lady Circe found the situation very amusing. Although she laughs about it now, BonaDea did not think it was very funny at the time. Given her reputation, Lady Circe could not have made a better entrance.

"She was quite an intimidating figure. She had a flair for the dramatic, and she was a very striking woman. Snow white hair. A tattoo of a spider under her eye. And I had heard a lot about her. I heard she was the Witch Queen of Toledo," said BonaDea.

"She was very nice. When we got ready to leave, I thanked her for getting to meet her and seeing her shop." With a knowing look, Circe replied, "Oh, don't worry. I'll be seeing you again."

The prediction turned out to be accurate. In the 1980s, while living as a professional artist, BonaDea crossed paths with Circe again. At the time, her art agent was helping her get artwork into various galleries and shops. Unbeknownst to BonaDea, the agent made an appointment with Circe. When BonaDea walked into the shop, Circe chuckled, as if to say, "I told you I'd see you again."

BonaDea later went on to study under Circe's supervision for over six years. "I had other mentors and went through other trainings, but she was my Wiccan mentor. She adopted me as one of her spiritual daughters. I was one of her priestesses for a long time. So, I'm very confident in my judgement of who she is."

During the Spencer Township investigation, a confidential informant identified Lady Circe as an instrumental figure in the alleged satanic cult. Although they never said her name publicly in connection with the investigation, investigators later came to believe that Leroy Freeman served as "High Warlock" under the guidance of Lady Circe. Those who knew her tell a different story.

"The cult thing just blows my mind," said BonaDea. "It was so not a cult."

By the 1990s, BonaDea had completed training in other locations. She knew she was destined to study under Lady Circe. One day, BonaDea entered the shop just after Circe had put out some fliers advertising the beginning of a new class. The confidential informant may have told the police that "cult members" were recruited, kidnapped, or brainwashed into joining, but BonaDea quickly learned that Circe was far more selective of her students.

She recalled, "I picked up the flier and went up to her counter where she was standing and said, 'I'm here to sign up for your class.' And she goes, 'Nope. You're not going to be in the class.' And, since I was still a mouse, I went back home. I was really sad and disappointed."

She returned to the shop a few days later and asked again to join the class. Circe turned her down a second time. At this point, BonaDea got angry. She thought to herself, "I know this was meant to be. I'm going to go back and demand to be let into her class. So, I went back and said, 'Look, I know it's supposed to be. You're supposed to teach me. I know that I'm supposed to learn from you. I'm going to be in your class.'"

Seeing this passion in her prospective student, Circe agreed.

"She wanted to see some fire in me. So, that started my training with her," said BonaDea.

The police's unnamed informant described a cult which recruited new members, completed thorough background checks, and maintained control through manipulation and the threats against friends and family. By contrast, Circe's classes were openly advertised on fliers.

The informant also claimed that cult initiates attended meetings multiple times per week where they were gradually broken down by hours of "mind-washing." These cult classes were designed to tell people exactly what to think and believe, using mind-altering drugs which were hidden in their food and drink.

When asked whether Lady Circe incorporated drugs and brainwashing, BonaDea replied, "That's ridiculous. No. She was a very good cook, and she would feed us, but nothing was ever drugged. I took my children and a couple of my grandchildren there occasionally. I wouldn't do that if I didn't feel it was safe. We met once a week for class. She never drugged us."

Circe's shop also surfaced in the informant's tales. Circe first opened her shop in Toledo around 1970. In 2003, she opened House of Circe in her own home, which became the final incarnation of the shop.[1] Circe's shop was very popular and well known, serving as the only occult shop in Toledo for many years.

The police informant claimed Circe's shop was a front for cult activities, with a secret passageway in the back which led to a massive underground temple. Allegedly, the informant had seen thousands of people gathered in this sacred space below the shop.

When asked about the secret underground temple, BonaDea laughed. "No. I knew that shop inside and out. I spent a lot of time there. That's ridiculous. She had a temple in her house, and we would attend there. No, there was no secret passageway. No underground temple."

Circe's movement may have been private at times, but it was not underground. "They would allow guests to come because she had nothing to hide. Guests could come to the rituals. There were some parts that were strictly for members only, but the regular rituals? Anybody could come."

What about the informant's allegations of "blood draining games" in the basement of a funeral parlor? About this alleged chamber of horrors below a funeral home, BonaDea said, "I heard that story a long time ago. I'd forgotten all about it. There's no truth to that." Such rituals would have gone against everything Circe taught.

BonaDea explained, "The Wiccan philosophy is, and the way Lady Circe taught us was, you respect all life. She even had a little prayer that we were supposed to say every time our foot touched the ground. Any time we touched grass or the dirt, and not cement. There was a little prayer we said to honor the life we might be stepping on. So, absolutely not. There were no sacrifices. Respect for life was number one."

Naturally, this respect for life extended to humans. The confidential informant may have told detailed stories of cult executions and human sacrifices, but no such practices occurred under Lady Circe. By the end of the investigation, officers had come to suspect that Circe had sacrificed her own daughter and buried her in a special plot designated for "sacred children" who were attached to the cult.

When Lady Circe passed away in 2004, her daughter, Sheryl Cather (who was very much alive and not buried in the woods) told reporters, "She was everything you'd ever want in a mother." Circe's daughter went on to continue the family tradition, taking on the name Lady Medea. Her mother never forced her to participate in Wicca.[2]

Self-proclaimed cult expert Dale Griffis told the Lucas County Sheriff's Department to be aware of specific dates on the calendar when the cult would carry out human sacrifices. Investigators went on to attach significance to various dates, including the twentieth day of any month, particular moon phases, and known holidays.

Although Circe's group did not engage in sacrifices, there is some truth to the idea that some dates hold special significance. BonaDea explained, "There are our eight holidays on the Wheel of the Year, and we have special rituals to honor these holidays. Those would be the ones where we would invite guests to come and see what it was all about."

"The equinoxes and solstices are definitely tied to the Earth's trip round the sun. Those are specific dates. There are some people who are such traditionalists, they wait until the exact minute, the exact moment, to do their celebration." BonaDea said there are other significant times of year related to alignment of the stars, the constellations in the sky, and cycles of planting and harvesting. "As far as specific dates for sacrifices, it may be that there is a cult that does that. I have no knowledge of that. It certainly wasn't what I was associated with."

To BonaDea, the stories about cult rituals and human sacrifice sounded more like something from a horror movie than real life. "When you're describing particular days and sacrifices, it sounds like somebody was watching *The Wicker Man*."

Was Circe the owner of numerous "cult houses" throughout the region, as the informant had alleged? Did Circe own the house with a domed roof which officers had surveilled? Was she involved in covering up her undocumented ownership of numerous ritual sites all over the county?

BonaDea sees no truth in these claims. "She lived in the Old West End for a long time. That's where she lived when I met her. She was not rich by any stretch of the imagination. I can't imagine she owned anything else, other than the house she lived in."

Did Lady Circe's rituals and practice center on devil worship? Did BonaDea and her fellow practitioners worship Satan?

BonaDea answered, "No. The devil is an Abrahamic concept. We don't have anything like that. There is reference to the Horned God, but the Horned God is the male energy of the forest. Horns as in antlers. He represents the raw energy and fertility of the forest... When Christians started bringing people into Christianity and groups started forming, they really wanted to sway people toward their philosophies. And so, they automatically labeled anything that didn't fit the Abrahamic view as being of the devil. There's no acknowledgment of Satan because there is no Satan in the Wiccan religion. There is nothing that portrays this concept."

And was Leroy Freeman a part of Circe's group? Was he a high priest under her teaching?

"I actually met Leroy," said BonaDea. "I met him several times. And I met his granddaughter several times because he lived in the area. I lived less than three miles from the place where the dig took place. This was before my training with Circe, so I wouldn't have known who her high priest was. I know now, and I knew when I started my training, because he's a very dear friend of mine. Leroy was not the high priest."

BonaDea knows Lady Circe was not involved in a secretive satanic cult. "There's no way she did any of that stuff. She was a wonderful, wonderful person. She was a very dear, loving person, who gave up her personal life so she could bring Wicca to Toledo and be a spiritual source for those of us who felt drawn to that."

Police records indicate that, by the time of the dig in Spencer Township, Lady Circe's criminal background check revealed nothing apart from an arrest in Georgia in September 1976, for "operating a business without a license, fortune-telling and palm-reading."

The confidential informant could not remember the name of the cult she had allegedly been a part of for years. The name of Circe's church, on the other hand, is well remembered. Her church was called the Sisterhood and Brotherhood of the Old Religion.

Always interested in healing, Lady Circe was a registered nurse at Parkview Hospital when she founded her church. In 1972, Circe told *The Toledo Blade* she knew she was a witch at age twelve.[3]

"She was a fifth-generation witch," said Connie Lorton, a church high priestess who was also known as Lady Meshlamthea. "She knew she had to set this path for us and to make it a recognized religion instead of a hidden religion. She was the most ageless, the sweetest, powerful woman. Her aura – her presence – was breathtaking."[4]

In 2021, BonaDea echoed this sentiment, saying, "One of the reasons she's well known, or was well known in the pagan community, was because she brought Wicca to Toledo. I'm sure there were Wiccan covens in the Toledo area that were underground, because we were discriminated against a lot during the 1990s when I was involved. But she was never hidden. She brought it out."

This public lifestyle was inspiring to many, but it also drew criticism and negative attention from people outside the Wiccan and pagan communities. "Circe was publicly declared. If there was going to be satanic stuff going on, and if people were going by the old Christian view, then anything that isn't Christian must be of Satan. Of course, she would be the first name that would pop into people's minds. I was not surprised when her name came up."

Sometimes, people would intentionally draw attention to Circe, by making unfounded claims about their personal connection with her. "Because she was well-known, and because she was famous for being who she was, people who really wanted a lot of attention would say, 'I've been to her house. I studied under her. She gave me a reading. She did spells for me.' And then they would get in trouble and blame it on Circe. I've run across people like that who use her as a cover."

One day, BonaDea asked Lady Circe what she thought about the stories people told about her. "I asked her about the satanic panic thing because rumors were still going around. It was still pretty fresh in Toledo's mind, the panic."

Circe rolled her eyes and replied, "You've known me a little while now. What do you think?" BonaDea answered, "I can't imagine that would ever be true." Circe asked why she felt that way, and BonaDea said, "Because this is not what you teach."

"She just smiled at me. I know she had no part in it. It was definitely not what she taught. I was at her house most days of the week. It's not like I just met her and made a snap judgement. She was my mentor in Wicca."

When Lady BonaDea started her own coven, she established three main goals. All of them came from the teachings of Lady Circe. The three goals were to dispel fear, educate the public, and do acts of community service.

There were plenty of rumors, but what was Lady Circe really like? BonaDea said, "She was a very deeply caring person." If she met someone who needed a place to live, Circe would often open her own home to them. Those who were closest to Circe would often worry about people robbing or taking advantage of her.

BonaDea remembers one day at Circe's house, when a gentleman knocked on the door and asked for food. Immediately, Circe instructed her group to find an empty grocery bag and fill it with as much food as possible, from Circe's own refrigerator and pantry. For Circe, this was a standard practice.

"She said that if anybody asks for food, you give it to them. No question."

Circe was also known for her wisdom and support. "If anybody had an issue and went to her and said, 'I don't know what to do,' she would give them a reading, and maybe give them some herbs for a nice tea. She was a big proponent of herbal teas to soothe the soul."

Lady Circe also had a reputation as a strict, no-nonsense teacher who had high expectations for her students. BonaDea said, "Circe told us, 'All of my students are the face of the Goddess and the face of Wicca. Any of my students who are out in public need to dress appropriately. They need to act appropriately, with manners and respect for all living things. They are not to talk about anybody. They are to show kindness to anybody who needs it.' And if we didn't toe the line, she would let us know. She was all about respect."

Circe also had a deep love for nature. The spider tattoo on her face was chosen to represent her arachnid ally in the natural world. When she passed away, her obituary invited mourners to honor her love for nature by making donations to local animal shelters or the Toledo Zoo.[5]

At the time of her death in 2004, Lady Circe's church had around fifty local participants, but thousands of students had passed through her doors. She was eighty-two when she passed away. In 2005, a special memorial gathering was held to honor Circe's life and legacy. The event was held at a sacred location in West Virginia. Hundreds of people attended the gathering, from all over the country.

Now, Lady BonaDea Lyonesse serves in a broader leadership role, having passed her own local coven into the hands of people she trained for more than fifteen years. "They're running it now. I was called to the greater community. I do a lot of public speaking at conventions and a lot of workshops and teaching within the pagan community."

Reflecting on her own experiences as a Wiccan, BonaDea recalled several incidents of discrimination against her and her coven. On one occasion, she organized a Beltane ritual in Oak Openings, a popular Preserve Metro Park in Lucas County. Even though they had permission to be there, a park ranger shut the ceremony down.

"He said somebody drove by and said there were a bunch of witches out here doing a ritual. They were afraid there was going to be a sacrifice. We got kicked out of the park, even though I had filed for a permit. We got kicked out of the park because one person didn't bother to stop and find out what was going on."

On another occasion, Lady BonaDea arranged a gathering on private property. The owner of a children's summer camp gave permission for the group to meet and hold rituals on the property during the off-season. BonaDea took great pains to ensure the privacy of the group.

"We set everything up and we had our celebration, and it was a very private place. There were big gates down at the end of the driveway, which was about a quarter of a mile long. Nobody would interfere with us when we got there."

Still, a maintenance man who was working on the property questioned the presence of the coven. As the coven ignited a campfire in an approved fire pit, the workman called the police.

Having been harassed at both a public park and a private campground, BonaDea took part in a third ceremony, this time in a woman's backyard. Surely, they would be free to practice their religion at a private residence. Shortly after the gathering began, a neighbor called the police. Officers arrived with lights and sirens, questioning attendees, and checking the area for potential wrongdoing. No arrests were made.

On the tendency of people to judge and stigmatize others, BonaDea said, "I think it's just kind of part of our human nature, unfortunately." She knows from firsthand experience that discrimination still occurs. People have lost custody of their children because of their Wiccan or pagan beliefs. People have lost their jobs, been denied housing. BonaDea concluded, "It still goes on. Not as bad as it was back then, but you can see how this satanic panic stuff gets started. Then it just snowballs."

25. Revisiting the Transcripts

Before she met with law enforcement officers, Sandy spoke to Mrs. Jones.

The unidentified church lady acted as intermediary, arranging all meetings with police. At least two of the interviews took place in Mrs. Jones' home, where she sat beside the confidential informant to offer words of reassurance, occasional prompts, and even some questions of her own. The two women evidently met at church.

The first mention of a satanic cult did not come from Sandy, but from Mrs. Jones. In her initial meeting with police, Mrs. Jones said she had watched a cable television special about devil worship. In a later conversation with Sandy, Mrs. Jones summarized what she had seen on television. Sandy revealed her own cult involvement in subsequent conversations.

Before the Lucas County Sheriff's Office became involved, Mrs. Jones had also carried out research of her own, taking detailed notes about satanic practices. During the recorded interview on April 22, Surprise asked if he could hold onto these notes for safekeeping. Although there is no record of the actual contents of these notes, Mrs. Jones told Surprise she would be honored if investigators used any of the information she had gathered.

Even though her alleged involvement in the cult spanned nearly two decades, and even though she said she had quickly risen in the ranks to the "third level" of the organization, Sandy could not remember the name of her cult.

The officers asked Sandy to identify the group by name on numerous occasions, even prompting her with examples. Despite these attempts, Sandy never once recalled the name of the cult. During her first meeting with officers on April 17, 1985, the transcript indicates Sandy called the cult "Occult group" and "Devil Worshipers."

When officers pressed her for details during another interview, Sandy slowly said, "The black sss," evidently trying to think of a word which began with the letter S. Surprise helpfully offered, "Something black?" Sandy replied, "Like Sundays, or black..." Later, she would say it was "just a group" without a real name.

Sandy openly acknowledged her inability to clearly remember the events in question. Throughout the transcripts, there are numerous instances of ambiguous language, using phrases like, "I think," or "could be," or "it seems." Often, Sandy said she could not remember. Despite these open admissions, and despite a lack of corroborating evidence, much of Sandy's testimony was repeated uncritically in the affidavit for the search warrant and shared with the media as the unvarnished truth.

The transcripts also reference Sandy's long history of drug use, which is linked to her ability to recall events. During the June 3 interview, Sandy said, "But I just can't remember, you know. Like I was telling her, it's... this is bad to say, but when you're doing drugs and different things, there's... a lot of things are hard." In the same conversation, Deputy Cashin acknowledged this difficulty, saying, "We realize ten, eleven, twelve, however many years is a long time, and especially doing drugs..."

Sandy's unreliable memory factored into the testimony in two ways. First, Sandy's testimony was inconsistent and sometimes contradictory. Second, Sandy displayed a high degree of suggestibility, often agreeing to ideas and details introduced by investigators, particularly in moments of uncertainty. The final narrative is often a product of collaborative storytelling, including some mixture of Sandy's comments and officer contributions.

During the May 17 interview, Surprise and Cashin questioned Sandy about the evening of April 20, when the officers believed they had overheard a satanic cult ritual taking place in the woods. When officers asked Sandy if she or her husband had been present at the alleged cult meeting, she said no. Cashin reminded Sandy, "You said between the last taping and this taping, you'd be able to find out what happened the twentieth. Were you able to?" Sandy replied, "No, I haven't been anywhere... I haven't had a car."

Even though she had not been present at the event on April 20, Sandy did not hesitate to list numerous individuals who were supposedly in attendance. She even commented on the turnout for the event, saying the gathering was "not real large," and, "I don't think there was over a hundred people out there."

Twice, Sandy said her husband had not been present at the suspected cult gathering because he had gone to work that evening.

Apparently unconvinced by this alibi, Surprise asked a third time if her husband had been involved. Sandy replied, "I know he didn't come home until about six o'clock in the morning." It was then Surprise, not Sandy, who placed the husband at the scene, bluntly saying, "Then he was there, okay."

This was not the only time Sandy was uncertain about event attendance. In the May 17 interview, Sandy told investigators she had witnessed the death of a woman named Judy. She said this woman had been tried and executed by the cult as a traitor. Sandy said Judy was the oldest victim she had personally witnessed being killed. During the June 3 interview, when officers asked her to identify Judy, Sandy contradicted her earlier testimony by saying she had not been present to witness Judy's death.

During the May 17 interview, Sandy told officers she and other cult members had kidnapped children from Mexico, Texas, Michigan, and other locations. At first, Sandy said she could not remember names or details for any of the children she had taken. Later, when Surprise implied that Sandy would need to provide details to capitalize on his promise of blanket immunity, Sandy changed her mind, saying she could probably remember the name of one child.

The boy was named Manuel. Sandy said she had kidnapped him from San Antonio with the help of an accomplice named Maria. Sandy said the boy had been standing in front of a convenience store when they lured him into their vehicle. She went on to share details about the abduction, including the boy crying in the backseat before they stopped to buy him something to help him calm down. When Surprise suggested they had drugged the boy, Sandy agreed, saying they put something in his drink. Sandy went on to say they used this exact method to abduct other children.

Later in the same interview, Sandy spoke about Manuel again, but the story changed. Surprise talked about money within the cult and said he "knew" there was an international ring of criminals buying and selling children. Referencing Manuel from San Antonio, he asked, "You had to buy that kid? Did you buy that kid?" This is the first time in the transcripts that anyone mentioned buying kids with money. Even though it conflicted with her earlier testimony, Sandy promptly answered, "Yeah."

In case it was unclear which child he was talking about, Surprise then asked, "How much money was Manuel?" Sandy said they probably spent around fifteen thousand down in Texas. When Surprise followed up by asking the price of the child "other than expenses," Sandy revised her answer to eleven thousand. She went on to say that a young girl would have cost about nine thousand. Sandy later agreed with Surprise when he suggested that the cult arranged the purchase of children in advance before giving her money to complete the transactions.

Sandy also talked about a young girl who had been stolen from a housing project in Texas. The girl was outside playing when Sandy and her accomplice asked the little girl to go for a ride. Sandy said the child climbed into the car with no physical struggle. Surprise asked if they had to physically pull the child into the car and Sandy said no. Surprise then suggested, "She was kicking and screaming a little?" Sandy changed her answer immediately, answering in the affirmative. When Surprise asked if they had drugged the girl, Sandy said, "Yes."

Manuel from San Antonio was either lured into a vehicle at a convenience store or purchased from a trafficking organization for eleven thousand dollars. The little girl stolen from a housing project either climbed into the car willingly, with no physical struggle, or she came kicking and screaming and had to be drugged, or she was purchased for around nine thousand dollars. Sandy's stories are full of inconsistencies.

In the June 3 interview, Manuel's name would come up again, only this time Sandy seemed to be saying he was not a kidnapped child, but a perpetrator. She said Manuel was the son of the mayor of Euclid, Minnesota who took a young boy into a cult house owned by "Weird Willie" where the child was given large amounts of alcohol until his "brain popped."

It is clear from the transcripts that Sandy felt immense pressure to share information with the officers, whether the information was accurate or not.

First, Sandy felt pressured to cooperate because she believed she might be treated with leniency in consideration of her own criminal record. When Sandy said she could not remember details, the officers reminded her of Surprise's promise of blanket immunity. At one point, Surprise pressured Sandy to share more details by reminding her, "We're trying to get you a fresh start in life, if we could just verify some of this stuff."

Surprise and Cashin frequently reiterated the importance of Sandy's testimony for their case. During the June 3 interview, Cashin said, "This is very important, Sandy. You have to think real hard on this one... But this might be the straw that broke the camel's back. If you can, think real hard on that."

There was an implication that Sandy's own legal jeopardy was hanging in the balance, depending on her level of cooperation. This idea resurfaced during a meeting between Cashin and Mrs. Jones, Sandy's religious friend. The conversation was recorded and fully transcribed. Although the transcript is not dated, comments from both parties indicate that the interaction happened sometime after the May 17 police interview.

During this conversation, Mrs. Jones shared her private concerns that Sandy was acting out of fear, and that Sandy may have misunderstood what police wanted from her. The following exchange comes from the transcript.

> MRS JONES: I think she knows her own record makes her vulnerable... in spite of all the assurances, you know.

> DEP CASHIN: Sure, I can't blame her. I'd feel the same way.

> MRS JONES: Confessions are pretty incriminating and that may be why she... she needs somebody. And also because she tends to misinterpret. Like, she thought the Lieutenant wanted her to set up a meeting with Leroy through the woman.

> DEP CASHIN: Oh, absolutely not.

Not only is it possible that Sandy misunderstood what officers wanted from her and what she stood to gain, it's also possible that she felt pressured to share information for her own personal safety. In the same conversation, Mrs. Jones told Deputy Cashin that Sandy feared officers would not protect her from her abusive husband unless she provided more information about the cult. From the transcript:

> MRS JONES: She said she was reacting. She felt like she's supposed to get information in exchange for her own protection.

> DEP CASHIN: You heard that all on tape. She's going to be protected.

Finally, Sandy felt pressured to provide information to the police because she falsely believed they had additional evidence from other informants. At times, Sandy confirmed key details because she falsely believed the information had already been corroborated by other sources or proven by physical evidence. Mrs. Jones' concerns were transcribed fully:

> MRS JONES: Kirk [Surprise] has pretty well bluffed her into thinking that he had other sources, and that he really knew more than he did. Because he was quite astute in some of the guesses that he was making, and the way he presented them. You know – you are aware – she said she thought it was confirmed...

Although it is not uncommon for informants to cooperate with police for personal gain, personal motivations may impact credibility. Sandy was backed into a corner. If she did not offer new information to the police, she feared she might face prosecution for her own past misdeeds. If she didn't play ball, she worried that officers would not protect her from her abusive husband. And, because she falsely believed the officers had already corroborated the information elsewhere, she may have felt she had no choice but to double down on her cult stories.

Throughout the police interviews, Sandy showed a high degree of suggestibility. While there are numerous instances when Sandy disagreed with the officers, corrected them, or added new details, there are lengthy sections where Sandy simply agreed with suggestions made by the officers. Often, she gave nothing more than a curt, "Yeah," or, "Uh-huh."

Sandy's story also morphed in response to questioning. Consider this brief interchange regarding requirements for cult members, taken from the April 22 transcript:

> LT SURPRISE: Are you required to do anything with your hair? Cut it, or wear it a particular way?

> SANDY: No, you only give a little bit of your hair.

LT SURPRISE: Okay. And that's a part of you, right?

SANDY: Uh-huh.

LT SURPRISE: But I mean, do... are you required, when you go to a meeting or ritual or whatever, do you have to wear your hair in a particular way, or does it matter?

SANDY: No.

LT SURPRISE: For example, a woman has to have it pulled back, or...

SANDY: Yeah. Seems to me that it is pulled back.

DEP CASHIN: Is that pulled back like a ponytail?

SANDY: No, just back down. It would be down, but back.

LT SURPRISE: What about men? No restrictions?

SANDY: No.

Sandy began by saying there were no requirements related to women's hair. Surprise followed up by suggesting an example. Sandy then agreed and said his answer seemed right. When Cashin suggested a ponytail, the informant said no, but incorporated both her previous answer and Surprise's suggestion by saying hair had to be both "down," as in not styled, and "back," as Surprise had suggested.

The discussion of hair regulations within the cult is ultimately inconsequential, but the exchange captures a dynamic that became common throughout the transcripts. Some aspects of the story did not come from Sandy alone, but from a back-and-forth collaboration between Sandy, the officers, and Mrs. Jones.

Another example can be found in Sandy's discussion of member recruitment. Sandy said the cult would watch new members closely before granting them full access. When the officers asked if this included background checks for family members, Sandy said yes. After Sandy mentioned that some cult members were police, Surprise suggested, "Maybe their contribution to the group would be police checks?" Sandy replied, "Probably." Cashin asked, "Is that their contribution to Satan?" Sandy replied, "Yeah."

When discussing the use of unidentified drugs during cult meals and ceremonies, Surprise and Cashin seemed to assist Sandy further. The following exchange appears in the transcript:

> DEP CASHIN: They're made-up drugs. Or are they behind a pharmaceutical counter?
>
> SANDY: No. You can't get them in there.
>
> LT SURPRISE: So, you have people in this group that are into the chemistry of making these types of...
>
> SANDY: Yeah. They make up their...
>
> LT SURPRISE: Alchemist. They're called alchemists. Have you heard that term?
>
> SANDY: No.
>
> LT SURPRISE: Or into alchemy.
>
> SANDY: They make all their own.
>
> LT SURPRISE: They make their own and you can go to Circe's and get what you need for supper tonight, right?
>
> SANDY: Yeah

Sandy had mentioned drugs being used during cult rituals and classes, but the officers initiated the discussion of drug manufacturing within the group. Rather than asking where the drugs came from, they instead made a series of specific suggestions, allowing their informant to go along with their explanation. A similar pattern can be seen in the section of

the interview when officers tried to determine whether they had overheard
a human sacrifice during their night of surveillance:

> LT SURPRISE: Would a goat have been used the other night? Or
> maybe a dog?

> SANDY: No, it would have been a goat.

> LT SURPRISE: It would have been a goat?

> DEP CASHIN: Wouldn't they have done a goat and a human at
> the same night?

> SANDY: They could have.

Once again, it was not the confidential informant who has
suggested a human sacrifice. Sandy indicated the cult "would have" used a
goat. The questioners introduced a human victim into the discussion.
Sandy then agreed it could be possible.

In one of the most bizarre and lurid portions of the conversation,
Mrs. Jones chimed in to contribute a question related to the alleged use of
goats during initiation ceremonies. Sandy had indicated that cult members
would use a sacrificial goat to play elaborate sex games. In the imaginative
conversation that followed, everyone contributed ideas:

> MRS JONES: You would know more about this, but I'm curious,
> does a goat cooperate with having sex with a human?

> SANDY: Huh-uh. [No.]

> LT SURPRISE: Why did you think I would know more about that?
> (laughter) No, I really don't know. What if they don't cooperate?
> Okay. Do they sedate this goat with potions or something?

> SANDY: Yes. They're drugged as well as a person.

> LT SURPRISE: Okay. I mean... 'cause a goat can get nasty with
> folks, you know.

SANDY: Yeah, they can. They're... they're...

MRS JONES: Does a goat have an orgasm with these people? With the humans?

SANDY: It depends on what they're going to do with them.

MRS JONES: You know what I'm talking about.

SANDY: Yeah.

DEP CASHIN: I would imagine if a woman was sucking on a goat, he would have an orgasm.

SANDY: Well, yeah. They do that.

Surprise sometimes expressed interest in deciphering hidden significance in aspects of the story. After Sandy said cult members attended classes for about three weeks, lasting from 8pm until 11pm, Surprise replied, "Three times a week, three hours a night, for three weeks. Does 3-3-3 mean anything?" When Sandy said she was not sure, Surprise answered, "It probably does."

It was also Surprise who attached significance to the twentieth day of the month. Because their recent surveillance in the woods had taken place on April 20, Surprise quickly came to believe the human sacrifice Sandy described must have also happened on the twentieth of the month. Surprise also told Sandy there was a new moon that evening.

Even though Surprise himself had attached significance to the twentieth day of the month, this element quickly became integrated into the story. During the May 17 interview, Surprise said, "I think we talked the last time, that it being April 20, it's an important date." Sandy replied, "Uh-huh." Surprise asked, "And that's a sacrifice date?" He then asked, "Would I be out of line to assume there was a sacrifice that night?"

It was also Surprise, not the informant, who placed the alleged cult execution in the month of October. During the April 22 interview, Sandy tried to remember when she had last witnessed a human sacrifice. Surprise zeroed in on the month of October based on Sandy's description of the weather being "not too hot and not too cold." Although the informant could not remember the month in question, Surprise quickly placed the event in October, seemingly to correspond with the discovery of Judith Ann Petrie's body a decade prior, on October 14, 1974.

When Sandy talked about a woman named Judy who had been executed by the cult, the officers took it as confirmation that Judith Petrie's death was connected to their current investigation. It is possible that Sandy, a longtime resident of the area, simply remembered the unsolved murder from years before and incorporated it in her story. Officers believed Sandy was leading them to a burial site for sacrificial victims at the end of Bemis Lane; perhaps she simply led them to the spot where she knew a body had been found in the past.

Surprise attached significance to the twentieth day of the month based on assumptions about sacred number patterns within the cult. He attached significance to the month of October based on an unsolved murder from the past. By the time the search warrant was issued, Surprise was stating unequivocally that the informant had indicated a child sacrifice happened on or about October 20, 1982, even though Sandy had never spoken those words.

Lt. Kirk Surprise had a personal agenda: he wanted to implicate and apprehend Leroy Freeman. The press conference on the morning of the dig seemed to suggest that Leroy Freeman had been a suspect from the beginning, but the transcripts tell a different story.

Sandy did not mention Leroy Freeman. It took the officers a long time to get Sandy to make any connection between Freeman and her cult allegations. Even then, she remained unwilling to speak his name aloud.

From the outset, Sandy identified "a Black man named Alex" as the leader of the supposed cult. She said Alex was responsible for the death of a young girl, who she claimed died of suffocation when the man sexually assaulted her during a ritual. Sandy described Alex as an imposing figure in the cult who was instrumental in "breaking" cult victims who were brought before him. As the investigation progressed, Alex faded from the story as investigators focused their attention on Leroy Freeman instead.

Surprise was the first person to mention Freeman. During his initial meeting with Sandy, Surprise showed her photos of both Leroy and Charity Freeman. Sandy said she did not recognize either of them. Early in the case report, both Surprise and Damasco suspected Sandy was lying. Surprise seemed to be trying to connect Charity Freeman to the child sacrifice story. Charity disappeared in 1982, but Sandy first claimed she had seen the cult murder a blonde-haired child sometime in the 1970s.

During the April 22 interview, Surprise again tried to connect Leroy Freeman to the cult. In a discussion about the identity of the cult High Priest, the following exchange took place:

LT SURPRISE: Have I showed you a picture of him before?

SANDY: No.

LT SURPRISE: Okay.

MRS JONES: Did anybody show you a picture of him before?

DEP CASHIN: Or a picture that looks like him?

MRS JONES: Yeah, something like him.

LT SURPRISE: Is it the picture that we had out there the other day? That is him?

SANDY: Something like him.

LT SURPRISE: You're telling me that's him, right?

SANDY: That could be.

Although Sandy had given no such indication, Surprise asked if the murdered child was related to the High Priest, perhaps even a daughter or granddaughter. Because he knew Leroy Freeman had absconded with his own granddaughter, Surprise apparently hoped to implicate Freeman by establishing a familial relationship between the alleged cult leader and victim.

Eventually, Sandy relented, saying "it could have been" Leroy Freeman. Surprise then revealed his earlier suspicions, saying, "I was watching you in the rear-view mirror, I knew it registered with you; but I knew you didn't... wouldn't want to say."

Surprise repeatedly tried to get Sandy to say Leroy's name. "Come on, Sandy. We're trying so hard," he said at one point.

Although the affidavit for the search warrant indicated the information had come from Sandy, Surprise was the one who crafted the theory about Freeman's evasive techniques. Before his informant had agreed that Freeman was hiding in Lucas County, Surprise told Sandy, "I know he went to New Mexico after Charity, and he got everybody thinking he took her with him and, last I heard, somebody thought they saw him. Maybe six, eight months ago. I don't believe that. I think he's been back here a long time because his checks are coming to Mama."

"He's the main guy, isn't he?" Surprise asked. He went on to list a variety of allegations, including corrective surgery to disguise himself. "How'd he changed his appearance? He must have done something. Has he had the eye taken care of? Surgery or something? Okay, so he's had that worked on, again trying to throw things off. He used to have dark hair. It's now white, or whatever?"

Similarly, Surprise suggested that Freeman was being hidden in a house with a stash of weapons. He said, "[Cult members] go to him because they still consider him the leader. They go to him not only for advice, but... what? Blessings? You tell me, you know. He's giving them instructions, to the members, what he wants done. For example, this April 20, we were laying out in the woods, and that... he planned that affair and he told them."

Sandy offered an occasional "yes" or "uh-huh" while Surprise spoke.

At one point, Surprise indicated just how far he was willing to go to capture Leroy Freeman. Surprise told his informant, "If we find Charity's remains, Leroy's gone. Leroy may not want to go, I'm almost sure of that. There may be problems with trying to arrest him, you know. The other people may not allow us or want us. I'm prepared for that. That doesn't concern me. And I'm sure, and you're telling me right now, that they will do whatever they gotta do to keep him… Whether it means killing all of us or not. That doesn't concern me. I don't know if you find that hard, or strange, but it doesn't."

During the May 17 interview, Surprise provided the most telling indication of his personal agenda when he said, in reference to Leroy, "I'll find him. They don't have any idea that I know he's still around. I once threw that up to my own bosses, because of the checks, and they said no. The FBI told me no. The FBI told me he was seen a few months ago in New Mexico. I know better. So, who knows, even the ones I've tried to tell I think is here, they don't believe it. That's why this is important. That's why. That's how you know nobody knows. I'm right."

Sandy eventually confirmed many of Surprise's suspicions. How could she deny it? The police officer interviewing her kept telling her what he knew to be true.

"I'm gonna take a guess here," Surprise said. "My guess is Circe is the leader for this section of the country. Leroy is the main man here." Again, Sandy said, "Uh-huh."

Mugshot of Leroy Freeman, taken in 1975. Courtesy of Lucas County Sheriff's Dept.

By the June 3 interview, Sandy had still not spoken Leroy's name. When Sandy referred to a cult leader, saying her son had seen "him" at a house, Cashin replied, "Nobody wants to say his name." Referring to a drawing she had made earlier, which showed the symbol of a cult member she called Dead-Eye, Surprise said, "You showed us his signature and, of course, we know his name is Leroy. What do you call him?"

As Surprise continued pressing her to say the name of Leroy Freeman, Sandy became emotional and continued to resist. When Surprise persisted, Sandy finally said she knew the man by the cult name of "BE-

ALS-A-BOP." Surprise interpreted this to be a reference to the Biblical figure Beelzebub. He also interpreted this person to be Leroy Freeman.

Surprise repeatedly used the "cult name" idea to drive Sandy toward identifying Freeman. At several points during the interviews, primarily on May 17 and June 3, Surprise appears to have deflected names he did not recognize by asserting the informant was sharing cult aliases instead of real names.

Sandy first brought up the topic of aliases during her initial interview with police on April 17, 1985. When asked to name the individuals involved in cult business, Sandy said her information may not be verifiable because, "A lot of the names you're gonna hear are not their names, because you don't use your own names a lot." Surprise then suggested the phrase "cult names." From that point forward, whenever Sandy provided a name that could not be verified, or a name that did not jive with police theories, Surprise explained the discrepancy by suggesting the snitch was using a cult alias.

In a private conversation between Trilby Cashin and Mrs. Jones, the topic of cult names came up again. Cashin and Surprise had been trying to get Sandy to confirm the identity of Charity Freeman's real parents. As Cashin discussed the situation with Mrs. Jones, the following exchange was transcribed:

> DEP CASHIN: We know who Charity's mother is, but Sandy's got to say it. Sandy's got to say it.
>
> MRS JONES: Has she got the first name wrong?
>
> DEP CASHIN: That's a cult name.
>
> MRS JONES: Oh.
>
> DEP CASHIN: If you say it again... Linda?
>
> MRS JONES: Kathleen.

DEP CASHIN: Kathleen, that's right. We've got to… I know Sandy knows the name. The real name.

In another exchange, Surprise asked Sandy to identify the woman in a photo. Her incorrect answers of Kathleen and Chris were dismissed by Surprise as cult nicknames. When Surprise pushed her to give "real names," Sandy seemed to sense that he was driving for a specific answer. After Surprise repeated the same question several times, Sandy interpreted his actions as a trick, saying, "You're being sneaky, aren't you?"

Ultimately, Surprise rejected the names Sandy had given and blurted out his own theory instead. When Sandy failed to connect the woman in the photo to Leroy Freeman, Surprise said, "Just for the record, 'Kathleen' and 'Chris' is Julie Freeman. That's the sister of the one on TV, posing as the real mother. Same one Leroy has been climbing on for years. Karen Freeman. Karen Creswell is not the real mother. She's posing. She's aware of the situation with Leroy and Kathleen. She's aware that the whole thing was staged, that the search for the daughter is garbage… it's over."

As Sandy cried, Cashin asked if Surprise's theory was correct. The informant said yes.

With so many names flying around, it was easy to get confused. Sandy was not the only one to experience consternation over the real name/cult name idea. In a private conversation, Mrs. Jones told Deputy Cashin that she needed to revise an earlier comment because of a misunderstanding. Jones said, "I hadn't been talking about 'Ralph' lately. You interjected his name and I agreed to it because I was thinking that was our pseudonym for Leroy, but it wasn't. No, 'Ralph' doesn't enter into this thing about Charity, that I know of."

Surprise's singular focus on Leroy Freeman is perhaps most evident in one segment of the May 17 transcript, when Sandy spoke about a cult member named Rose, who allegedly lived at the corner of Angola and Crissey Roads. By the end of the exchange, Surprise had shifted the focus from Sandy's tip about a woman living in the house on the northeast corner of Angola and Crissey to a man in the house on the southeast corner:

SANDY: (*speaking of "Rose," the female cult member*) She lives on the corner house of Angola and Crissey.

LT SURPRISE: Angola and Crissey.

SANDY: There's a store, and right behind that there's a house that she lives in.

LT SURPRISE: Okay. The store's on... you picture this on the northeast corner?

SANDY: Yeah.

LT SURPRISE: Okay, you have a dead end... let me show you here. (*draws diagram*) Angola and Crissey, the store's right here.

SANDY: Yeah. And right behind that is the house.

LT SURPRISE: (*pointing to diagram*) Back this way?

SANDY: Yeah, that would be her house.

LT SURPRISE: (*pointing to the house on the southeast corner*) Who lives in this house, do you know? On that corner.

SANDY: The big house?

LT SURPRISE: Yeah. Come on, you know. Who lives there?

SANDY: I don't know.

LT SURPRISE: Come on.

SANDY: I don't know.

LT SURPRISE: That's where the goats are kept. Come on, Sandy. Who is it?

SANDY: I don't know.

(*moments later, still pointing to the southeast corner of the diagram*)

LT SURPRISE: Who? Who stays there?

SANDY: I don't remember.

LT SURPRISE: Alright. But they're part of this.

SANDY: Could be.

LT SURPRISE: Could be. They are, okay?

MRS JONES: Are you afraid?

LT SURPRISE: Why are you afraid of those people? Are they biggies?

SANDY: Yeah, they could be.

LT SURPRISE: Could be. Well, you've already told me [redacted]. You've already told me [redacted]. I know about Leroy. Is there anyone bigger than Leroy there?

SANDY: Might be.

Numerous times, Sandy said a woman named Rose lived in a house behind the store on the north side of the street, but Surprise drew her attention to a different house on the south side of the street. By their next meeting on June 3, Surprise began incorporating both houses in his questioning.

"They're hiding Leroy, aren't they? They're hiding Leroy in that house," Surprise said.

Surprise's hand-drawn diagram of Angola and Crissey Roads, referenced in the transcript, was later displayed at a press conference, and printed in the local newspaper. Laretta

Kirk Surprise speaking at press conference, showing hand-drawn map. © *The Toledo Blade*.

Harris Never's home, behind the store, was circled and labeled as a "cult house." The house across the street was labeled "Leroy's house."[1]

On June 20, 1985, law enforcement officers did not raid the home Sandy circled, on the northeast corner of Angola and Crissey. Instead, they raided the Litton residence, which Surprise had pointed to, on the southeast corner.

✶

Deputy Trilby Cashin also had strong personal reasons for working this case. In a moment of candor during the May 17 interview, Cashin relayed a story to Sandy about a terrifying personal experience involving her daughter.

Cashin said, "I had a two-year-old. She was in the front yard. There was a man, dressed from head to toe in black. Back and forth in front of my house. I was keeping an eye on him, but I was also keeping an eye on my daughter. The man headed up in my front yard. I went out there and leveled a .380 at him. I turned around; I got the police. I had four police crews in a matter of, say, four minutes. We drove the entire area. The man was gone."

Cashin then asked the informant, "Was he coming after my daughter?" Sandy replied, "Probably." When Cashin asked why the man was wearing black, Sandy replied, "They always wear black."

193

Cashin went on to ask a series of questions, trying to identify the man who had approached her young daughter. Wondering if he might be a member of the cult, Cashin asked Sandy if she could name the man based on the description given. She said she hoped to look through a book of mugshots to find the man. Although Sandy had not been present during the incident, Surprise asked if the mysterious man would have had a car waiting nearby to steal the child. Sandy said yes.

About Cashin's line of questioning, Surprise said, "Alright, I know she's been wanting to get that question out for a while. That's why you picked up on this personal interest she has in this." Cashin added, "That's why, if it takes me to my grave, I'm gonna do what I do to find out about this."

Later in the interview, Cashin reminded Sandy of her personal quest, saying, "I have one personal favor. If there is any way possible, without jeopardizing yourself, if you could come up with a name so I can look at a mug shot book and know whether it was the man, I would much appreciate it. I know you're scared, and I know you understand."

As Surprise brought the May 17 interview to a close, he concluded, "It's a matter of me putting this whole package together and doing what I have to do. And now you understand why Trilby's involved in it. Personal grudge. Didn't realize it at the time... and I personally think she didn't realize the depth of it when it happened, or until very recently."

Sandy said, "I know."

Signs of paranoia and conspiracy thinking appear early in the case notes. When Cashin and Surprise visited the alleged burial site to surreptitiously take photographs, they became convinced they were being tailed by a woman in a blue Chevette. As they hid in the woods to observe the suspected cult house, they grew concerned that every passing car might be driven by a sentry from the cult. And when there seemed to be a radio malfunction during the surveillance operation, Surprise ominously wrote, "There is no explanation for that fact."

Concerned that cult members might try to infiltrate their investigation, Surprise and Cashin tried to keep the operation as confidential as possible. Regarding the police officer Sandy claimed to have seen in the area two to three years prior, Cashin said, "If you can think of the deputy's name, it would be really important to us... the reason being is, there's only four of us involved, but we definitely want to make sure he's no part of this investigation. Which, nobody else will be."

At the beginning of the May 17 interview, Surprise tried to identify any police officers who might be involved in the cult. Surprise named one of his colleagues from Lucas County, Deputy James Meredith. By asking a former cult member to identify co-conspirators within his own department, Surprise demonstrated to some extent the concern he was experiencing.

This same concern contributed to Surprise's decision to cancel his request to use Dr. Robert Culver's airplane to carry out aerial surveillance on April 23, 1985. At some point, deputies became suspicious of the area pilot, believing he had secretly been a devil worshiper for more than twenty years.

The suspected conspiracy went beyond Lucas County. When Sandy discussed selling drugs on behalf of the cult, Surprise introduced the idea of child trafficking. Explaining his reasoning, he told Sandy, "Because I know there's a network of kids being sold around the country. You go snatch one, you can sell it to Philadelphia for ten thousand dollars, whatever." He went on to ask if the satanic cult paid for children to be "stolen, made to order."

"Your cult work hand in hand with the kiddie porn group?" he asked.

"Sure," replied Sandy.

"Moving kids through the country," added Surprise.

"All that works together," said Sandy. "Even the mafia works together with us."

"Well," said Surprise, without batting an eye. "That's organized crime."

In Lucas County, there was evidence of one missing child, who at that time was already known to have been abducted by a family member, but Surprise entertained and seemingly endorsed a theory which involved groups of organized child pornographers, mafia bosses, and deranged Satan worshipers, all working together undetected.

Mrs. Jones later initiated a conversation about celebrities who were involved in the cult. In response, the officers asked Sandy if she could identify which wealthy and powerful individuals worshiped Satan. Cashin said, "If I name them, just say yes or no." According to Sandy, the founder of Playboy magazine, Hugh Hefner, was secretly a cult member. When asked for more details, Sandy said Hefner was a "big contributor" of money, drugs, and girls for use by the cult.

When Sandy said the woman who "plays Rhoda on TV" was also part of the cult, Surprise supplied the name of the actress, Valerie Harper. He went on to ask if Valerie Harper had visited the cult, and Sandy replied that she had personally seen the actress at cult meetings. Sandy also mentioned Freddy Friendly, who Surprise identified as a singer.

As the investigation went on, the satanic conspiracy grew wider and wider. Even something innocuous and mundane could be considered evidence of conspiracy. About one suspected cult house, Cashin asked, "Early in the morning, when I went by there, there was people sitting on the front porch. Does that mean anything?" Sandy replied, "Sometimes."

Surprise asked, "Are those people all up and down 295 spotters?" Sandy said most of them were. Surprise repeated, "Those are all cult people?" By the end of the conversation, every person along State Route 295, all the way up to Old State Line Road, was either a member of the cult, a spotter for the cult, or a participant in a grand conspiracy of silence.

During the June 3 interview with Sandy, Cashin pulled out a blanket she had acquired from a friend, which had allegedly been purchased at Lady Circe's shop. It had a stain on it, which Cashin suspected was evidence that the blanket had been used during a human sacrifice. Cashin said she was going to get the stain tested in a lab. The following exchange is recorded in the transcript:

DEP CASHIN: Why? It must mean something.

LT SURPRISE: Is that used on an altar?

SANDY: (*answer inaudible*)

LT SURPRISE: Remember what I told you I thought was on there?

DEP CASHIN: That stain. Because I have to believe my girlfriend. She said she's never used it. She packed it away 'cause it was so pretty. And there is a stain on there.

MRS JONES: They thought if they sold it, it couldn't be traced. I mean no one... they get money for it, but no one would ever bring it back.

DEP CASHIN: Well, my next step is to have that stain analyzed and find out what it is.

After they discussed their suspicions, Sandy suddenly remembered that the blanket used to hang on the wall at Lady Circe's house. "Whoever carried it was very special," she added. Surprise suggested, "It was used to cover someone after they'd be sacrificed." Sandy added, "More than likely, it was her daughter."

The blanket was not the only piece of evidence Cashin introduced. During the May 17 interview, Cashin said, "Several years ago, there was a little boy down in, I believe, the Lion's Store, or LaSalle's, or Tiedtke's, or one of the stores downtown. Mama let him go to the bathroom himself. Didn't come out... didn't come out... didn't come out. Finally, they went in and found him with his penis cut off."

"Uh-huh," Sandy replied.

"Who did that?" asked Cashin.

"Um, a man named David."

Cashin went on to talk about the way the perpetrators left the young victim to bleed to death. When Sandy asked if the boy died, Cashin said she thought he did, but she would need to go back and check. Surprise mentioned two other names Sandy had given, asking if they were the ones who had castrated the little boy in the public restroom. She said yes, they were involved.

Just a few months prior to the Spencer Township investigation, in March of 1985, *The Columbus Dispatch* ran an article which relayed Cashin's story nearly word for word.[2] Professor Ralph Rosnow of Temple University in Philadelphia described the "castration story" as the ultimate anxiety-based rumor. Researchers found that the earliest tales of public restroom castration attacks gained traction in the Detroit area during the race riots of 1967. Interestingly, when white people told the story, the alleged perpetrator was always said to be Black; when a Black person told the story, the alleged perpetrator was always said to be white.

Newspapers quickly debunked the rumor as untrue, and scholars considered it a byproduct of social anxieties of the time. There are no documented cases of castration attacks in public restrooms in the Toledo area during this time. None of this stopped Sandy from identifying three individuals in connection with the crime.

On one occasion, Deputy Cashin did cite her sources. During their final interview with the informant, Cashin asked Sandy, "Did you see *20/20* the night it was on? A couple weeks ago?" She then went on to describe a portion of the infamous "Devil Worshippers" segment which had aired on May 16, 1985.

"Remember when *20/20* was on? Did you see it when they were talking about satanic worshiping? At the end of the show, an expert from California, who I believe was named Sandi..."

"I know who you're talking about," said Surprise.

"Okay," continued Cashin. "She said that the reason they can't put any of these cases together is because usually the children are cremated, and then their ashes and bones are used for whatever reason."

Deputy Cashin went on to ask the informant why this case was different from the cases shown on television.

There is no question that Kirk Surprise and Trilby Cashin were acting with sincerity and conviction. Months into an investigation, and potentially surrounded by co-conspirators on all sides, Cashin and Surprise found themselves in a lonely place. In a private conversation with Mrs. Jones, Cashin described their situation, leaving no doubt about her belief in Sandy:

DEP CASHIN: I wholeheartedly believed in her, but... you've got to understand, because you're a normal person, that you've got to convince a judge this isn't BS.

MRS JONES: Uh-huh.

DEP CASHIN: And in my mind, in my Lieutenant's mind, and in your mind, we know it's not BS. We see the fear in Sandy. But they haven't seen that, so you've got to understand where they're coming from.

MRS JONES: Yeah.

DEP CASHIN: You know. You saw *20/20* tonight? How police departments are trying to say not my police, not my country.

MRS JONES: Yeah.

DEP CASHIN: Things like that, you know... and that's basically what's going on. We just can't confide in anybody, because they laugh at us. They think we're nuts.

MRS JONES: Yeah.

DEP CASHIN: And if they could only be there to see Sandy talk. They would know...

MRS JONES: Yeah.

DEP CASHIN: We're not nuts.

26. An Interview with Dr. G. Michael Pratt

In 2021, thirty-six years after he was asked to consult on the Spencer Township dig, Dr. G. Michael Pratt agreed to sit down for an interview. Reflecting on his experience, he said, "I worked on several cold cases where we found nothing, and I worked on several other cases where we did find remains that were connected to murder cases. But this one, I have a lot of memories of, just because it seemed both chaotic and bizarre."

A native of Middletown, Ohio, Pratt enrolled at Miami University Middletown before relocating to the Oxford campus, where he completed his bachelor's degree in Anthropology in 1973. He went on to earn his master's and doctoral degrees from Case Western Reserve University. While completing his doctorate, Pratt was adjunct faculty at the University of Toledo and served as a Regional Archaeologist for the Ohio Historic Preservation Office at the Ohio Historical Society in Columbus. He also led numerous archaeological surveys, focusing his research on the prehistory of the Western Lake Erie Basin.

From 1983 until 2010, Pratt held faculty and administrative positions at Heidelberg University (formerly Heidelberg College) in Tiffin, Ohio, where he achieved tenure and promotion to Professor of Anthropology. He directed the Heidelberg Archaeological Survey and later the Center for Historic and Military Archaeology. Pratt's archaeological research resulted in two battlefield sites becoming National Park Service units, including Fallen Timbers-1794 and River Raisin-1813.

Sometimes construction or other digging projects turn up human bones which are archaeological in nature, such as ancient Native American remains or abandoned gravesites. Investigators from the coroner's office often consult with an archaeologist to determine whether the case is forensic in nature. Throughout his career, Pratt worked with law enforcement in this capacity, as a forensic anthropologist. Later in his career, Pratt went on to become a member of DMORT (a federal disaster, mass fatalities response team), and taught forensic anthropology courses at Heidelberg and a Continuing Education course in Forensic Anthropology at Ohio Peace Officers Training Academy in London, Ohio.

At the time of the Spencer Township investigation, Pratt had been contracted by Lucas County to organize and execute the relocation of Sunshine Cemetery, which had been a potter's field or indigent graveyard.

200

The cemetery had been legally declared abandoned and the county had initiated plans to build a senior center on the land. They expected to move between seven hundred and fifteen hundred graves; by the end of the project, Pratt's team had found nearly four thousand graves.

Pratt's first contact with the Spencer Township investigation stemmed from his ongoing work in Lucas County. The relocation of Sunshine Cemetery had drawn significant media attention and colleagues in the coroner's office had already found Pratt to be professional and reliable. When the Prosecutor's office and Sheriff's Department were looking for someone to consult on the satanic cult case, Pratt's name came up.

Pratt remembers being approached by someone from Lucas County, who he believes may have been associated with the prosecutor's office. "He just showed up out at the Sunshine Cemetery, where we were working, and told me he thought they could use my help in a police investigation."

Willing to offer whatever help he could, Pratt got in a car and was driven to the suspected burial site in Spencer Township. During the ride, he recalls, "At that time, they thought there was some kind of satanic operation going on, with the sacrificing of children. They thought there were perhaps a lot of children sacrificed over a long period of time. They weren't looking for a mass grave with a lot of people in it. They were looking for a series of graves or burials."

On this initial visit, which police files specify took place on April 19, 1985, Pratt viewed the site from the road. Investigators withheld specific details, but Pratt was able to survey the general area and provide basic information about how a search for burials would need to be conducted.

"Those are old lake margin areas out there, and it's almost entirely sand. You have topsoil over the sand, and that's usually dark black or brown in color. The sand itself is kind of yellowish or goldish or light brown. Lake Erie beach sand is what it is. If you scrape the top off and anybody's dug a hole, then it will be easy to see."

Whenever someone digs a hole, they fundamentally change the site. Pratt explained, "When you fill it back up, you can never fill it back exactly the way it was. This is an archaeological principle. The dirt that goes back in is always a mixture of what was taken out. It's never as densely packed as it originally was. You fill the hole up and you end up with a mound over the top of the hole. If somebody is trying to conceal a grave, they're going to scrape that away. But as the body decomposes, that is going to settle, and you get a depression."

Along with other factors, such as the decomposition of organic materials causing discoloration of the soil, these depressions make recent burials easier to spot. Pratt recommended the use of bulldozers to scrape away the top layers of soil to expose any possible graves.

"I said you're going to have to look over a big area, because if this has been going on for several years, it's only the people that have been buried in the last year or so where you would actually see settling in the area where the grave had been dug."

When he finished giving his advice on the matter, investigators drove Pratt back to Sunshine Cemetery. Pratt heard nothing else about the investigation until the morning of June 20, two months later, when deputies raided the Litton residence in Springfield Township.

Always a habitual news-watcher, Pratt remembers turning on the television that morning and watching the event unfold in real time. "I remember seeing the news coverage and saying, 'I know what they're talking about. That is where they took me.' So then, this thing blows up on TV. It's all over the morning news. They were standing outside the house they had raided, and I got phone calls that they were going to start excavating. They sent a detective's car to pick me up."

As he heard early reports of the raid, Pratt recalls his initial impressions. "They were kind of shooting at a moving target. I remember Ozzy Osbourne albums and a *Raiders of the Lost Ark* poster. As an archaeologist, we'd all seen *Raiders of the Lost Ark*. And goats. That was what came up in the search. I didn't think any of those were particularly convincing."

Media reports mention a *Raiders of the Lost Ark* poster seized from the Litton residence, but police records indicate that the poster depicted Mola Ram, the villain of the *Raiders* sequel, *Indiana Jones and the Temple of Doom*.

Pratt acknowledges he was not privy to the investigative work done behind the scenes, but the decision to start digging came across as rather abrupt. "I thought we were going to schedule a time. I thought we'd set everything up and go out there. Instead, they served a warrant on this house and then immediately went into the field."

When he arrived at the scene of the dig, the lack of clarity did not improve.

"We got out there and it was chaotic. It's the only way I can describe it to you. They had obtained a backhoe, with a backhoe operator. And they were digging a big, deep hole, which was the opposite of how I thought they should do it. I thought they would scrape off the topsoil over a wide area.

"There was no perimeter control. The press people were literally standing around the wheels of the backhoe, and around the tractor. And the backhoe driver was nearly in a panic."

Pratt remembers the look of terror on the poor man's face as he tried to maneuver the heavy digging apparatus without hitting anyone. Reporters and photographers were surrounding him on all sides, and many were standing in places where the operator could not see them.

"He was really nervous. People were shouting questions at him. He dug down, and then he needed to move the tractor to dig another big, deep hole right next to it. He was sweating buckets and he was exhausted. He'd probably been out there for an hour or two before I got there. I remember standing around and thinking, why aren't they getting people away from this guy?"

The backhoe in action. Photo courtesy of Lucas County Sheriff's Dept.

Pratt repeated his advice, suggesting the use of a bulldozer instead of a backhoe. "The police were in control of this excavation. Nobody said who I was or told me what to do. And at some point, they discontinued that backhoe. I don't remember who called it off. It was going to be unsuccessful, in my opinion. They had dug deeper than anybody could have with a hand tool. Unless the perpetrators of all the murders had power equipment out there, that was way too deep."

At one point, police knocked the cover off an old septic tank. They asked Pratt to look inside to make sure no bodies had been hidden inside.

Pratt noted that the tank was old, dry, and had no smell, indicating it was probably empty. He and officers shone flashlights into the tank without climbing inside.

The Columbus Dispatch reported that the backhoe dug in three areas, ranging in size from about five by twenty feet to thirty by fifty feet, by one reporter's estimation.[1] After a few hours, when the dig yielded no signs of human remains, investigators stopped using the backhoe and shifted their focus to several nearby houses. Pratt recalls, "Then they decided to go across the street. There were a couple of abandoned houses, and the police went in there to look around, and they wanted me to come with them.

"These houses, in my opinion, had a lot of junk. There were paint cans, there were Ball jars, there was clothing scattered around. It didn't look like there was any organization. I think one of those houses is where they found a doll that was nailed to a board."

Pratt remembers entering the cellar area of one of the abandoned houses. "Maybe some people were using it as a hangout for booze or drugs or something. I didn't even think it was being used by the homeless. There wasn't a lot of stuff that looked like it was occupied by anybody. It just had a lot of junk in it."

At the time, Pratt told reporters from *The Columbus Dispatch* that the dirt-floored cellar had several stakes driven into the ground, with a mound of sand in the center. There was nothing buried in the sand.[2]

Most of the items identified by investigators as evidence of satanic activity came from within the abandoned houses. Investigators ascribed satanic significance to a variety of objects from within the buildings, including rags, paint cans, clothing, written symbols on walls and papers, and other items.

Pratt recalls one knife, which investigators found in the cellar among a collection of old, discarded paint cans. "I remember one of the knives they found. I remember specifically because they showed it to me. I've seen them in antique stores before. One of those cake or bread knives that's got a wavy blade and an open wire handle. And it was thickly covered with paint. It wouldn't be able to cut anything. I thought somebody had used this old knife as a paint stirrer."

Investigators search the basement of an abandoned building near the dig site. Photos courtesy of Lucas County Sheriff's Dept.

Knowing Pratt was a forensic anthropologist, investigators sometimes asked him to comment on items they found. "People bring things to archeologists all the time and say, 'I found this, it fits in my hand. If I were going to use it, I'd use it for this.' And most of the time, that's not an accurate assessment of what it is. The police said to me, 'What is this?' And I said it looks like they've used it for stirring paint."

Eventually, another expert would comment on the significance of the knife. Pratt recalls, "Later, Dale Griffis came out. That was one of the things he thought was related to sacrifice. He said the paint was put on the blade to simulate blood, because it might not have been a real sacrificial knife. It didn't look like it was anything other than an old knife that had been used to stir paint. But I wasn't going to contradict the guy. I'm not a witchcraft expert."

When Griffis arrived on the scene, it created quite a stir. "He came in a medical helicopter, and the news was all surrounding the area. It was a big deal when he landed there in that helicopter. And he identified as satanic some things I hadn't thought were significant."

Pratt has always wondered about the necessity of this dramatic entrance. "Why were they using a medical helicopter to bring this guy up from Tiffin? He could have driven. I often drove from Tiffin. It's close to an hour drive."

The arrival of the occult expert changed the general dynamic of the search, shifting the focus away from the excavation and onto Griffis' commentary about items found in and around the abandoned houses. "After that, nobody asked me what I thought, and that was fine with me. I kept waiting for the bulldozer to show up and I kept waiting to go back over to the other field and look for where there might be graves. That's what I had the expertise to look for.

"He alighted from the helicopter and the press started asking him questions, and so that kind of put him in control of where they wanted to dig. I had no opinion. My job was to help the police to investigate and dig where they wanted to dig."

In the end, Pratt said, "They didn't find the bodies they were looking for. They thought there were scores of missing children, or missing people anyway. The other question then is, how were all these missing children supposed to be buried out there?"

If they had found human remains in Spencer Township, Pratt would have been willing to assist further. "I came back the next day with a carload of archaeological equipment. The people who were working at Sunshine Cemetery had been removing graves for months. By that time, I had a crew of ten who were working on that project for the county. We easily could have shifted out there and recovered what was out there."

Still, Pratt had known this outcome was unlikely. "I was happy to be done with it. What I thought all along was, if this was true, we would hit human remains right away, because there was supposed to be a lot of them out there."

Commenting in 2021, Pratt's recollection closely resembles the assessment he gave on the first day of the dig. He was quoted in *The Akron Beacon Journal*, saying the exploration of the cellar had yielded nothing but a bunch of junk.[3] When Dale Griffis identified a ten-foot-square area covered with fencing and cinder blocks as "highly unusual," Pratt told reporters from *The Columbus Dispatch*, "It looked to me like some fence fell over and a groundhog dug a hole under it."[4]

Pratt concluded, "I have worked on a number of police searches, successful and unsuccessful. This one was probably the most chaotic and uncontrolled, at least on the first day. If somebody wanted to look there, I'm an archaeologist. If you want to dig in the ground, we'll find it. If there's nothing there, we'll be able to tell you there's nothing there. And there, we didn't find it."

27. Riding a White Horse

Other than the confidential informant, perhaps no other person shaped the trajectory of the Spencer Township investigation more than Dale Griffis. Within days of the initial report, Public Relations Officer Marvin Reams contacted the Tiffin Police Department and asked to consult with the self-proclaimed cult expert. Griffis briefed investigators in matters of black magic and the occult, provided guidance on surveillance techniques, and even rode along with officers during a stake out. It was also Griffis who discerned various pieces of evidence and supposed signs of cult activity which surfaced throughout the investigation.

Who was Dale Griffis? How did he become an expert in the occult? And just how credible was the information he passed along?

Later in his career, Griffis' qualifications faced renewed scrutiny, particularly after he testified as an expert witness in the widely publicized West Memphis Three trial in 1994. In the infamous case, three teenagers were convicted of the brutal murder of three young boys, in what was purported to be a satanic ritual. Damien Echols was sentenced to death, while Jesse Misskelley Jr. and Jason Baldwin were sentenced to life imprisonment. Although his credentials faced rigorous scrutiny during the trial, Griffis was permitted to testify as an expert in the occult. This decision was later upheld by the Arkansas Supreme Court.

Due to the dubious nature of the evidence and suspected presence of emotional bias in the courtroom, the case generated widespread controversy and later became the subject of several documentaries. In 2011, after the Arkansas Supreme Court ordered new hearings on claims of jury misconduct and newly produced DNA evidence, all three defendants were released from prison after entering Alford pleas, a legal mechanism which allows a person to assert their innocence while acknowledging the prosecution has enough evidence to convict.

When he testified in 1994, Griffis claimed his knowledge of the occult came from over 4800 books he had read since 1976. For the timeline involved, this would mean Griffis read at least one book every day, all while serving as a full-time police officer and managing a private consulting business. During the two-year period when he gained his doctoral degree, he claimed to read three hundred books.[1] Griffis also cited the various training seminars he had attended throughout his twenty-six-year career, which ranged in topics from intelligence work to forensic hypnosis.[2]

208

In a 2015 interview, Griffis said he had encountered his first occult-related case when he was "barely out of Heidelberg, just a few weeks," after he graduated from college. In that case, a teenage boy died by suicide.[3] Griffis explained, "I started it after a kid committed suicide, offering his body up to Satan. And nobody in this whole area of Ohio had any idea what the heck was going on."[4]

Griffis was also fond of saying he had spent time with law enforcement agencies on the West Coast to learn about cults, through a process he called "lateral transfer." In 2015, Griffis said he spent one week with the San Francisco Police Department and one week with the Los Angeles Police Department, "just so that I knew what was going on in California, and so forth."[5] When he testified as an expert witness in 1994, Griffis said he had spent two weeks in San Francisco and two weeks in Los Angeles.[6]

Griffis described the West Coast trip, saying, "I had the opportunity to go into some traditional occult groups where they were where they carried out their services, I had a chance to go into their bookstores. I met members, talked with them. And really worked the street, right, walking and talking with them into their coffeehouses."[7] It is unclear whether the trip lasted two weeks or four weeks, but Griffis often cited the experience as being instrumental in opening his eyes to matters of the occult.

Dale Griffis had both a master's and doctoral degree which came under scrutiny during the West Memphis Three trial. On the stand, Griffis said his degrees were in criminal justice.[8] He sometimes said his degrees were in psychology. A letter from Columbia Pacific University specified that Griffis received a Doctor of Philosophy degree with a major in Law Enforcement and Psychology.[9]

Griffis received his master's and doctoral degrees in three years while maintaining his full-time position as deputy police chief in Tiffin, Ohio. He completed both degree programs by mail and never attended any classes. Griffis indicated that he did not need formal classrooms to become an expert, saying, "I was in the classroom about every day when I was on the street."[10]

The state of California ordered Columbia Pacific University to close in 1995, citing among other reasons a failure to employ duly qualified faculty, failure to meet various requirements for issuing PhD degrees, and awarding excessive credits for prior experiential learning. In the suit which ultimately led to the permanent closure of the institution in 1999, the Deputy Attorney General of California referred to Columbia Pacific University as "a diploma mill which has been preying on California consumers for too many years" and "a consumer fraud, a complete scam." The suit also referred to Columbia Pacific University as a "phony operation" offering "totally worthless [degrees]...to enrich its unprincipled promoters."

In a written statement, Griffis defended his credentials, pointing out that the state of California had determined that degrees issued by Columbia Pacific University prior to 1997 should be considered legally valid. "While I was going to CPU, it was in corresponding status for accreditation."[11] He later added, "This was not some place that my dog graduated from."[12]

Even late in life, Griffis never doubted the validity of his work in the occult. He wrote, "Yes, I am retired, and I quiver when I hear that in the 1980's some misguided individuals started the Satanic Panic. The truth is that I reported on and discussed cases on which I worked or obtained firsthand knowledge. I even withdrew some claims for which I questioned the documentation. Were there people spreading some questionable data? I think so. But I never associated with them, and I tried hard never to be associated with them."[13]

In the same letter, he added, "Although some media portrayals depict me as a charlatan, I was qualified by the judge as an expert based on my credentials, training, and experience. I testified about my opinions, and I never perjured myself. MY integrity is unscathed."

To his credit, many people who worked with Griffis agreed with his assessment, at least early in his career. In 1984, after attending Griffis' training seminar on the dangers of cults, Belmont County Sheriff Richard Stobbs said, "He knows the subject and gave us some good insights." A colleague from the Ohio Peace Officer's Training Academy, Jeff Rossi, said, "I think it's important knowledge. I worry sometimes about the issue of church-state separation, but we keep the information pretty moderate and don't accuse all cults of criminal activities."[14]

Jerry Kiser of the Seneca County Prosecutor's office praised Griffis for his work on the occult, saying, "He can differentiate between suspected cult activities and a person who is trying to make a crime look like the work of a cult as a cover-up."

As calls flooded his office from concerned parents who had attended his training seminars, Griffis emphasized above all his desire to help others. "I have difficulty sleeping at times. I keep wishing I could do more for these people."[15]

To many he advised, Griffis was seen as one who tried to impart method and reason to seemingly senseless acts of violence.[16] This view was not universally shared.

Discussing Griffis' complicated legacy, one journalist wrote, "To some reporters and the law enforcement community, he is an intelligent analyst of an increasing source of criminal activities. To others, he is an obsessive gatherer of useless information." Later in the same article, the journalist wrote, "He is sometimes remembered by Tiffin residents as the guy who got shot in the derriere during a police training exercise, or for the time he blasted a hole in the roof of his police cruiser while fiddling with a shotgun."[17]

Griffis also alienated some people at home who believed his first duty was to manage Tiffin's thirty-two-member police force. Although he was second in command at the time of the Spencer Township dig, other officers complained that Griffis was detached from day-to-day activities. Most of his working day, they claimed, was spent chasing down claims of cult crimes.[18] Mayor of Tiffin Tom Yager said, "What is he doing for us? That's what I want to know."[19]

Mayor Yager had been at odds with Griffis since May of 1985, when Griffis agreed to appear on the television program *20/20*. After the broadcast, Yager wrote a letter to ABC, which also appeared in the local newspaper. In the letter, Yager called the *20/20* segment, "one of the most irresponsible and sensationalistic pieces of journalism I have ever seen." He went on to attack Griffis' motivations and education, saying, "Dale Griffis is hardly known locally for absolute credibility, and his motives in continually attempting to obtain publicity for himself and his 'cult' field have to be suspect."[20]

In response to these criticisms, Griffis admitted that his thoughts often wandered from conventional police work to his own specific concerns. While he sometimes had trouble separating his private interests from his local obligations, Griffis insisted his heart was in the right place. "All I want to do is help people."[21]

Tiffin Police Chief David A. Martien also said it was sometimes difficult to distinguish between duties for the police force and Griffis' own personal consulting business. Griffis had been warned numerous times about his large phone bills, from frequent long-distance calls around the country to discuss cults. Although Griffis was on-the-clock for the police department when he consulted with Lucas and Union Counties on suspected cult crimes, he was also paid for his services through his private consulting business.[22]

Although he had praised Griffis earlier in his career, Jeff Rossi of the Ohio Peace Officer's Training Academy in London, Ohio later changed his assessment. According to Rossi, the academy was considering dropping Griffis from its part-time faculty due to student complaints. Griffis had been hired to teach students from small police departments how to handle complicated investigations. Instead, students alleged Griffis became preoccupied telling stories about his cult-related exploits. In 1985, Rossi told reporters, "I would rather not have him back."[23]

When it came to Griffis' work on the occult, there was an undercurrent of skepticism throughout the law enforcement community. In both the Lucas County dig and the Union County animal mutilation cases, Griffis corroborated claims of satanic activity. Both cases were widely publicized but led to no arrests. Rossi gave voice to many of his colleagues when he said, "I'm a skeptic. I want to see evidence. Where's the evidence? This creates a false image of baby killers. But there's never been a documented case of human sacrifice in this country."[24]

Some officers disliked working with Griffis because his appearance at a crime scene often resulted in media attention, professional animosity, and a disregard for standard investigative procedures. Colleagues in Tiffin reportedly nicknamed Griffis "The Riddler," because, "You can never get a straight answer out of him."[25]

A federal agent from the Cleveland area who had worked with Griffis criticized his police work as ineffective. Speaking anonymously to reporters, the agent said, "He does a lot of flow charts, but nobody goes to jail. The guy is apparently interested in media attention rather than putting people in the can."[26]

Griffis also found himself at the center of a few local scandals during his time on the Tiffin Police Department. Funders provided a significant amount of grant money with the understanding it would be spent on police equipment, computers, and for drug-buy money. Computer equipment purchased with grant money ended up at Griffis' home, where he used it for his personal consulting business. Drug-buy money went unaccounted for. The state auditor's office and Seneca County prosecutors investigated alleged misuse of thousands of dollars which had been destined for Tiffin's Furtherance of Justice Fund. Griffis justified his actions by saying he never promised the grant money would be used within the police department. "I got a grant for me," he said.[27]

Seventeen members of the Tiffin Police Department also sued the city to void Griffis' 1985 appointment to the newly created position of Deputy Chief. The suit claimed Griffis was appointed to the position without a competitive examination and that other officers were passed over for the opportunity.[28] Shortly after, Griffis retired from the police department to focus on his consulting business.

It should be noted that most of the agencies who worked with Griffis had no public record of complaints about him. In some cases, Griffis was praised for his contributions, including his involvement in the investigation of Dr. Michael Swango, a former OSU Hospital resident who was found guilty of poisoning his colleagues in Adams County, Illinois. The mayor's public criticism of Griffis also ignited a debate about his value in the community. Griffis' personnel file was filled with good deeds done for the local citizenry and his supporters were quick to denounce the mayor in letters and paid advertisements in the local paper.[29] Griffis was certainly well-loved.

Griffis often wore a ring with the inlay of a Roman Centurion, who he considered to be the police of ancient Rome. When speaking with reporters, he sometimes sat at his desk, surrounded by the framed certificates of his completed coursework and training seminars.[30] Although he spoke about his humble beginnings as a small-town cop, Griffis tended to cast himself in the heroic role, suggesting he could offer unique services which few others could duplicate.

In 1984, he said, "I can think of maybe four other people in law enforcement with the same knowledge. It is an extremely limited field."[31] He later told a Toledo-area reporter, "I like going to an area where I can do my thing and leave, and ride out on a white horse, and never been seen again."[32]

Griffis acknowledged that he was sometimes a last resort for investigators who had their backs against the wall. During an interview with *The Columbus Dispatch* in 1984, Griffis said, "You've got to remember there're a lot of sheriffs and a lot of police chiefs under a hell of a lot of pressure when I get there. I'm there to help my brother police officers. I report to them, not to the public."[33]

Because Griffis remained tight-lipped about the details of past consultations, it was difficult to track the number of occult cases he had worked on. Although Griffis publicly said, "It is also essential that we look for validation markers, and document, document, document," the cult expert was notoriously evasive when it came to corroborating details.[34]

When describing his experience with the occult, Griffis frequently mentioned his years of experience on the Tiffin Police Force, a twenty-six-year tenure which is well-documented and undisputed. While serving as a full-time officer in his small-town police department, Griffis claimed to have knowledge of over 1500 occult-related cases by 1994. In a written letter, Griffis later said he personally worked on over two thousand cult cases before he retired. For the years involved, Griffis' estimates would equate to eighty-three new cult cases per year, or one to two cases per week, all in addition to his full-time responsibilities in Tiffin.[35]

In his training seminars and in numerous interviews, Griffis was fond of sharing a particular story, which he said had circulated among law enforcement agencies. Allegedly, two police officers were murdered by devil worshipers after they crossed the boundary of a five-pointed star. When Griffis shared this story, he usually included a warning about the risks of interrupting a cult ritual in progress. "Their spells aren't dangerous," he said. "But when their spells don't work, they tend to make them work."[36]

In a 2015 interview, Griffis said he learned about the incident for the first time during one of his training seminars. According to Griffis, someone told him the story right before he gave a lecture. He passed the story along to his audience, saying, "I've just been informed this happened. Be careful in the field." When a seminar participant asked where and when the incident had occurred, Griffis looked around the room, hoping to find the person who had told him the story. The alleged source was gone. "They had skedaddled," Griffis claimed.[37]

After describing the dubious origin story of his cult cop-killer anecdote, Griffis went on to cite the seminar incident as a reason why he always insisted on properly sourcing information. He did not explain why he continued sharing this story for years after his lone source skedaddled.

During the Spencer Township dig, Dale Griffis pointed to several signs which he said were indicative of cult activity. The media is often accused of sensationalizing or fabricating stories for the sake of gaining a wider audience, but even in the earliest reports, many journalists responded to Griffis' evidence with a skeptical tone

For example, several news outlets reported on mysterious writings inside a vacant house which were said to be satanic in nature. The writing was found on a sheet of tin, but investigators could not decipher the specific meaning. Some journalists pointed out that this "satanic writing" appeared to be normal letters of the alphabet which had been written in reverse.[38]

Investigators also found a knife with a wooden handle in one of the vacant buildings. To the journalists present, it appeared to be a common household kitchen knife. Griffis told the press it was a "ritual dagger" called an "athame." When reporters asked how he could tell it was a ritual dagger as opposed to a discarded knife, Griffis replied, "Any kind of knife can be an athame, even a steak knife."[39]

Later, Griffis showed reporters a small plot of land which had been sectioned off with wooden stakes and red string. Several reporters noted that it appeared to be a small vegetable garden which had been poorly tended. Griffis insisted the plot served a ceremonial purpose. He pointed to a tin can near the middle, which he said would be used for burning items during a ritual. Reporters noted that the can was empty.[40]

At one point, Griffis called attention to a piece of red string which was hanging at eye level from a tree branch. Nearly fifty television reporters gathered to listen while Griffis explained the significance of the string, which he claimed had been used during satanic rituals. The journalists were unimpressed, noting in their reporting that the string was only about six inches long, draped over the branch with no discernable knotting, shape, or pattern.[41]

When investigators found a headless doll with a toy phone tied to its wrist, Griffis all but admitted that he was piecing together his theories as he went along. As reporters shouted questions at him, asking what the doll might mean in connection to the mysterious cult, Griffis candidly replied, "I'm trying to work that out."[42]

This devil-may-care approach to clue identification would resurface throughout Griffis' career. In 1994, during his testimony in the West Memphis Three trial, Griffis emphasized his expertise in "non-traditional groups." These groups, according to Griffis, followed their own leaders and were not bound by any structures, systems, or manuals. When asked to describe signs of satanic crime, Griffis said, "It could be anything."[43]

Since non-traditional groups were not bound by rules or norms, any action could be attributed to them. If elements of a crime scene fit the pattern, they could be called textbook examples of devil worship. If elements of a crime scene did not fit the pattern, they could be written off as the idiosyncrasies of a non-traditional group. Anything and everything could be considered a sign of satanic crime.

During his testimony in the 1994 trial, Griffis even took time to "correct" some of the evidence. When asked to comment on the significance of symbols written in one of the defendants' journals, Griffis said the boy must have been confused because he had blended several types of witchcraft in his writings. The defendants were alleged to be practitioners of witchcraft and active members of a cult, but Griffis claimed the symbols they drew were incorrect because they did not match his expectations. In essence, he claimed to know more about devil worship than the devil worshipers themselves.[44]

In a similar example during the trial, Griffis said cult members would always wear tattoos and markings on the left hand in one of two specific places... unless the cult member was mixed up, in which case they would put the tattoo elsewhere. For Griffis, if an alleged cult signifier did not fit the preconceived pattern, it was simply explained away as a deviation by non-traditional actors.[45]

Despite the apparent fluidity and unpredictability of non-traditional satanic groups, Griffis had no trouble identifying "clear signs" of their presence in virtually every case he worked. Any plain steak knife could be a ritual dagger. Any combination of numbers could hold significance. Any tattoo in any location could signify secret cult involvement. In essence, Griffis had created a dynamic where anything and everything could be evidence of satanic activity, and he was the only person in the room who was perceptive enough to see the signs.

Throughout his career, Griffis demonstrated a proclivity for storytelling, even if the details were vague, undocumented, or impossible to falsify. Although it is not directly related to the Spencer Township investigation, Griffis' involvement in the highly publicized West Memphis Three trial is worth examining because it provides critical insights about his credibility and reliability as an expert.

According to Griffis, officers from West Memphis, Arkansas had attended one of his seminars on cult crime. Concerned about possible satanic activity among teenagers, the officers had asked Griffis for advice. What could be done to stop a satanic cult from recruiting teens in their area?[46]

Griffis told them to watch out for animal mutilations. He told them to be aware of any cult holidays, or special dates which might hold significance. He said any text underlined in red might signify cult involvement.[47] Finally, Griffis gave a series of suggestions to protect teens, including monitoring the type of music teens enjoyed, observing the types of clothing they wore, and checking with local schools to see if anyone had written about satanic themes in English class or created any artwork with satanic imagery.[48]

Eighteen months after he made these suggestions, three boys were murdered in West Memphis. If they had only listened to him, Griffis claimed, those boys would still be alive. In a 2015 interview, Griffis lamented that teachers and principals had not acted on his advice, saying, "I had no knowledge these people had not followed the instructions I had given them. And as a result, three kids died. And I felt very bad for the parents. I feel bad for the victims. It wasn't exactly my job to follow through with it, but on the other hand, I sure wish people had listened."[49]

After the arrests had already been made, investigators sent information about the case to Griffis by fax machine, asking if anything at the crime scene pointed to a satanic motivation. Griffis never visited the crime scene, never examined the victims, and never met any of the defendants. He only became involved when prosecutors decided to incorporate a possible satanic motivation into their case.

When it was time for him to testify, Griffis flew into the area the night before. He returned home as soon as his testimony ended. Griffis later claimed he was grilled for over six hours. Of the time he spent on the stand, he claimed defense attorneys spent five and a half hours questioning his credentials.[50] Griffis' testimony was recorded and fully transcribed. His time on the stand truly lasted a little over two hours.

Despite his small and focused role, Griffis later went on to paint himself as a central figure in the case. In a 2007 newspaper interview, Griffis claimed that Damien Echols, one of the defendants who stood accused of murdering three boys, could be seen staring at the photo of Griffis during the trial. Griffis said, "When he got done testifying, what you didn't see on television, what you didn't see in the [HBO documentary] *Paradise Lost*, was the fact that Damien Echols said, 'I got three. I had ten more to go for my coven, but that damn cop from Ohio stopped me.'"[51]

By his own admission, Griffis played no role in the arrest or prosecution of Damien Echols. Investigators did not reach out to Griffis until the trial was underway, and even then, he only corresponded by fax. Griffis openly lamented that law enforcement officers had failed to follow his suggestions to root out devil worshipers. If Griffis was not involved in the case, and if officers had ignored the only advice he had given, why would Echols credit the "damn cop from Ohio" as the one who stopped him?

Even if Echols somehow believed Dale Griffis was responsible for stopping his alleged murder spree, when would he have been able to make the statement Griffis claimed to overhear? Why would he make such an incriminating statement within earshot of others, particularly in the courtroom during his own murder trial? How had television cameras and audio recorders missed it? And since the records show that Griffis left as soon as his testimony ended, when could he possibly have heard Echols make such an admission?[52]

While on the stand, Griffis claimed he had been qualified as an expert witness in other occult-related cases. He could not recall any names or locations for these cases. In one instance, Griffis said he had been an expert witness for the defense in a case which involved a husband and wife who murdered and dismembered a body inside a large pentagram, as part of a satanic ritual. He could not remember the full name of the defendant but said the case had happened somewhere near Flint, Michigan.[53] No reports could be found which matched the description given by Griffis.

Griffis later wrote, "The defense counsel became highly agitated and charged the witness box, angrily asking if it was true that Columbia Pacific University was not a state accredited college."[54] In a 2015 interview,

Griffis repeated this claim, saying Damien Echols' defense attorney was screaming "within six inches of my face."

Griffis said the attorney went "berserk," asking the same question "fifty to seventy-five times." Because the lawyer was "screaming and yelling his head off," the judge intervened, taking the attorney into his chambers, and threatening to throw him in jail if he persisted in the line of questioning. Undaunted by this threat, Griffis said the attorney continued questioning his credentials anyway.[55]

Court transcripts show no evidence that the same question was asked "fifty to seventy-five times." Griffis' testimony was captured on camera by filmmakers and segments of the testimony were included in a series of HBO documentaries called *Paradise Lost*. Footage of the defense counsel's line of questioning does not match Griffis' characterization of events.

Further, the entirety of Griffis' testimony is fully transcribed and available as an audio recording. None of the recordings captured attorneys "screaming and yelling" at Griffis. There is also no indication that the judge threatened to send the defense team to jail, or that they withdrew to his chambers for a conference.[56]

Griffis also claimed he narrowly escaped death during his testimony in the West Memphis Three trial. He wrote, "I finished and was about to step down from the witness box, and the doors opened, and a SWAT team approached me, and I was escorted from the courtroom. The media never show these security measures that were required to protect me, nor the group of Damien Echols groupies in the courtroom."[57]

Griffis repeated this story in a 2015 podcast interview. He claimed that Damien Echols had "followers" who sat in the courtroom, all dressed in black. These people stared at him, trying to intimidate him into silence. After finishing his testimony, Griffis claimed a group of SWAT officers burst into the courtroom, covered him with a bomb blanket, and rushed him to safety before the devil worshipers could do him harm.[58]

No media reports mention this incident. The audio recording of Griffis' testimony gives no indication that such an incident transpired. In the recording, both attorneys can be heard saying they have no further questions. The judge can be heard asking, "Can we let him go?" After that, the judge can be heard telling Griffis that a state police officer will drive him to the airport to catch his plane. Griffis can be heard thanking the judge. After a pause, the judge can be heard calmly saying, "Let's take a short recess."[59]

In fairness, Griffis did claim that media outlets never reported on his near-death experience in the courtroom. Perhaps there was a cover-up. Maybe the documentary filmmakers missed the incident or chose not to include the harrowing footage in their final cut.

In a 2021 email, Joe Berlinger, one of the filmmakers behind the HBO documentary series *Paradise Lost*, commented on the anecdote. Berlinger was in the room when Dale Griffis took the stand, and he filmed the whole thing. Was Dale Griffis threatened? Was he grilled on the stand for six hours, while the defense attorneys shouted in his face? Was he whisked to safety by a SWAT team as devil worshipers attacked?

"None of that happened," said Berlinger. "He gave his testimony and that was that. You can rest assured, if it really happened, it would've ended up in *Paradise Lost*."

28. Bibles and Badges

Law enforcement expert Robert Hicks researched and wrote extensively on the police model of satanic crime, collecting dozens of handouts, books, and other training materials distributed throughout the country at police training seminars. Based on his observations, Hicks wrote a thorough critique of the cult crime model in his book, *In Pursuit of Satan: The Police and the Occult.*

Hicks noted that seminar presenters rarely defined their terms. There was a strong tendency in police training sessions to blend words like satanism, cult, witchcraft, and occult without clarity. While many police training manuals warned of the danger posed by "Satanists" or "devil worshipers," no distinction was made between members of alleged underground, child-murdering cults, and law-abiding practitioners of non-Christian religions, such as satanism, Wicca, or other pagan traditions.[1]

Further, Hicks noticed a strong bias in cult-cop presentations toward Anglo-Christian viewpoints. In many police training sessions, presenters referenced an attack on traditional Christian values and framed cult-related crime as an attempt to undermine faith in God. Even when the presentation did not overtly reference the Christian faith, virtually all seminars on satanic crime came from a Christian perspective.[2]

In a survey of police officers who specialized in satanic crime, Hicks determined that the field was ninety-one percent male and ninety-six percent white. Almost all cult cops reported believing in God, although some said they did not believe in the Devil.[3] Cult-crime seminar presenters tended to be conservative Christians who identified their own cultural experience as normative.[4]

Although presenters claimed to respect the First Amendment right of religious freedom, many seemed to target anything that was not expressly Christian. During one seminar, Sandi Gallant of the San Francisco Police Department said, "Satan's goal is to defeat God's plan of grace and to establish his kingdom of evil in order to ruin man. Satan needs men and women alive to accomplish his work for him, because he is a disembodied spirit."[5] In another session, Gallant said everything Satanists might do "is done to defame the name of God and Christ."[6]

In the absence of criminal evidence, cult-crime experts encouraged officers to investigate a growing list of non-criminal behaviors. Under the satanic crime model, listening to certain music, wearing certain clothing or jewelry, or practicing non-Christian (particularly Afro-Caribbean) religious beliefs were listed as "reg flags."

Using this model, law enforcement agencies across the country began procuring noncriminal intelligence on suspected cult members.[7] Occult expert Dale Griffis frequently told educators, parents, and police officers to check music, books, and artwork for signs of possible satanic crime. Griffis even named wearing black clothing, tattoos, or painted fingernails as signs of satanic involvement.[8]

Political bias also factored into many cult-crime seminars. One FBI conference on satanic crime "taught its participants questions to ask children in ritual abuse cases, and it instructed prosecutors in what was virtually a tenet of the economically cutthroat Reaganite 1980s: that people who lacked high-powered jobs and large salaries were failures, even morally defective." Officer Sandi Gallant told conference participants that Satanists were "working class" people or "underachievers" who led "mediocre lifestyles."[9]

Most of all, Hicks criticized the satanic crime model for its complete lack of prosecutable evidence. Hicks noted a tendency for some cult experts to disguise the absence of verifiable substance with the use of scientific, technical, or occult-related jargon. There was often a strong emphasis on anecdotal evidence, with a tendency to repeat undocumented or unconfirmed stories of cult crime rather than verifiable facts. Many training seminars claimed satanic crimes were on the rise, but there was no data to support this claim.[10]

Satanic crime seminars required a pre-existing belief in satanic cults. Conference attendees were asked to begin with the assumption that their town was full of devil worshipers, then "root out" evidence to support this conclusion. Hicks criticized the cult-cop model for relying on the suspension of critical faculties and abandonment of standard investigative techniques. Hicks wrote, "When cult cops find no evidence, they intensify efforts to uncover wrongdoing. An absence of criminal behavior merely indicates success at eluding the police."[11]

In most cases, officers were able to choose which training seminars to attend. Robert Hicks surveyed participants at a prominent satanic crime conference, asking officers what had triggered their initial interest in the occult.

Some reported graffiti or vandalism in their community as an inciting incident. A few mentioned an unsolved local crime, such as kidnapping or murder. Others said they had attended previous workshops on satanism or read about the topic. A small number of conference attendees said they became interested in the occult because they noticed local teens dabbling, or because they had discovered mutilated animals in their community. A few officers cited personal reasons.[12]

Regardless of their reason for attending, many law enforcement officers attended well-organized, slickly produced, and often sensational training seminars which promoted conspiracy theories about a massive underground network of devil worshipers. There have always been stories of devils. In the 1980s and 1990s, certain American law enforcement entities validated such stories by searching for those devils in public.

The satanic crime model, which became the standard model in police training seminars across the country, described four levels of satanic involvement. The lowest level, called dabblers, referred to teens and young adults who listened to rock music with occult themes, showed interest in satanic imagery or ideas, or became involved in fantasy role-playing games. The second level of satanic involvement was "self-styled satanism." This level of satanic crime was populated mostly by psychopathic or sociopathic criminals who engaged in dangerous and deviant behavior. The third level of satanism was called "organized satanism," referring to people who are public Satanists, as part of an organized movement. The fourth and final level is "covert satanism," which refers to involvement in secretive, criminal cults.

Although the model for satanic crime remained virtually unchanged for nearly a decade, Hicks noted several problems with the approach. The four-tiered model implied a progression, with people beginning their involvement in low-level dabbling before rising through the ranks. Changes between the various proposed levels would require radical changes in personality, predilection, and social status. The model theorized that under-achieving teenagers could progress from occult-themed rock music to increasingly antisocial behavior, but how could a sociopathic deviant go on to become part of the organized, very public Church of Satan? Further, how might this same person be suited for service in a highly secretive, delicately calibrated network of child traffickers that spanned the globe?[13]

223

FBI investigator Ken Lanning spent the better part of a decade looking into claims of satanic crime. Of the popular police model, he wrote, "The implication often is that all are part of a continuum of behavior, a single problem or some common conspiracy. The information is a mixture of fact, theory, opinion, fantasy, and paranoia, and because some of it can be proven or corroborated (desecration of cemeteries, vandalism, etc.), the implication is that it is all true and documented."[14]

Although he thoroughly investigated claims, using virtually every resource available to him as a federal agent, Lanning never found any evidence of the massive child-sacrificing network described by the police model. "I can't find even one documented case, and I've been looking for seven years or more," said Lanning in the early 1990s. "I personally have investigated some three hundred cases – and there is not a shred of evidence. There are no bodies and there is not one conviction."[15]

Ken Lanning first began asking polite yet skeptical questions about satanic crime in 1984, while attending occult conferences alongside his colleagues from the FBI. As his questioning grew more direct and as he made his skepticism more publicly known, cult-crime proponents promptly attacked him, implying Lanning was part of a cover-up launched by cult members to conceal the satanic conspiracy.[16]

Lanning described the satanic crime panic as an updated version of the "stranger danger" panic of the 1950s. He believed the theory gained popularity because it put complex issues into simple terms. "One of the oldest theories of crime is demonology. The devil makes you do it."[17]

Lanning ultimately concluded that cult ritual abuse did not exist, at least in the form of a massive, global network of devil worshipers. Similarly, Lanning found no compelling reason to confirm any instances of satanic murder. He wrote, "A satanic murder should be defined as one committed by two or more individuals who rationally plan the crime and whose primary motivation is to fulfill a prescribed satanic ritual calling for murder. By this definition, I have been unable to identify even one satanic murder in the United States."[18]

After the panic died down in Salem, there were apologies and reparations. In 1697, Samuel Sewall, who had presided over many witch trials, asked that a formal apology be read before the congregation in Boston's South Church so he could "take the blame and shame" for the harm done to their neighbors. Twelve trial jurors also came forward to publicly seek forgiveness.[19] Although numerous people lost their families, reputations, and livelihoods, and although many stood trial and some were wrongly convicted in connection with satanic conspiracy theories, no such apologies followed the satanic rumor-panic of the 1980s and 1990s.

29. Rumor Has It

In 1610, Basque villagers began hearing rumors, filtered down through their closest friends and relatives, that French judges in the north had discovered witches in the region.

Soon after, Franciscan friars warned about the aquelarre, or diabolical assembly, also known as the Witches' Sabbat. According to the friars, witches would gather on special dates to indulge in their own perverse rites and rituals, including orgies, desecration of Christian sacraments, and obscene contracts with the Devil.

And the witches would feast on the flesh of infants.

Children in the villages began to say they had witnessed these dark rituals taking place. When the children began naming people they had seen, lynch mobs were formed to round up the accused. Local judiciaries imprisoned and tortured those suspected of witchcraft. By 1611, a formal inquisition was called in response to the outcry of villagers seeking help in their fight against the witchy threat.

Using the most authoritative texts of the time, inquisitors extracted confessions, tortured, and burned to death hundreds of people as they sought out members of the supposed satanic conspiracy. These events in the Basque region became a microcosm of the broader witch panic that swept Europe between the fifteenth and seventeenth centuries.[1]

There are many examples of similar rumor panics throughout history. There is the centuries-old antisemitic blood libel myth, which has falsely accused Jewish people of murdering Christian children to use their blood in rituals. Ancient Romans accused the early Christians of taking part in orgies and elaborate infant-feasts. In the 1990s, a region in Kenya broke into a witchcraft panic following a widespread preaching campaign which equated traditional witchcraft ideas with satanic power as citizens grappled with power dynamics related to government and new wealth.[2]

When the Lucas County Sheriff's Department initiated their investigation in Spencer Township, satanic cult rumors were not unique to their community. In the mid-1980s and early 1990s, rumors of harmful satanic cults spread throughout the United States, and eventually into Canada and Europe. People were arrested and put on trial, and scores of alleged devil worshipers were accused of all sorts of heinous acts, including cannibalism, sexual abuse, and human sacrifice.

What is it that makes ugly rumors seem so attractive? Where do rumors come from and how do they spread? Why are these stories so persistent? And what can the average truth-seeker do to curb the spread of misinformation?

If history is any indication, there will be rumors of witches again.

A rumor can be defined as a story shared in conversations between people, containing assertions of truth that cannot be confirmed by incontrovertible evidence at the time, which is widely regarded as being true or plausible anyway. Rumors are usually shared by word of mouth but can also be disseminated by other means. Rumors are usually short-lived, locally situated, and specific in content.[3] In his book *The Watercooler Effect*, Nicholas DiFonzo describes rumors as unverified information which circulate about topics people care about, which often arise in situations of ambiguity or threat, and attempt to make sense of circumstances or manage risk.[4]

In the formation of rumors, truth is not the issue. A story can be considered a rumor if it collectively creates a shared perception of reality, without any manifestly obvious evidence to substantiate it. Rumors usually arise when something unusual or unexpected happens. When a rumor offers a plausible or satisfactory explanation for shared anxieties or concerns, it is more likely to persist over time.

Describing the explanatory power of rumors, DiFonzo wrote, "In short order, a causal chain of events is concocted so as to explain the current state of affairs. Rumors may start as isolated bits of information but soon evolved into cause-and-effect sequences."[5]

Why is the child missing? Because she was taken by a cult. Why did the cult take the child? Because they wanted to sacrifice her. Rumors gain credibility when they offer specific answers about an uncertain or anxiety-inducing situation.

As people contribute supporting details to the collective story, rumors can grow through the "snowball" effect. If the details of the rumor are specific, listeners may perceive great explanatory power within the rumor. The most crucial "evidence" for a rumor usually comes from eyewitness testimony.[6]

Like nightmares, satanic cult rumors reveal much about the fears and anxieties of the time. As parents and civic leaders grappled with a

227

changing society, some having lost faith in the "traditional" moral order of American society, many embraced simple answers. Richard Beck posited that the "Satanic Panic" era was largely an attempt of some minds to protect themselves by repressing two ideas: the traditional conception of the nuclear family was dying, and no one wanted to save it.[7] The satanic cult rumor could be translated to mean, "Our world is falling apart, because all things good and decent are under attack by evil forces beyond our control."

In scary times, people often find comfort in the explanation such rumors provide: the hidden evildoers are to blame.[8] The term memorate is used by folklorists to describe the process whereby individuals incorporate popular legends to explain puzzling or ambiguous circumstances. This often includes supernatural explanations, such as unseen ghosts or aliens. Because these explanations are a mixture of deeply rooted lore and modern-day anxieties, these types of rumors can be quite powerful.[9]

Rumors are "reality construction." As rumors are repeated, skepticism can erode. Researchers investigating claims of devil worship in rural Montana in the 1990s discovered just how powerful rumors can be. Even for the hardened non-believers in the group, the persistent repetition of rumors had an effect.

One investigator said, "Although we never found objective evidence to support the Satanist theory, we had no obvious basis for rejecting it either." As researchers investigated the origin of the devil worshiper stories, many residents explained their belief, saying, "Everyone was talking about it, so I thought there must have been truth to the stories."[10]

There are three broad motivations for spreading rumors: fact-finding, relationship-building, and self-enhancement. To the extent that a rumor satisfies one or more of these motivations, it will spread. The most persistent or stubborn rumors often satisfy more than one motivation.[11]

The motivation of fact-finding highlights the role of uncertainty, ambiguity, and cognitive unclarity in the spread of rumors. Uncertainty undermines an individual's ability to effectively deal with their environment. This leads to feelings of loss of control and anxiety, which motivates action to reduce the sense of uncertainty. By listening to and sharing rumors, people can assuage their feelings of insecurity in the absence of concrete information.[12]

Although rumors often arise during ambiguous circumstances, they do not always reduce uncertainty. Sometimes, rumors create or fuel uncertainty. Still, rumors may persist because the exchange of theories serves as a problem-solving process aimed at reducing uncertainty.[13]

In the absence of information from official channels, or when official channels are not trusted, people often turn to each other for answers. The exchange of rumors could be framed as an informal process for collective problem solving, satiating the need for understanding and predictability. In addition to granting an opportunity to vent anxiety, rumors often help people focus on an impending threat and rally others to take preemptive or retaliatory action.[14]

People often engage in social comparison of information before deciding what to believe. At some point, people must discuss information of questionable veracity, to verify whether other people share their uncertainty. Because people exchange rumors to find trustworthy information, the information that propagates most widely may not be that which is most believed, but rather that which is most in question. Partially believed or controversial rumors are more likely to be discussed. If information is obviously true or obviously false, it is less likely to become the subject of conversation.[15]

Rumors can also satisfy the motivation of relationship-building. Most rumors are shared during social encounters. People are conscious of the impressions they create in others and act to manage these impressions. During social interactions, people may share rumors to grab attention, to appear to be "in the know" on a particular topic, or to create and maintain a sense of status difference between themselves and others.

The act of spreading rumors can also assist in the manipulation of the inclusion vs. exclusion dynamic in the group by making a particular narrative only understandable to select people within the group.[16] People may share rumors to express social solidarity against a disliked or elite group, or to be favored over others in the eyes of their peers.[17]

Rumors may seem implausible at first, but the more a rumor is repeated, and the more it is taken seriously within their social network, the more likely a person is to adopt it as true. Most rumors disappear after a short time as relevance fades, but some rumors may persist to such an extent that they are folded into local mythology, where they can be drawn from the collective social rumor bank for incorporation into future rumors.[18]

In social encounters, individuals often come forward to verify or attest to even the most bizarre details of a rumor. There are a variety of personal motivations for endorsing a rumor in social settings, including attention or prestige, expression of one's own fantastical fears, attack on someone they dislike, as a joke or a prank, or as an expression of confusion or mental delusion.[19]

The primary motivation for spreading rumors is not always to find truth. Sometimes the rumor is shared purely to seek connection. This might explain why a friend stops speaking to someone after that person corrects or debunks a rumor, or why someone might find themselves blocked on social media after fact-checking the content of a post. Some people are not interested in the accuracy of information, but rather the connections they may gain from sharing said information.[20]

People are also more likely to spread a rumor when they personally believe it to be true. Maintaining credibility in the eyes of peers is a strong motivator for most people. Information is the currency of power and influence. If a person frequently shares information which is later proven to be inaccurate, their input is likely to hold less value in the future.[21]

The final motivation for rumor-spreading is self-enhancement. When judging the value of a rumor, many people do not engage in rational hypothesis testing. Instead, they tend to evaluate a rumor in light of their existing worldviews. To the extent that a rumor resonates with their pre-existing worldview, it is more likely to be believed. Rather than functioning as "reality construction," rumors for some people can function as "justification construction," or the collection of stories which most agree with prior attitudes.[22]

There are a variety of cognitive biases which focus on self-affirming hypotheses while promoting stereotypical or derogatory hypotheses about others. This contributes to many wedge-driving rumors which are designed to demonize or attack other groups. Rumors rarely contain negative or critical information about the teller's own in-group.[23] Successful rumors tend to be consistent with prevailing cultural themes, and the more a rumor aligns with a group or person's beliefs, the more persistent the rumor will become.[24]

One component of negativity bias involves the general tendency for people to take note of bad things that could happen to them more than good things. People are more likely to latch onto rumors of possible harm than rumors of good fortune. For example, people are more likely to act on a rumor that says they will lose $100 if they do not call their utility company right away, than a rumor that suggests they might win $100 if they call into a radio station during a contest.[25]

When parents heard shocking, detailed accounts of abuse and murder at the hands of bloodthirsty devil worshipers, for many it felt safer to assume the rumors were true. If the rumors were later proven to be false, their children would still be safe. If the rumors were true and parents failed to act, the consequences could be dire.

Research on rumors found that people were more likely to believe stories when they were shared by sources which seemed official or authoritative. Also, people were more likely to remember the most sensational aspects of news reports while forgetting any later corrections, retractions, or published denials.[26] Even when charges of devil worship were dropped or specific claims were debunked, these stories did not receive the same fanfare as the initial sensational coverage.[27]

One study found that lurid, disturbing, or disgusting stories were more likely to be spread than mundane or less detailed accounts. Researchers presented three different variations of the same story, then tracked how often the rumor was passed along. In the first version, a person opened a new bottle of soda and found a dead rat inside. In the second version, a person opened a bottle of soda and drank half of it before noticing the dead rat inside. In the third version, the person opened a bottle of soda, drank half, and only noticed the rat when he felt something solid in his mouth. The third story, clearly the most disgusting, was found to be passed along to others more frequently than the other two versions.[28]

Stories of satanic cults throughout the United States in the 1980s and 1990s were not perpetuated solely by individuals or small, isolated groups. These claims were made by prominent people. The rumor-spreaders were often child protective workers, therapists, social workers, teachers, clergymen, and in the case of Spencer Township, law enforcement personnel. Almost all were quite sincere.[29]

When rumors gain traction and move beyond a particular in-group, they can become community or regional rumor-panics. In 1972, noted sociologist Stanley Cohen described the progression of a moral rumor-panic in the following terms: "A condition, episode, person, or group of persons emerges to be defined as a threat to societal values and interests; its nature is presented in stylized and stereotypical fashion by the mass media; the moral barricades are manned by editors, bishops, politicians, and other right-thinking people; socially accredited experts pronounce their diagnoses and solutions; ways of coping are evolved or (more often) resorted to; the condition then disappears, submerges, or deteriorates and becomes more visible."[30]

In 1993, author Jeffrey Victor studied regional rumor-panics related to satanism. Looking back through police records and media reports, Victor identified sixty-three separate panics around the United States between 1982 and 1993. More incidents followed in the United States and abroad. Victor noted that the peak years for satanic rumor-panics were 1988 and 1989.[31]

Reports of satanic rumors usually mentioned one or more antecedents, or "triggering events." A survey of newspaper reports highlighted several commonly cited triggering incidents. Thirty-nine percent of cases mentioned graffiti in the community. Twenty-nine percent of cases referred to instances of cemetery vandalism, while nearly half of all cases pointed to a recent instance of violence, including murder or suicide.

Local church meetings or recent seminars related to satanism were also commonly cited as a triggering incident, along with mass media presentations on the topic. Some communities also mentioned previous crime among young people, conflict between groups, and the discovery of mutilated animals. Some communities cited a specific date, like Friday the 13th, a particular lunar phase, or the winter or summer solstice as other possible triggers.[32]

In the Spencer Township case, nearly all of these triggers were present. A local girl had gone missing in the years leading up to investigation, and a homicide victim had been discovered in Spencer Township a few years before. The prominent murder case of Sister Margaret Ann Pahl was fresh on the minds of many Toledo residents. Reports of satanic graffiti and cases of animal mutilation were pouring in from surrounding counties. A local church had recently been vandalized under mysterious circumstances. Police officers attended a briefing with occult expert Dale Griffis, who gave special significance to several dates on the calendar.

Jeffrey Victor also found a higher rate of prevalence of rumor-panics in rural settings, where underlying socioeconomic stresses were more pronounced.[33] At the time of the dig, Spencer Township had the lowest per capita income in Lucas County.[34]

In hindsight, it is easy to look back on the Spencer Township dig as an overreaction, but the incident did not happen in a vacuum. When persistent, snowballing rumors mixed with preexisting beliefs and unchecked biases following a series of triggering events, conditions were ripe for a full-blown rumor-panic.

Why did rumors of satanic cults take hold throughout the 1980s and 1990s? Jeffery Victor identified three key reasons for the persistence of the satanic cult conspiracy.[35]

First, the satanic cult legend had mass media appeal. The term "satanic cult" was so vague, it could be attached to anyone. They could be child molesters, violent gang members, psychotic serial murderers, teens swept up in makeshift rituals, or harmless practitioners of non-Christian religions. Regardless of their identity, the cult could serve as a scapegoat for all societal ills.

Second, the satanic cult legend persisted because it was frequently legitimized by authority figures. Police experts, religious leaders, and child protection experts all lent credibility to the rumors. In the Spencer Township case, Sheriff James Telb offered one such example when he stepped in front of television cameras and said, "This is not a hoax."[36] Even though the dig yielded no hard evidence, newspapers were citing Telb's investigation as verification of cult crime as late as 1989.[37]

This sort of verification was offered by authorities in numerous rumor-panics around Ohio, from the Union County Sheriff's Department confirming rumors of satanic cults during their animal mutilation investigation to the church leaders in the Kenmore neighborhood of Akron validating stories of devil worshipers in the local park.

People do not implicitly trust all authority figures, but authorities can have a tremendous impact on the spread of rumors. When a story comes from a respected source, the information is often held in higher esteem. In 1991, during the height of the Procter & Gamble logo scandal, one church member explained why he believed the rumors about devil worshipers in the company, saying, "Our pastor presented it to us. And if a person of trust presents something to you, you believe it."[38]

Finally, the satanic cult legend persisted because it promoted certain vested interests. Various people and organizations stood to make great gains from the spread of rumors. Satanic cult stories revived waning interest in anti-cult groups who had lost steam and needed new members. The satanic threat brought increased funding, volunteer workers, and receptive audiences who wanted to "do something" to fight the Devil.

Occult experts and cult survivors attracted large audiences. Many profited from lucrative lecture fees. The satanic threat sold books, fueled movies, and created a television goldmine. Some religious ministries even gained new access to public school children as they launched programs designed to warn against the dangers associated with devil worship while openly proselytizing.[39]

Christian comedian and evangelist Mike Warnke spent decades touring the country, sharing his life story as a former satanic high priest. Investigators at a Christian magazine publicly debunked Warnke's story in the early 1990s, providing thorough documentation proving his fictional accounts never took place, but Warnke still profited. By 1991, he had performed in over two hundred locations around the country. In the seven years leading up to his public downfall, Warnke and his two partners profited over $3.6 million.[40] Warnke still operates a ministry to this day.

If Warnke's outlandish stories were so easy to falsify, why had so many churches promoted his ministry? The answer is simple. "Warnke got results. He sold records; he made converts." Caught up in the rise of various communications industries, including Christian radio, television evangelism on cable, and the burgeoning Christian publishing industry, Warnke helped propel many others to greater heights. "The comedy sugar-coated the paranoid satanic cult theory and so spread its influence."[41]

Although he wrote the words in 1993, author Jeffrey Victor made a telling prediction when he wrote, "It will also be necessary for some politicians, perhaps in primarily rural states, to find that appeals to a fear of criminal Satanists have the potential for attracting many voters."[42] Years later, numerous U.S. politicians capitalized on the Q-Anon movement and other conspiracy theories to mobilize millions of voters and donors, reviving old tales about a secretive group of devil worshipers who actively prey on children. The satanic panic never went away.

✹

Sheik was a popular eatery in Detroit. On September 12, 2001, someone sent out an anonymous email claiming they had seen everyone in the restaurant cheer when two hijacked airplanes crashed into the World Trade Center one day earlier. The email told people to boycott the restaurant and take their business to other, more patriotic establishments. Significant public outcry followed.

Of course, the rumor was not true. No one in the restaurant had cheered for a terrorist attack. The owner even provided security camera footage from the restaurant during the incident. Civic leaders and local supporters stood up for Sheik and denounced the anonymous email as a lie. None of it mattered. The damage was done. Business in the restaurant tanked, reporting significant financial losses well into 2005.[43]

Misinformation is not harmless. Intentionally or unintentionally, rumors can heighten distrust or animosity between people and groups. Cunning manipulators or savvy opportunists can weaponize rumors for gain, targeting opponents and seeking personal advantage through misinformation. From unfounded claims of election fraud, to rumors that life-saving vaccines causing significant health problems, to allegations of a secret child-trafficking ring in the basement of a pizza restaurant, rumors have the potential to do great harm.

When the average person comes across a piece of misinformation, what is the best way to respond? Rumor researcher Nicholas DiFonzo provided several guidelines for how best to refute a rumor.

Effective refutations must be based in truth. It does no good to replace one mistruth with another. Facts and verifiable evidence are more effective than counter-rumors. It also helps when a refutation comes from a trusted source. Rumor-believers will be more likely to consider refutations from respected friends or family members, or reputable sources which they know and respect.

The best refutations come early in the rumor process, not later. If possible, it is always best to stop a rumor in its tracks at the outset, without giving the story time to grow and take hold. The most effective refutations usually come with context, or an explanation for the motivations involved in refuting the rumor. It may be helpful to convey a sense of concern, care, or an appreciation for the person's quest for truth. Also, the best refutations are clearly communicated. Providing a careful, detailed, and easy-to-understand explanation will go further than a flat denial.

In the closing section of their book about the topic, Carl Bergstrom and Jevin D. West perhaps said it best when they gave this concluding charge, "The rise of misinformation and disinformation keeps us up at night. No law or fancy new AI is going to solve the problem. We all have to be a little more vigilant, a little more thoughtful, a little more careful when sharing information – and every once in a while, we need to call bullshit when we see it."[44]

30. The Real Enemy

In his book *Suspicious Minds: Why We Believe Conspiracy Theories*, Rob Brotherton defines a conspiracy theory as an unanswered question that assumes nothing is as it seems. The theory usually portrays conspirators as preternaturally competent and shockingly evil. Conspiracy theories are founded on anomaly hunting and ultimately irrefutable.[1]

Building on this broad definition, Anthony Oberschall presented five cognitive attributes of the internal logic present in most conspiracy narratives.[2] First, a specific agent or group is named, and they are ascribed a clear motivation. Second, this agent or group is said to be evil, and their acts are said to be destructive. This is usually accompanied by a simple, uncomplicated assertion that this agent or group is to blame for complex events.

Third, the evil agent or group is said to have the capacity for some big event. The alleged conspirators may be said to control resources or act in secret with powerful allies. Fourth, the conspiracy thinker will often point to real-world examples of actual conspiracies as corroboration for their own theory. Finally, because some learned, respected, prominent individuals promote conspiracy theories, even for self-serving reasons, the conspiracy thinker will often incorporate these endorsements into the narrative.

The conspiracy thinker can easily blame hidden puppeteers for undermining, attacking, or infiltrating an otherwise healthy and wholesome society. They can blame the government for killing Kennedy, covering up the existence of extraterrestrials, or even hiding the identity of Jack the Ripper. Satanic cult stories warned about next-door-neighbors who secretly dabbled in the dark arts, but also doctors, lawyers, businessmen, and politicians who piloted the evil organism from the top. In the mind of the satanic conspiracy thinker, "they" are evil and powerful, and only a select few have the perceptive abilities to discern their pernicious threat.[3]

Insider or outsider, commoner or elite, the enemy does not need to truly exist for a conspiracy theory to take hold. Or if they do exist, the perceived enemy does not need to pose an actual threat. They are a social construct. Society has grown adept at inventing evil enemies.[4]

During the 1980s and 1990s, as conspiracy thinkers sought out new internal enemies to blame, devil worshipers became the fashionable choice. This new imaginary menace became particularly useful at a time when previous enemies, such as Communist subversives, were no longer compelling to talk about. The threat of hidden Satanists brought together different groups, who suddenly overcame their differences to form a united front. Catholics found ways to work alongside Protestants, secular child welfare advocates and feminists learned to tolerate religious leaders, and law enforcement agencies, mental health professionals, and social workers learned to mobilize God-fearing congregations against evil.[5]

Who is the conspiracy thinker? Anyone can succumb to the allure of tidy explanations for ambiguous circumstances, and anyone can be tempted to "connect the dots" or seek out patterns in moments of uncertainty. We can all be conspiracy thinkers from time to time. However, decades of psychological research have identified certain common characteristics of people who frequently buy into conspiracy theories.

As part of their wider mission to promote healthy and evidence-based treatment in the mental health field, Grey Faction, a project of the Satanic Temple, has compiled many resources on the topic of conspiracy thinking. Their work centers on raising awareness and advocating against mental health practitioners who incorporate satanic conspiracy thinking into their practices. Grey Faction compiled a list of studies, which are linked on their website, which reveal various characteristics of conspiracy thinkers, such as the need to feel unique, a need for certainty, rejection of authoritative accounts of events, a hypersensitive "agency detection" system, reduced analytical thinking, increased paranoia, lack of interpersonal trust, and more.[6]

Rumors of clandestine plots from secret organizations reinforce the sense of helplessness, and sometimes victimhood, in the conspiracy thinker. Conspiracy narratives are often underlined by a general sense of powerlessness in the face of daunting circumstances. People who believe conspiracy theories generally have low trust of others and often doubt that groups or institutions have their best interest at heart.[7]

Although it is sometimes popular to ridicule conspiracy thinkers, writing off their contributions as hare-brained or wacky, it is helpful to note that they do not generally view themselves as deficient. As Psychologist Jovan Byford pointed out, "Conspiracy theorists do not see themselves as raconteurs of alluring stories, but as investigators and researchers."[8] In most cases, they genuinely believe there is a mystery to be solved or a plot to be uncovered, and they genuinely believe their research to be compelling, regardless of the validity or replicability of their methodology.

Anomalies, or little details the main story cannot evidently account for, are the lifeblood of conspiracies. By identifying odd details, quirks, or peculiarities and weaving them into a larger, coherent narrative, conspiracy thinkers can often construct conspiracies which account for elements left out of official explanations. Because they "make all the pieces fit," some people may find conspiracy stories more appealing because of their apparent completeness.[9]

Anxiety can be better managed when it is channeled into fear or anger against someone or something that can be blamed. The conspiracy thinker can occupy a self-promoted role of significance. They must heroically battle both the malice of the conspirators and the ignorance or unbelief of their own in-group.[10] Many conspiracy thinkers, consciously or unconsciously, cast themselves as the protagonist in their own story. Not only do they need to expose evil enemies in their midst, but they must also rally resistance against the interlopers against all odds.

Because they believe they are uncovering the truth, and because they are doing so as the heroes of the story, conspiracy thinkers often exude confidence. Refutations or facts which contradict the theory may be dismissed as disinformation meant to throw them off the scent. Similarly, the absence of evidence does not disqualify a theory, but is rather asserted as proof of their powerful enemy's ability to conceal themselves or an indication of the gullibility of the masses.

Thus, conspiracy thinkers create their own world, where no matter what information comes to light, their theory cannot be proven false. "If it looks like a conspiracy, it was a conspiracy. If it doesn't look like a conspiracy, it was *definitely* a conspiracy. Evidence against a conspiracy theory becomes evidence of a conspiracy. Heads I win, tails you lose."[11]

Satanic conspiracy theorists lamented the demise of hundreds, sometimes thousands, of children who had been abused and murdered at the hands of cult members. When no evidence turned up, they credited the cult for cunning skills of deception. When the estimates in their stories did not match the actual data on missing children, they theorized about "breeders" who gave birth to undocumented babies for use in cult rituals. The absence of evidence did not deflate the conspiracy but further bolstered the narrative.

The FBI, state investigators, and his own supervisors at the Lucas County Sheriff's Department told Kirk Surprise that Leroy Freeman was out of state, but the lieutenant told his informant he *knew* a group of devil worshipers had secretly altered his appearance and hidden him underground. There was no evidence that various animal deaths in Union County were connected, but Sheriff Overly and Deputy Lala *knew* a satanic cult was behind the slayings.

Sound investigations consider the evidence, seek verification, and draw conclusions. Conspiracy theorists begin with their conclusion, then find ways to make the evidence fit. Brotherton cautioned against this type of approach. "This is how confirmation bias sets in. Merely finding evidence that appears to fit our preconceptions doesn't always mean we're right, but if we don't check for evidence that we're wrong, we have no reason to question our beliefs."[12]

Brotherton also wrote that conspiracy theories "come with a tacit admission that the ultimate truth is just out of reach, behind the next curtain, able to be glimpsed but not yet grasped. The conspiracy is forever being unraveled, but the holy grail of incontrovertible proof – the undeniable evidence that will alert the masses and finally topple the house of cards – has not yet been produced. Whether they turn out to be true or not, conspiracy theories, deep down, are unanswered questions."[13]

Conspiracy theorists often have a startling amount of faith in the capabilities of their enemies. The conspirators always seem to be able to pull together toward a singular goal, with unyielding obedience, almost like a single organism as opposed to a disparate group of individuals.

At their worst, conspiracy theories make their enemies all powerful, verging on omnipotent. In *The Paranoid Style of American Politics*, Hofstadter pointed out how unseen conspirators could be held responsible for all the world's ills, saying the secret organization "makes crises, starts runs on the banks, causes depressions, manufactures disasters, and profits from the misery." By extension, this means events are not merely the sequence of history, but "the consequences of someone's will."[14]

Loren Collins pointed out that the cabal always seems to be "exactly as competent and powerful as the conspiracy theorist needs it to be."[15] This points to the paradox at the center of many such conspiracy theories. Satanic cults allegedly had tightly organized, powerful, infallible networks that leave no evidence of their large scale abduction, breeding, and human sacrifice activity, yet these same people also leave behind an easily spotted trail of clues which invite official investigation.[16] The Satanists had covered their tracks so well, police could make no arrests. Yet, local cult hunters pointed to dead animals, opened graves, and easily visible graffiti as proof of their existence.

The cult was allegedly too cunning to be detected, but anyone who had watched a *20/20* special or attended a seminar at their church could easily expose their evil deeds by playing a rock album in reverse. The satanic cult was somehow both insidious and incompetent, secretive and conspicuous. When Lt. Surprise spoke with his confidential informant about the highly secretive cult on May 17, 1985, he even scoffed that cult members were "not very good at hiding their bonfires," because he had clearly seen their gathering from his vantage point on a public road.

Devil worshipers had to maintain secrecy and perfect discipline, despite their disparate membership of teenage dabblers, unhinged sociopathic criminals, public Satanists, and prominent and powerful individuals. Despite the alleged existence of an elaborate organized network, no organizational apparatus has ever been discovered. No investigation turned up correspondence, membership lists, phone logs, travel records, bank accounts, buildings, or meeting places (or underground temples), ritual implements, crematoriums, filming equipment, photos, or films. These satanic cults were apparently so secretive, no one could ever definitively prove they existed.[17]

Of course, conspiracy theorists have demonstrated a great capacity for weaving the absence of evidence into the larger narrative. The Satanists must have hidden the bodies in clever ways, such as double graves or portable high-temperature ovens. Perhaps the perpetrators ate the remains of their victims, or hid them, or used the power of Satan to make them disappear.[18] But by relying on a lack of confirming evidence, conspiracy theorists cheat in one final way: they shift the burden of proof from themselves, the ones making the claim, to the skeptics, or those who question the claim.[19]

In 1987, Geraldo Rivera told his vast television audience, "There are over one million Satanists in this country. The majority of them are

241

linked in a highly organized, very secret network. The odds are that this is happening in your town."[20]

Crime is common. If crime can be linked to satanism, then satanism warrants serious attention. As Jeffrey Victor wrote, "When moral values are in dispute in a society, a witch hunt for moral subversives serves the purpose of clarifying and redefining the limits of moral conduct."[21] In this process of seeking out so-called subversives, it is not uncommon for people to target minorities.

During one of the many daycare abuse trials which followed the McMartin Preschool case, an openly gay man named Bernard Baran was convicted and sentenced to consecutive life terms for his alleged abuse. Baran's case spanned twenty-five years, from the first allegations in 1984 until June 2009, when all charges were dropped. Baran maintained his innocence until his dying day.

During his trial, the prosecutor told the jury that hiring a gay man to work in a daycare was like putting "a chocoholic in a candy store." This brazen display of homophobia perpetuated the false and harmful notion that gay men were deviants.[22]

Throughout the satanic rumor-panic of the 1980s and 1990s, homophobia and transphobia were common features of conspiracy stories. During the animal mutilation investigation in Union County, Deputy Lala went out of his way to tell reporters that most of the satanic cult members were homosexuals. He cited no evidence.[23]

The Spencer Township investigation was no different. According to the transcript of the May 17 interview, Lt. Surprise made several references to gender expression. Asking if a male cult member dressed as a woman, Surprise added, "You never know. That would be perfect. Has he grown a beard?" Later in the same conversation, Surprise responded to Sandy's indication that a man sometimes wore a dress by saying, "I knew there had to be one of those in there somewhere!"

Research into trends in American racism illustrates the social dynamic of "internal enemy" conspiracies. One study found that Black people were scapegoated more often during periods of economic stress. There were increased lynching incidents and racial attacks when area farmers faced economic hardship, for example. Another study found greater racist behavior in areas of the country where there was greater income inequality between white and Black people.[24]

The satanic rumor-panic of the 1980s and 1990s led to an increase in scapegoating behaviors against minorities. Researchers noted a rise in attacks on homosexual people, with assaults and murders more than doubling between 1985 and 1987. There was also a sharp rise in anti-Semitic hate crimes, with reports of a sudden spike between 1986 and 1988 after a period of decline. By 1990, the Anti-Defamation League had recorded the highest number of hate crimes since they began tracking such data in 1979.[25]

There are dangerous consequences to moral witch hunts. When unfounded conspiracy theories are acted upon, people suffer. The social pressure to dramatize the purging of evil by making public examples of enemies further exacerbates the situation.[26] All too often, when conspiracy-minded moral crusaders act against those they accuse of monstrous acts, they become monsters themselves.

Ancient novels about evil cults and witchfinding manuals share a common feature: voyeurism. The process of rooting out evildoers is frequently filled with graphic descriptions of violent, sexual acts, detailed testimonials of varied atrocities, and intense interrogatives about alleged activities. The satanic conspiracy believer claims to be repulsed by the actions of the cult, but also seems perfectly satisfied to linger on every bloody detail.[27]

David Frankfurter wrote that, even though our most pious Satan hunters would express abject horror at the exploits of the cult, "that horror comes partly from our fascination... with these transgressive impulses to invert the moral order. The Other, the Savage, who bears our projections and inversions is now in our neighborhoods; and this new location requires that we repudiate it sharply."[28]

Conspiracy thinkers imagine inverted versions of themselves, then sharply condemn the shadow people they've created. By attributing ritual and religious motivations to the cultists, the invented conspiracy myth both simplifies and exoticizes the acts of the conspirators. "Real or imagined maleficence in the community now derives not from envy, social tensions, or hereditary malign powers like the evil eye, but rather from internal motivation: dedication to Satan."[29]

And so, the actions of the evil cult members become a kind of parody of the conspiracy thinker's own rituals. "We" have baptism, special vestments, dance, chanting, meal-sharing, and Eucharist. "They" have their own disgusting reversals of everything we love. Those treacherous monsters have stolen what is ours. We can easily imagine how evil they are because they are simply the opposite of all that we choose to be.

People crave the rhetoric of evil and the sense of certainty which follows. The concept of evil signifies what is inhuman, beyond the pale of comprehensible behavior, and of a nature that transcends individual atrocity. There is a certain comfort in the clarity offered by the word evil. But evil is a discourse, not a thing that exists out there, somewhere, as a concrete force in itself.[30]

Many satanic cult rumors derive from ancient myths, which involve innocent children being kidnapped and murdered by strangers for use in some elaborate blood ritual.[31] Although children were often incorporated as innocents and victims, there have been historical instances when children were used as scapegoats too. In 1595, Nicholas Rémy's witchfinding manual discussed at length the reasons why seven-year-old children should be executed for associating with the Devil. The German city of Augsburg saw mass incarceration of children as witches, most of which were accused by their own parents.[32]

As Frankfurter wrote, "The real atrocities of history seem to take place not in the perverse ceremonies of some evil cult but rather in the course of purging such cults from the world. Real evil happens when people speak of evil."[33]

Most experts agree that conspiracy theories aren't going anywhere. In many ways, conspiracy thinking is central to what it means to be human. We must learn to cope with it.

"A lot of our beliefs, conspiracy theories included, are based on how well they fit with our intuition," Rob Brotherton wrote in an email. "So, one strategy for making people a little more resistant to conspiracy theories would be to get them to slow down and process the claims more analytically, and to realize that their brain might be being biased. Of course, that's easier said than done."[34]

The philosopher David Hume commented on our human tendencies when he said, "We find human faces in the moon, armies in the clouds; and by natural propensity, if not corrected by experience and reflection, ascribe malice and good will to everything that hurts or pleases us."[35]

Jesse Walker, in his book *The United States of Paranoia,* said it best when he wrote, "The conspiracy theorist will always be with us, because he will always be us. We will never stop finding patterns. We will never stop spinning stories. We will always be capable of jumping to conclusions, particularly when we're dealing with other nations, factions, subcultures, or layers of the social hierarchy. And conspiracies, unlike many of the monsters that haunt our folklore, actually exist, so we won't always be wrong to fear them. As long as our species survives, so will paranoia.

"Yet we can limit the damage that paranoia does. We can try to empathize with people who seem alien. We can be aware of the cultural myths that shape our fears. And we can be open to evidence that might undermine the patterns we think we see in the world. We should be skeptical, yes, of people who might be conspiring against us. But we should also be skeptical – deeply, deeply skeptical – of our fearful, fallible selves."[36]

Epitaph

In October 1985, nearly three months after he permanently called off the dig in Spencer Township, Sheriff James Telb began a new project.

Telb announced he would be coordinating a special anti-terrorism task force. Working alongside the FBI, the Secret Service, the U.S. Treasury Department's Bureau of Alcohol, Tobacco, and Firearms, the Toledo-Lucas County Port Authority, and the Toledo Police division, Telb would work in Lucas and Wood Counties to prepare for potential threats. The task force would also serve parts of southern Michigan, and possibly Ottawa County, which housed the Davis-Besse nuclear power station.

Telb told reporters, "We don't want to someday say, 'If we only had planned for it,' when a terrorist group puts something in your water systems, or burns your buildings, or attempts to firebomb the jail or police headquarters. You have to be able to move and react."[1]

Neither Telb nor his associates at the FBI would say whether there was any evidence of terrorist activity in the region, but the task force had already identified possible targets.

"The airport is always a major interest to terrorist groups, perhaps the water supply, and railroad yards, and of course the nuclear power plant..."

Appendix: Timeline of Events

October 14, 1974 – A skeleton is discovered in Spencer Township, on a vacant lot near Bemis Lane, off Meilke Road. The victim is identified as 22-year-old Judith Ann Petrie of Oregon, Ohio. In 1985, a confidential informant would claim cult victims were buried in this same area.

August 1976 – Reports of animal mutilation in Logan, Ohio ignite speculation about satanic cult activity. Gun sales skyrocket in the area and groups of local vigilantes patrol in vans, hunting for signs of a secret cult.

October 1978 – Rumors begin to circulate that McDonald's restaurants support the Church of Satan. The rumors are traced to a church in Akron, Ohio. Similar allegations against Procter & Gamble and Liz Claiborne soon follow.

April 4, 1980 – Sister Margaret Ann Pahl is murdered in the chapel at Mercy Hospital in Toledo. Due to the shocking nature of the crime and various elements at the crime scene, some speculate that the crime is occult-related.

November 1, 1980 – Dr. Lawrence Pazder and Michelle Proby publish their book, *Michelle Remembers*. The influential cult survivor story details various gruesome and lurid allegations of satanic ritual abuse. Millions of copies are sold, drawing widespread media attention.

Spring 1982 – Anonymous fliers and letters begin circulating, alleging that the Ohio-based company Procter & Gamble supports the Church of Satan. Rumors about satanic imagery in the company logo intensify over the next decade, persisting into the 1990s.

September 5, 1982 – Seven-year-old Charity Freeman is reported missing from her home in Lucas County.

October 1983 – Reports of alleged animal mutilations begin to surface in Fairfield and Shelby Counties. The incidents are covered in major newspapers across Ohio.

December 23, 1983 – Arrest warrant is issued for Leroy Freeman, following an indictment for one count of child-stealing in connection with the disappearance of Charity Freeman.

February 1984 – The McMartin Preschool case gains national attention. With lurid accusations of child exploitation, satanic ritual abuse, and murder, the McMartin trial would receive widespread media coverage for nearly a decade.

July 15, 1984 – *The Columbus Dispatch* prints a multi-page article profiling Tiffin Police Captain Dale Griffis and his work investigating cults and occult-related crime. The article features a chilling story from an anonymous Jane Doe who claims to have witnessed a human sacrifice in a field somewhere in northwestern Ohio. The story bears striking resemblance to allegations which would later arise in Spencer Township.

December 1984 – First documented cases of alleged animal mutilation surface in Union County, Ohio. Sheriff John Overly and Deputy John Lala launch an investigation. Deputy Lala begins speaking in local schools about the dangers of satanic cults.

March 1985 – Reports of unsolved animal mutilations begin to surface in the Kenmore neighborhood of Akron, Ohio.

April 15, 1985 – Deputy John Lala reports more than one thousand hours spent investigating animal mutilations and vandalism in Union County, Ohio. Reports of satanic activity appear in newspapers all over the region.

April 17, 1985 – Mrs. Jones makes her initial phone call to the Lucas County Sheriff's Office, reporting allegations of a satanic cult in Spencer Township. That same day, officers conduct their first meeting with the confidential informant, Sandy.

April 20, 1985 – Lucas County Sheriff's Department meets with occult expert Dale Griffis and conducts nighttime surveillance of possible cult locations in Spencer Township. Officers report hearing "chanting" in the woods.

April 22, 1985 – Officers conduct first recorded interview with confidential informant, Sandy.

May 8, 1985 – Official report from occult expert Dale Griffis confirms "cult activity" in Lucas County.

May 16, 1985 – National news program 20/20 airs segment entitled "The Devil Worshippers," detailing many cases of alleged satanic crime all over the nation. Tiffin police officer Dale Griffis appears in the segment as a law enforcement expert in the occult. The program is viewed by millions.

May 17, 1985 – Officers conduct a second recorded interview with confidential informant, Sandy.

June 3, 1985 – Officers conduct a third recorded interview with confidential informant, Sandy.

June 10, 1985 – A community meeting is held in Akron, Ohio regarding unsolved animal mutilations. Hundreds of residents gather to hear presentation about alleged satanic activity and watch a video recording of the recent *20/20* segment on satanic crime. The event draws widespread media attention, appearing in local newspapers throughout the region.

June 16, 1985 – Unknown parties break into and vandalize Wilkins Methodist Church, approximately six miles from the suspected burial site in Spencer Township.

June 17, 1985 – A second community meeting is held in Akron, Ohio regarding the dangers of alleged satanic activity. The event features numerous local leaders and politicians, drawing widespread media attention.

June 20, 1985 – Lucas County Sheriff James Telb holds a press conference, publicly sharing allegations of human sacrifice by a satanic cult. Officers raid a home in Springfield Township and begin excavating locations in Spencer Township, expecting to find fifty to seventy-five bodies. The incident ignites a national media frenzy. No bodies are found.

June 21, 1985 – Investigators conduct a second day of digging in Spencer Township. No bodies are found. The search is called off indefinitely.

June 23, 1985- *The Akron Beacon Journal* reports on a group of local vigilantes patrolling the Kenmore neighborhood of Akron with baseball bats, hunting for signs of crime and devil worship.

July 2, 1985 – Sheriff Telb secretly returns to Spencer Township to dig again, angering local leaders. No bodies are found.

July 10, 1985 – Sheriff Telb attends Spencer Township Trustee meeting to defend his investigation. No further digging is planned, and the formal investigation is ended.

October 21, 1988 – Charity Freeman is discovered alive and well in Huntington Beach, California. Her grandfather, Leroy Freeman, is arrested for child-stealing.

NOTES

Chapter 1: Stop the Presses

[1] Cross, Sue. (1985, July 15). Rural township tries to return to normal after search for bodies. *AP News*. Retrieved from https://apnews.com/article/adb05be6c18665cca0b640ba6613260b

[2] Baessler, J. (1985, June 20). Sheriff's Dept. starts Spencer Twp. dig for 50 reported killed by Satanic cult. *The Toledo Blade*, pp. 1, 7.

[3] Evans, C., & Wendling, T. (1985, June 21). Hunt near Toledo fails to find human sacrifices. *The Plain Dealer*, pp. 1, 16.

[4] Baessler, Sheriff's Dept. starts dig, *The Toledo Blade*.

[5] Baessler, Sheriff's Dept. starts dig, *The Toledo Blade*.

[6] Baessler, Sheriff's Dept. starts dig, *The Toledo Blade*.

[7] Evans & Wendling, Hunt near Toledo, *The Plain Dealer*.

[8] Baird, D. (1984, July 15). Sympathy for the devil. *The Columbus Dispatch*, pp. 338-342. Available from NewsBank: Access World News – Historical and Current database.

Chapter 2: Search and Seizure

[1] Breiner, J. (1985, June 21). No bodies found yet in cult probe. *The Columbus Dispatch*, p. 18.

[2] Baessler, Sheriff's Dept. starts dig, *The Toledo Blade*.

[3] Evans, C., & Wendling, T. (1985, June 22). Bedeviled searchers call it off. *The Plain Dealer*, pp. 1, 14.

[4] Evans & Wendling, Hunt near Toledo, *The Plain Dealer*.

[5] Cross, Sue. (1985, July 15). Rural township tries to return to normal after search for bodies. *AP News*. Retrieved from https://apnews.com/article/adb05be6c18665cca0b640ba6613260b

[6] Evans & Wendling, Hunt near Toledo, *The Plain Dealer*. And Associated Press. (1985, July 27). Satanic search victims sue for $1.52 million. *The Plain Dealer*. p. 1B.

[7] Evans & Wendling, Hunt near Toledo, *The Plain Dealer*.

[8] Baessler, Sheriff's Dept. starts dig, *The Toledo Blade*.

[9] Richardson, J.T., Best, J., & Bromley D.G. (1991). Satanism as a social problem. In J.T. Richardson, J. Best, & D.G. Bromley (Eds.), *The Satanism Scare*. Aldine De Gruyter, p. 10.

[10] Richardson, Best, & Bromley, Satanism as a social problem, p. 10.

[11] Nathan, D. (1991). Satanism and child molestation: Constructing the ritual abuse scare. In J.T. Richardson, J. Best, & D.G. Bromley (Eds.), *The Satanism Scare*. Aldine De Gruyter, p. 79.

[12] Beck, R. (2015). *We believe the children: A moral panic in the 1980s*. PublicAffairs, p. xii.

[13] Nathan, D. & Snedeker, M. (1995). *Satan's silence: Ritual abuse and the making of a modern American witch hunt*. BasicBooks, HarperCollins Publishers, p. 127.

[14] Victor, J.S. (1993). *Satanic panic: The creation of a contemporary legend*. Open Court Press, p. 125.

[15] Victor, *Satanic Panic*, p. 123.

[16] Richardson, Best, & Bromley, Satanism as a social problem, p. 10.

[17] Bromley, D.G. (1991). Satanism: The new cult scare. In J.T. Richardson, J. Best, & D.G. Bromley (Eds.), *The Satanism Scare*. Aldine De Gruyter, p. 62.

[18] Nathan & Snedeker, *Satan's Silence*, p. 30.

[19] Best, J. (1991). Endangered children in antisatanist rhetoric. In J.T. Richardson, J. Best, & D.G. Bromley (Eds.), *The Satanism Scare*. Aldine De Gruyter. pp. 98.

[20] Nathan & Snedeker, *Satan's Silence*, pp. 29-30.

[21] Walker, J. (2013). *The United States of paranoia*. Harper Perennial, p. 216.

[22] Best, Endangered children in antisatanist rhetoric, p. 97.

[23] Bromley, Satanism: The new cult scare, p. 53.

[24] Nathan, Satanism and child molestation, p. 75.

[25] Bromley, Satanism: The new cult scare, p. 66.

[26] Bromley, Satanism: The new cult scare, p. 66.

[27] Stevens, P. (1991). The demonology of satanism: An anthropological view. In J.T. Richardson, J. Best, & D.G. Bromley (Eds.), *The Satanism Scare*. Aldine De Gruyter, p. 29.

[28] Bromley, Satanism: The new cult scare, pp. 68-69.

[29] Victor, J.S. (1991). The dynamics of rumor-panics about satanic cults. In J.T. Richardson, J. Best, & D.G. Bromley (Eds.), *The Satanism Scare*. Aldine De Gruyter, p. 221.

[30] Frankfurter, D. (2006). *Evil incarnate: Rumors of demonic conspiracy and satanic abuse in history*. Princeton University Press, p. 100.

[31] Victor, The dynamics of rumor-panics, p. 221.

Chapter 3: Tight Knit

[1] Wall, J. (1985, June 21). Area residents skeptical of sacrifice stories. *The Toledo Blade*, p. 4.

[2] Wall, Area residents skeptical, *The Toledo Blade*.

[3] Wall, Area residents skeptical, *The Toledo Blade*.

[4] Wall, Area residents skeptical, *The Toledo Blade*.

[5] Evans & Wendling, Hunt near Toledo, *The Plain Dealer*.

[6] Evans & Wendling, Hunt near Toledo, *The Plain Dealer*.

[7] Evans & Wendling, Hunt near Toledo, *The Plain Dealer*.

Chapter 4: On Portents and Being Earnest

[1] Albrecht, B. (1984, December 30). Rumors swirl over animal mutilations in rural Ohio county.
The Plain Dealer, pp. 1, 8.

[2] Albrecht, Rumors swirl over animal mutilations, *The Plain Dealer*.

[3] Baird, D. (1985, April 14). Unmasking the devil. *The Columbus Dispatch*, p. 2B.

[4] Albrecht, Rumors swirl over animal mutilations, *The Plain Dealer*.

[5] Baird, Unmasking the devil, *The Columbus Dispatch*.

[6] Albrecht, Rumors swirl over animal mutilations, *The Plain Dealer*.

[7] Baird, Unmasking the devil, *The Columbus Dispatch*.

[8] Associated Press. (1985, April 15). Deputy says Union County is a satanic center. *AP News*. Retrieved from https://apnews.com/article/d7221d0cca4265edb63afe91e7b892ae

[9] Associated Press, Deputy says Union County is a satanic center, *AP News*.

[10] Baird, Unmasking the devil, *The Columbus Dispatch*.

[11] Miller, W.C. (1985, June 21). Satanic worship is no joke: Lucas County officials praised for taking occult seriously. *The Plain Dealer*, p. 19.

[12] Associated Press, Deputy says Union County is a satanic center, *AP News*.

[13] Baird, Unmasking the devil, *The Columbus Dispatch*.

[14] Associated Press, Deputy says Union County is a satanic center, *AP News*.

[15] Baird, Unmasking the devil, *The Columbus Dispatch*.

[16] Miller, Satanic worship is no joke, *The Plain Dealer*.

[17] Miller, Satanic worship is no joke, *The Plain Dealer*.

[18] Associated Press, Deputy says Union County is a satanic center, *AP News*.

[19] Baird, D. (1985, April 14). Satanists suspected in animal mutilations. *The Columbus Dispatch*, p. 1.

[20] Albrecht, Rumors swirl over animal mutilations, *The Plain Dealer*.

[21] Miller, Satanic worship is no joke, *The Plain Dealer*.

[22] Baird, D. (1985, May 13). OSU professor says satanism is an escape from the turmoil. *The Columbus Dispatch*, p. 26.

[23] Scott, D. (1985, June 23). A cult in Kenmore – or just 'ornery kids?' *The Akron Beacon Journal*, pp. A1, A4.

[24] Rhoden, Y. (1985, June 11). Cult warning is sounded in Kenmore: animal mutilations spur information session. *The Akron Beacon Journal*, pp. C1, C2.

[25] Scott, A cult in Kenmore, *The Akron Beacon Journal*.

[26] Rhoden, Cult warning is sounded in Kenmore, *The Akron Beacon Journal*.

[27] Rhoden, Cult warning is sounded in Kenmore, *The Akron Beacon Journal*.

[28] Miller, Satanic worship is no joke, *The Plain Dealer*.

[29] Rhoden, Cult warning is sounded in Kenmore, *The Akron Beacon Journal*.

[30] Haferd, L. (1985, June 21). Satanism in Ohio – is it horror or hoax: Devil worship feeds on fear. *The Akron Beacon Journal*, pp. A1, A9.

[31] Haferd, Satanism in Ohio, *The Akron Beacon Journal*.

[32] Rhoden, Cult warning is sounded in Kenmore, *The Akron Beacon Journal*.

[33] Canterbury, W. (1985, June 19). Animal mutilation probe stepped up in Kenmore. *The Akron Beacon Journal*, pp. D1, D4.

[34] Canterbury, Animal mutilation probe stepped up, *The Akron Beacon Journal*.

[35] Canterbury, Animal mutilation probe stepped up, *The Akron Beacon Journal*.

[36] Canterbury, Animal mutilation probe stepped up, *The Akron Beacon Journal*.

[37] Canterbury, Animal mutilation probe stepped up, *The Akron Beacon Journal*.

[38] Scott, A cult in Kenmore, *The Akron Beacon Journal*.

[39] Scott, A cult in Kenmore, *The Akron Beacon Journal*.

[40] Scott, A cult in Kenmore, *The Akron Beacon Journal*.

[41] Scott, A cult in Kenmore, *The Akron Beacon Journal*.

[42] Scott, A cult in Kenmore, *The Akron Beacon Journal*.

[43] Scott, A cult in Kenmore, *The Akron Beacon Journal*.

[44] Scott, A cult in Kenmore, *The Akron Beacon Journal*.

[45] Scott, A cult in Kenmore, *The Akron Beacon Journal*.

[46] Scott, A cult in Kenmore, *The Akron Beacon Journal*.

[47] Baird, D. (1984, July 15). Sympathy for the devil. *The Columbus Dispatch*, pp. 338-342. Available from NewsBank: Access World News – Historical and Current database.

[48] Baird, Unmasking the devil, *The Columbus Dispatch*.

[49] Baird, Sympathy for the devil, *The Columbus Dispatch*.

[50] Associated Press. (1976, August 5). Vigilantes seek 'sect' in animal mutilations. *The Akron Beacon Journal*, p. 20.

Chapter 5: Raiders of the Cult House

[1] Baessler, Sheriff's Dept. starts dig, *The Toledo Blade*.

[2] Associated Press. (1986, June 22). Fruitless dig for victims of cult leaves family angry. *The Plain Dealer*. p. 22.

[3] Evans & Wendling, Hunt near Toledo, *The Plain Dealer*.

[4] Brown, M. (1985, June 21). Satanism in Ohio – is it horror or hoax: Lucas County clues vague. *The Akron Beacon Journal*, pp. A1, A9.

[5] Breiner, J. (1985, June 21). No bodies found yet in cult probe. *The Columbus Dispatch*, p. 18.

[6] Brown, Satanism in Ohio, *The Akron Beacon Journal*.

[7] Baessler, Sheriff's Dept. starts dig, *The Toledo Blade*.

[8] Evans & Wendling, Bedeviled searchers call it off, *The Plain Dealer*.

[9] Brown, Satanism in Ohio, *The Akron Beacon Journal*.

[10] Brown, Satanism in Ohio, *The Akron Beacon Journal*.

[11] Breiner, No bodies found yet in cult probe, *The Columbus Dispatch*.

[12] Baessler, Sheriff's Dept. starts dig, *The Toledo Blade*. And Associated Press, Satanic search victims sue, *The Plain Dealer*.

[13] Case, G. (2016). *Here's to my sweet Satan: How the occult haunted music, movies, and pop culture, 1966-1980*. Quill Driver Books, p. 13.

[14] Case, *Here's to my sweet Satan*, p. 16.

[15] Rusnak, S. (2015). Scapegoat of a nation: The demonization of MTV and the music video. In K. Janisse & P. Corupe (Eds.), *Satanic panic: Pop-cultural paranoia in the 1980s*. FAB Press, p. 173.

[16] Case, *Here's to my sweet Satan*, p. 16.

[17] Victor, *Satanic Panic*, p. 163.

[18] Best, Endangered children in antisatanist rhetoric, p. 103.

[19] Walker, *The United States of Paranoia*, p. 203.

[20] Case, *Here's to my sweet Satan*, p. 11.

[21] Denisoff, R. (1988). *Inside MTV*. Transaction, p. 289.

[22] Walker, *The United States of Paranoia*, p. 203.

[23] Walker, *The United States of Paranoia*, p. 203.

[24] Searcey, D. (2006, January 9). Behind the music: Sleuths seek messages in lyrical backspin. *The Wall Street Journal*. Retrieved from https://www.wsj.com/articles/SB113677367081541303

[25] Case, *Here's to my sweet Satan*, p. 138.

[26] Ladouceur, L. (2015). The filthy fifteen: When Venom and King Diamond met the Washington wives. In K. Janisse & P. Corupe (Eds.), *Satanic panic: Pop-cultural paranoia in the 1980s*. FAB Press. p. 167.

[27] Case, *Here's to my sweet Satan*, p. 32.

[28] Case, *Here's to my sweet Satan*, p. 148.

[29] Victor, *Satanic Panic*, p. 172.

[30] Hicks, R. (1991). The police model of satanic crime. In J.T. Richardson, J. Best, & D.G. Bromley (Eds.), *The Satanism Scare*. Aldine De Gruyter. p. 185.

[31] Phillips, P. (1986). *Turmoil in the toybox*. Starburst Publishers.

[32] Phillips, *Turmoil in the toybox*, p. 147.

[1] Nichols, J. (1985, June 21). Lights, camera, action! Media flurry catches residents by surprise. *The Toledo Blade*, pp. 1, 4.

[2] Baessler, Sheriff's Dept. starts dig, *The Toledo Blade*.

[3] Baessler, Sheriff's Dept. starts dig, *The Toledo Blade*.

[4] Baessler, J. (1985, June 21). Dig resumes for alleged victims of Satanic cult: Initial search uncovers eight-inch dagger, doll associated with occult. *The Toledo Blade*, pp. 1, 4.

[5] Breiner, No bodies found yet in cult probe, *The Columbus Dispatch*.

[6] Evans & Wendling, Hunt near Toledo, *The Plain Dealer*. And Brown, Satanism in Ohio, *The Akron Beacon Journal*. And Sielicki, J. (1985, June 22). Report could have been 'fairy tale'. *UPI Archives*. Retrieved from https://www.upi.com/Archives/1985/06/22/Report-could-have-been-fairy-tale/2901488260800

[7] Sielicki, Report could have been 'fairy tale,' *UPI Archives*.

[8] Richardson, Best, & Bromley, Satanism as a social problem, p. 6.

[9] Frankfurter, *Evil Incarnate*, p. 54.

[10] Beck, *We believe the children*, p. 265.

[11] Case, *Here's to my sweet Satan*, p. 135.

[12] Beck, *We believe the children*, p. 265.

[13] Heller-Nicholas, A. (2015). "The only word in the world is mine": Remembering 'Michelle remembers.' In K. Janisse & P. Corupe (Eds.), *Satanic panic: Pop-cultural paranoia in the 1980s*. FAB Press. p. 25.

[14] Richardson, Best, & Bromley, Satanism as a social problem, p. 7.

[15] Victor, *Satanic Panic*, p. 9.

[16] Victor, *Satanic Panic*, p. 237.

[17] Victor, *Satanic Panic*, p. 8.

[18] Hertenstein, M. & Trott, J. (1993). *Selling Satan*. Cornerstone Press, p. 3.

[19] Victor, *Satanic Panic*, p. 230.

[20] Hertenstein & Trott, *Selling Satan*, p. 255.

[21] Bowling Green speaker mixes comedy, religion [Advertisement]. (1984, January 30). *Defiance Crescent News*, p. 19.

[22] The Satan Seller Christian comedian will entertain [Advertisement]. (1985, April 20). *New Castle News*, p. 8.

[23] Comedian-evangelist scheduled [Advertisement]. (1985, October 26). *East Liverpool Evening News*.

Chapter 7: Media Circus

[1] Baessler, Sheriff's Dept. starts dig, *The Toledo Blade*.

[2] Nichols, Lights, camera, action! *The Toledo Blade*.

[3] Nichols, Lights, camera, action! *The Toledo Blade*.

[4] Evans & Wendling, Bedeviled searchers call it off, *The Plain Dealer*.

[5] Nichols, Lights, camera, action! *The Toledo Blade*.

[6] Evans & Wendling, Bedeviled searchers call it off, *The Plain Dealer*.

[7] Nichols, Lights, camera, action! *The Toledo Blade*.

[8] Evans & Wendling, Bedeviled searchers call it off, *The Plain Dealer*.

[9] Nichols, Lights, camera, action! *The Toledo Blade*.

[10] Nichols, Lights, camera, action! *The Toledo Blade*.

[11] Nichols, Lights, camera, action! *The Toledo Blade*.

[12] Nichols, Lights, camera, action! *The Toledo Blade*.

[13] Evans & Wendling, Bedeviled searchers call it off, *The Plain Dealer*.

[14] Nichols, Lights, camera, action! *The Toledo Blade*.

[15] Evans & Wendling, Bedeviled searchers call it off, *The Plain Dealer*.

[16] Case, *Here's to my sweet Satan*, p. 145.

[17] Hatton, L. (2015). All hail the acid king: The Ricky Kasso case in popular culture. In K. Janisse & P. Corupe (Eds.), *Satanic panic: Pop-cultural paranoia in the 1980s*. FAB Press. pp. 130.

[18] Case, *Here's to my sweet Satan*, p. 145.

[19] Shaw, D. (1990, January 20). Reporter's early exclusives triggered a media frenzy. *Los Angeles Times*. Retrieved from https://www.latimes.com/food/la-900120mcmartin_lat-story.html

[20] Walker, *The United States of Paranoia*, p. 212.

[21] Shaw, Reporter's early exclusives triggered, *Los Angeles Times*.

[22] Victor, *Satanic Panic*, p. 117.

[23] Victor, *Satanic Panic*, p. 116.

[24] Beck, *We believe the children*, p. 117.

[25] Richardson, Best, & Bromley, Satanism as a social problem, p. 12.

[26] Walker, *The United States of Paranoia*, p. 10.

[27] Richardson, Best, & Bromley, Satanism as a social problem, p. 12.

[28] Hertenstein & Trott, *Selling Satan*, p. 255.

[29] Victor, *Satanic Panic*, p. 10.

[30] Haferd, Satanism in Ohio, *The Akron Beacon Journal*.

[31] Wooden, K. & Kunhardt, P.W. (Producers). (1985, May 16). *20/20: The Devil Worshippers* [Television broadcast]. ABC News.

Chapter 8: Location, Location, Location

[1] Evans & Wendling, Hunt near Toledo, *The Plain Dealer*.

[2] Brown, Satanism in Ohio, *The Akron Beacon Journal*.

[3] Brown, Satanism in Ohio, *The Akron Beacon Journal*.

[4] Evans & Wendling, Bedeviled searchers call it off, *The Plain Dealer*.

[5] Evans & Wendling, Hunt near Toledo, *The Plain Dealer*.

[6] Evans & Wendling, Hunt near Toledo, *The Plain Dealer*.

[7] Baessler, Dig resumes for alleged victims, *The Toledo Blade*.

[8] Baessler, Dig resumes for alleged victims, *The Toledo Blade*. And Sielicki, Report could have been 'fairy tale,' *UPI Archives*.

[9] Sielicki, Report could have been 'fairy tale,' *UPI Archives*.

[10] Brown, Satanism in Ohio, *The Akron Beacon Journal*.

[11] Hicks, The police model of satanic crime, p. 175.

[12] Richardson, Best, & Bromley, Satanism as a social problem, p. 12.

[13] Mulhern, S. (1991). Satanism and psychotherapy: A rumor in search of an inquisition. In J.T. Richardson, J. Best, & D.G. Bromley (Eds.), *The Satanism Scare*. Aldine De Gruyter, p. 160.

[14] Victor, The dynamic of rumor-panics, p. 229.

[15] Mulhern, Satanism and psychotherapy, p. 166.

[16] Hicks, The police model of satanic crime, p. 179.

[17] Hicks, The police model of satanic crime, p. 176.

[18] Hicks, The police model of satanic crime, p. 177.

[19] Hicks, The police model of satanic crime, p. 176.

[20] Victor, *Satanic Panic*, p. 233.

[21] Hicks, The police model of satanic crime, p. 178.

[22] Beck, *We believe the children*, p. 120.

[23] Beck, *We believe the children*, p. 120.

[24] Frankfurter, *Evil Incarnate*, p. 71.

[25] Frankfurter, *Evil Incarnate*, pp. 43-44.

Chapter 9: Explainer of Evil, Discerner of Demons

[1] Baessler, Dig resumes for alleged victims, *The Toledo Blade*.

[2] Wooden & Kunhardt, *20/20: The Devil Worshippers,* ABC News.

[3] Baessler, Dig resumes for alleged victims, *The Toledo Blade*. And Brown, Satanism in Ohio, *The Akron Beacon Journal*.

[4] Nichols, Lights, camera, action! *The Toledo Blade*.

[5] Evans & Wendling, Bedeviled searchers call it off, *The Plain Dealer*.

[6] Nichols, Lights, camera, action! *The Toledo Blade*.

[7] Evans & Wendling, Bedeviled searchers call it off, *The Plain Dealer*.

[8] Evans & Wendling, Hunt near Toledo, *The Plain Dealer*.

[9] Evans & Wendling, Hunt near Toledo, *The Plain Dealer*.

[10] Breiner, J. (1985, June 23). Satanic murders: A great story that just wasn't there. *The Columbus Dispatch*, p. 9C.

[11] Wall, J. (1985, June 22). Sheriff calls off digging at site in Spencer Twp. *The Toledo Blade*, p. 1. And Cross, Sue. (1985, July 15). Rural township tries to return to normal

after search for bodies. *AP News*. Retrieved from
https://apnews.com/article/adb05be6c18665cca0b640ba6613260b

[12] Yonke, D. (2006). *Sin, shame, secrets: The murder of a nun, the conviction of a priest, and cover-up in the Catholic church*. Continuum International Publishing Group, p. 91.

[13] Evans & Wendling, Bedeviled searchers call it off, *The Plain Dealer*.

[14] Evans & Wendling, Hunt near Toledo, *The Plain Dealer*.

[15] Nichols, Lights, camera, action! *The Toledo Blade*.

[16] Evans & Wendling, Bedeviled searchers call it off, *The Plain Dealer*.

[17] Evans & Wendling, Bedeviled searchers call it off, *The Plain Dealer*.

[18] Brown, Satanism in Ohio, *The Akron Beacon Journal*.

[19] Baird, Sympathy for the devil, *The Columbus Dispatch*.

[20] *Testimony of Dale Griffis*. (2017, February 15). West Memphis Three Case Document Archive. Retrieved October 25, 2021, from http://www.callahan.mysite.com/wm3/ebtrial/dalegriffis.html

[21] Baird, Sympathy for the devil, *The Columbus Dispatch*.

[22] Baird, Sympathy for the devil, *The Columbus Dispatch*.

[23] Wooden & Kunhardt, *20/20: The Devil Worshippers,* ABC News.

[24] Baird, Sympathy for the devil, *The Columbus Dispatch*.

[25] Baird, D. (1985, May 22). Viewers who saw... *The Columbus Dispatch*, p. 19.

[26] Victor, *Satanic Panic*, p. 232.

[27] Ellis, B. (1991). Legend-tripping and satanism: Adolescents' ostensive traditions as 'cult' activity. In J.T. Richardson, J. Best, & D.G. Bromley (Eds.), *The Satanism Scare*. Aldine De Gruyter, p. 289.

[28] Mason, D. (1987, February 20). Ex-addicts may try satanism. *The Columbus Dispatch*, p. 3C.

[29] Ellis, Legend-tripping and satanism, p. 289.

[30] Baird, Sympathy for the devil, *The Columbus Dispatch*.

[31] Baird, Sympathy for the devil, *The Columbus Dispatch*.

[32] Baird, Sympathy for the devil, *The Columbus Dispatch*.

[33] Ellis, Legend-tripping and satanism, p. 289.

[34] Baird, Sympathy for the devil, *The Columbus Dispatch*.

[35] Baird, Sympathy for the devil, *The Columbus Dispatch*.

[36] Frankfurter, *Evil Incarnate*, p. 53.

[37] Frankfurter, *Evil Incarnate*, p. 20.

[38] Frankfurter, *Evil Incarnate*, p. 20.

[39] Frankfurter, *Evil Incarnate*, p. 32.

[40] Frankfurter, *Evil Incarnate*, p. 70.

[41] Frankfurter, *Evil Incarnate*, p. 39.

[42] Frankfurter, *Evil Incarnate*, p. 70.

Chapter 10: Closing Time
[1] Evans & Wendling, Hunt near Toledo, *The Plain Dealer*.
[2] Wall, Sheriff calls off digging, *The Toledo Blade*.
[3] Evans & Wendling, Hunt near Toledo, *The Plain Dealer*.
[4] Evans & Wendling, Bedeviled searchers call it off, *The Plain Dealer*.
[5] Baessler, Dig resumes for alleged victims, *The Toledo Blade*.
[6] Breiner, Satanic murders, *The Columbus Dispatch*.
[7] Evans & Wendling, Hunt near Toledo, *The Plain Dealer*.
[8] Baessler, Dig resumes for alleged victims, *The Toledo Blade*.
[9] Baessler, Dig resumes for alleged victims, *The Toledo Blade*.
[10] Wall, Sheriff calls off digging, *The Toledo Blade*.
[11] Miller, Satanic worship is no joke, *The Plain Dealer*.
[12] Brown, Satanism in Ohio, *The Akron Beacon Journal*.
[13] Wall, Sheriff calls off digging, *The Toledo Blade*.
[14] De Boer, R. (1985, June 21). Area witches express doubt of sacrifices by Satanic cult. *The Toledo Blade*, p. 4.
[15] De Boer, Area witches express doubt, *The Toledo Blade*.
[16] De Boer, Area witches express doubt, *The Toledo Blade*.
[17] De Boer, Area witches express doubt, *The Toledo Blade*.
[18] Baird, D. (1985, June 21). Satanic ritual murders aren't witches' style. *The Columbus Dispatch*, p. 18.
[19] Baird, Satanic ritual murders aren't witches' style, *The Columbus Dispatch*.
[20] Baird, Satanic ritual murders aren't witches' style, *The Columbus Dispatch*.
[21] Baird, Satanic ritual murders aren't witches' style, *The Columbus Dispatch*.
[22] Victor, *Satanic Panic*, p. 197.
[23] Victor, The dynamics of rumor-panics, pp. 231-233.
[24] Victor, *Satanic Panic*, p. 197.
[25] Victor, *Satanic Panic*, p. 198.
[26] Frankfurter, *Evil Incarnate*, p. 5.
[27] Walker, *The United States of Paranoia*, p. 55.
[28] Walker, *The United States of Paranoia*, p. 101.
[29] Walker, *The United States of Paranoia*, p. 129.
[30] Baessler, Dig resumes for alleged victims, *The Toledo Blade*.
[31] Evans & Wendling, Hunt near Toledo, *The Plain Dealer*.
[32] Hertenstein & Trott, *Selling Satan*, p. 289.

Chapter 11: TGIF

[1] Baessler, Dig resumes for alleged victims, *The Toledo Blade*.

[2] Nichols, Lights, camera, action! *The Toledo Blade*.

[3] Nichols, Lights, camera, action! *The Toledo Blade*. And Evans & Wendling, Bedeviled searchers call it off, *The Plain Dealer*.

[4] Baessler, Dig resumes for alleged victims, *The Toledo Blade*.

[5] Sielicki, Report could have been 'fairy tale,' *UPI Archives*.

[6] Wall, Sheriff calls off digging, *The Toledo Blade*.

[7] Evans & Wendling, Hunt near Toledo, *The Plain Dealer*.

[8] Sielicki, Report could have been 'fairy tale,' *UPI Archives*.

[9] Sielicki, Report could have been 'fairy tale,' *UPI Archives*.

[10] Bromley, Satanism: The new cult scare, pp. 52.

[11] Bromley, Satanism: The new cult scare, pp. 56.

[12] Bromley, Satanism: The new cult scare, pp. 57.

[13] Campion-Vincent, V. (2005). From evil others to evil elites: A dominant pattern in conspiracy theories today. In G.A. Fine, V. Campion-Vincent, & C. Heath (Eds.), *Rumor mills: The social impact of rumor and legend*. Transaction Publishers, p. 111.

[14] Frankfurter, *Evil Incarnate*, p. 5.

Chapter 12: In the Wake

[1] Associated Press. (1985, June 24). Sheriff to continue probe of alleged satanic deaths despite criticism. *AP News*. Retrieved from https://apnews.com/article/7f8380666eaf1d86d25970379ef376ff

[2] Associated Press, Sheriff to continue probe, *AP News*.

[3] Associated Press. (1985, June 25). Spencer Twp. official upset by cult search. *The Plain Dealer*. p. 15.

[4] Associated Press, Sheriff to continue probe, *AP News*.

[5] Wendling, T. (1985, July 7). The devil, you say: begone, sheriff! Dig for bodies infuriates trustee. *The Plain Dealer*, pp. 1, 19.

[6] Wendling, The devil, you say, *The Plain Dealer*.

[7] Associated Press, Sheriff to continue probe, *AP News*.

[8] Associated Press, Spencer Twp. official upset, *The Plain Dealer*.

[9] Associated Press, Spencer Twp. official upset, *The Plain Dealer*. And Associated Press, Sheriff to continue probe, *AP News*.

[10] Cross, Sue. (1985, July 15). Rural township tries to return to normal after search for bodies. *AP News*. Retrieved from https://apnews.com/article/adb05be6c18665cca0b640ba6613260b

[11] Cross, Rural township tries to return to normal, *AP News*.

[12] Baessler, Dig resumes for alleged victims, *The Toledo Blade*.

[13] Baessler, Dig resumes for alleged victims, *The Toledo Blade*.

[14] Breiner, No bodies found yet in cult probe, *The Columbus Dispatch*.

[15] Clements, C. (1985, June 24). Political notebook. *The Toledo Blade*, p. 3.

[16] Clements, Political notebook, *The Toledo Blade*.

[17] Johnson, R. (Ed.) (1985, June 25). The great cult caper. *The Toledo Blade*, p. 16.

[18] Johnson, The great cult caper, *The Toledo Blade*.

Chapter 13: Unforgetting the Forgotten

[1] Yonke, *Sin, shame, secrets*, p. 3.

[2] Yonke, *Sin, shame, secrets*, p. 14.

[3] Yonke, *Sin, shame, secrets*, p. 39.

[4] Yonke, *Sin, shame, secrets*, p. 63.

[5] Yonke, *Sin, shame, secrets*, p. 63.

[6] Yonke, *Sin, shame, secrets*, p. 64.

[7] Yonke, *Sin, shame, secrets*, p. 66.

[8] Yonke, *Sin, shame, secrets*, pp. 66-67.

[9] Yonke, *Sin, shame, secrets*, p. 70.

[10] Yonke, *Sin, shame, secrets*, pp. 73-75.

[11] Yonke, *Sin, shame, secrets*, p. 103.

[12] Yonke, *Sin, shame, secrets*, p. 114.

[13] Yonke, *Sin, shame, secrets*, p. 228.

[14] Mulhern, Satanism and psychotherapy, p. 147.

[15] Jenkins & Maier-Katkin, Occult survivors, p. 133.

[16] Victor, *Satanic Panic*, p. 81.

[17] Victor, *Satanic Panic*, p. 82.

[18] Beck, *We believe the children*, p. 24.

[19] Beck, *We believe the children*, p. 29.

[20] Victor, *Satanic Panic*, p. 82.

[21] Nathan, Satanism and child molestation, p. 81.

[22] Frankfurter, *Evil Incarnate*, p. 56.

[23] Bromley, Satanism: The new cult scare, pp. 53.

[24] Mulhern, Satanism and psychotherapy, p. 154.

[25] Mulhern, Satanism and psychotherapy, p. 155.

[26] Beck, *We believe the children*, p. 231.

[27] Richardson, Best, & Bromley, Satanism as a social problem, p. 11.

[28] Nathan, Satanism and child molestation, p. 81.

[29] Nathan, Satanism and child molestation, p. 82.

[30] Jenkins & Maier-Katkin, Occult survivors, p. 139.

[31] Yonke, *Sin, shame, secrets,* p. 103.

[32] Yonke, *Sin, shame, secrets,* pp. 103-104.

[33] Bromley, Satanism: The new cult scare, pp. 63.

[34] Mulhern, Satanism and psychotherapy, pp. 158-159.

[35] Victor, *Satanic Panic*, p. 81.

[36] Heller-Nicholas, "The only word in the world is mine," p. 28.

Chapter 14: Branded and Besmirched

[1] McGruder, R. (Ed.). (1985, July 3). Lucas sheriff resumes dig for alleged sacrifice victims: Eight hours of excavation finds no evidence of foul play. *The Plain Dealer*, p. 1B.

[2] McGruder, Lucas sheriff resumes dig, *The Plain Dealer*.

[3] McGruder, Lucas sheriff resumes dig, *The Plain Dealer*.

[4] Wendling, The devil, you say, *The Plain Dealer*.

[5] Wendling, The devil, you say, *The Plain Dealer*.

[6] Wendling, The devil, you say, *The Plain Dealer*.

[7] Associated Press. (1985, July 11). Spencer told it can't halt dig for Satan. *The Plain Dealer*. p. 1B.

[8] Wendling, The devil, you say, *The Plain Dealer*.

[9] McGruder, Lucas sheriff resumes dig, *The Plain Dealer*.

[10] Evans & Wendling, Hunt near Toledo, *The Plain Dealer*.

[11] Wendling, The devil, you say, *The Plain Dealer*.

[12] Wendling, The devil, you say, *The Plain Dealer*.

[13] Skvarla, When the 1980s Satanic Panic targeted Procter & Gamble, *Atlas Obscura*.

[14] Skvarla, When the 1980s Satanic Panic targeted Procter & Gamble, *Atlas Obscura*.

[15] Blumenfeld, L. (1991, July 15). Procter & Gamble's devil of a problem. *The Washington Post*. Retrieved from https://www.washingtonpost.com/archive/lifestyle/1991/07/15/procter-gambles-devil-of-a-problem/36f27641-e679-40f4-ac02-9d12c59a2f3b/

[16] Blumenfeld, Procter & Gamble's devil of a problem, *The Washington Post*.

[17] Skvarla, When the 1980s Satanic Panic targeted Procter & Gamble, *Atlas Obscura*.

[18] Skvarla, When the 1980s Satanic Panic targeted Procter & Gamble, *Atlas Obscura*.

[19] Belkin, L. (1985, April 18). Procter & Gamble fights Satan story. *The New York Times*. Retrieved from https://www.nytimes.com/1985/04/18/garden/procter-gamble-fights-satan-story.html

[20] Belkin, Procter & Gamble fights Satan story, *The New York Times*.

[21] Belkin, Procter & Gamble fights Satan story, *The New York Times*.

[22] Blumenfeld, Procter & Gamble's devil of a problem, *The Washington Post*.

[23] Belkin, Procter & Gamble fights Satan story, *The New York Times*.

[24] Belkin, Procter & Gamble fights Satan story, *The New York Times*.

[25] Belkin, Procter & Gamble fights Satan story, *The New York Times*.

[26] Belkin, Procter & Gamble fights Satan story, *The New York Times*.

[27] Associated Press. (1985, May 30). Devilish contest upsets Procter & Gamble. *The Akron Beacon Journal*, p. 7.

[28] Belkin, Procter & Gamble fights Satan story, *The New York Times*.

[29] DiFonzo, N. (2008). *The watercooler effect: An indispensable guide to understanding and harnessing the power of rumors*. Penguin Group, p. 18.

[30] Blumenfeld, Procter & Gamble's devil of a problem, *The Washington Post*.

[31] Blumenfeld, Procter & Gamble's devil of a problem, *The Washington Post*.

[32] Blumenfeld, Procter & Gamble's devil of a problem, *The Washington Post*.

[33] Blumenfeld, Procter & Gamble's devil of a problem, *The Washington Post*.

[34] Blumenfeld, Procter & Gamble's devil of a problem, *The Washington Post*.

[35] Blumenfeld, Procter & Gamble's devil of a problem, *The Washington Post*.

[36] Blumenfeld, Procter & Gamble's devil of a problem, *The Washington Post*.

[37] Blumenfeld, Procter & Gamble's devil of a problem, *The Washington Post*.

[38] Belkin, Procter & Gamble fights Satan story, *The New York Times*.

[39] Associated Press. (2007, March 20). Procter & Gamble wins satanic civil suit. *CBS News*. Retrieved from https://www.cbsnews.com/news/procter-gamble-wins-satanic-civil-suit/

[40] Skvarla, When the 1980s Satanic Panic targeted Procter & Gamble, *Atlas Obscura*.

[41] Price, M. (2012, October 29). Local history: Akron's devilish rumor causes national scandal in 1970s. *The Akron Beacon Journal*. Retrieved from https://www.beaconjournal.com/article/20121029/NEWS/310299420

[42] Price, Local History: Akron's devilish rumor, *The Akron Beacon Journal*.

[43] Price, Local History: Akron's devilish rumor, *The Akron Beacon Journal*.

Chapter 15: Burying the Hatchet

[1] Associated Press. (1985, July 12). Sheriff explains devil dig to township. *The Plain Dealer*. p. 10C.

[2] Cross, Rural township tries to return to normal, *AP News*.

[3] Associated Press, Sheriff explains devil dig, *The Plain Dealer*.

[4] Associated Press, Sheriff explains devil dig, *The Plain Dealer*.

[5] Associated Press, Sheriff explains devil dig, *The Plain Dealer*.

[6] Associated Press, Sheriff explains devil dig, *The Plain Dealer*.

[7] Associated Press, Sheriff explains devil dig, *The Plain Dealer*.

Chapter 16: From the Case Files of Lt. Kirk Surprise
[1] Surprise, K.R. (1985, June 8). *Investigation into local cult activities*. RB002113-85. Lucas County Sheriff's Department Record Bureau.

Chapter 21: The Affidavit for the Search Warrant
[1] Surprise, K.R. (1985, June). *Affidavit for search warrant*. RB002113-85. Lucas County Sheriff's Department Record Bureau.

Chapter 22: An Interview with Trilby Cashin
[1] Skeleton is discovered in Spencer Twp field. (1974, October 14). *The Toledo Blade.* Retrieved from: https://news.google.com/newspapers?id=ovNOAAAAIBAJ&sjid=HgIEAAAAI BAJ&pg=6513%2C96606
[2] Dental records confirm identity of slain woman. (1974, October 15). *The Toledo Blade*. Retrieved from: https://news.google.com/newspapers?id=o_NOAAAAIBAJ&sjid=HgIEAAAAIBAJ& pg=5661%2C645080
[3] Skeleton is discovered in Spencer Twp field, *The Toledo Blade*.

Chapter 23: Tying Up Loose Ends
[1] Churm, S. & Carlton, J. (1988, October 23). Ohio girl, 13, found in Southland after 6-year search. *Los Angeles Times*. Retrieved from https://www.latimes.com/archives/la-xpm-1988-10-23-mn-463-story.html
[2] Smith, L. (1988, October 26). Family of man held in kidnapping of granddaughter flees apartment. *Los Angeles Times*. Retrieved from https://www.latimes.com/archives/la-xpm-1988-10-26-me-38-story.html
[3] United Press International. (1988, December). Grandfather pleads guilty in kidnapping. *UPI Archives*. Retrieved from https://www.upi.com/Archives/1988/12/14/Grandfather-pleads-guilty-in-kidnapping/9629598078800/
[4] Smith, Family of man held in kidnapping, *UPI Archives*.
[5] Smith, Family of man held in kidnapping, *UPI Archives*.
[6] Churm & Carlton, Ohio Girl, 13, found in Southland, *Los Angeles Times*.
[7] Smith, Family of man held in kidnapping, *UPI Archives*.
[8] Smith, Family of man held in kidnapping, *UPI Archives*.
[9] United Press International, Grandfather pleads guilty, *UPI Archives*.
[10] Mills, D. (1985, June 18). *Criminal Report for Franklin J. Frazier*. Record Sections Number 002960-85. Lucas County Sheriff's Department Record Bureau.
[11] Evans & Wendling, Hunt near Toledo, *The Plain Dealer*.
[12] Associated Press. (1985, July 27). Satanic search victims sue for $1.52 million. *The Plain Dealer*. p. 1B.

13 Associated Press. (1986, June 22). Fruitless dig for victims of cult leaves family angry. *The Plain Dealer*. p. 22.

14 Associated Press, Fruitless dig for victims, *The Plain Dealer*.

15 Associated Press, Fruitless dig for victims, *The Plain Dealer*.

16 Associated Press, Fruitless dig for victims, *The Plain Dealer*.

17 Associated Press, Fruitless dig for victims, *The Plain Dealer*.

18 Associated Press, Fruitless dig for victims, *The Plain Dealer*.

19 Associated Press, Fruitless dig for victims, *The Plain Dealer*.

20 Associated Press, Fruitless dig for victims, *The Plain Dealer*.

21 Wendling, The devil, you say, *The Plain Dealer*.

22 Wendling, The devil, you say, *The Plain Dealer*.

23 Wendling, The devil, you say, *The Plain Dealer*.

24 Wendling, The devil, you say, *The Plain Dealer*.

25 Wendling, The devil, you say, *The Plain Dealer*.

26 Wendling, The devil, you say, *The Plain Dealer*.

27 Wendling, The devil, you say, *The Plain Dealer*.

28 Wendling, The devil, you say, *The Plain Dealer*.

29 Ellis, Legend-tripping and satanism, p. 279.

30 Ellis, Legend-tripping and satanism, p. 279.

31 Ellis, Legend-tripping and satanism, p. 287.

32 Ellis, Legend-tripping and satanism, p. 288.

33 Elizabeth, L. (2018, July 18). *CHILLING: Cult Activity* [Video]. YouTube. URL https://www.youtube.com/watch?v=rGpBbHMt1_I

34 Baird, Unmasking the devil, *The Columbus Dispatch*.

35 Baird, Unmasking the devil, *The Columbus Dispatch*.

36 Baird, Sympathy for the devil, *The Columbus Dispatch*.

Chapter 24: In the Lineage of Lady Circe
1 Toledo 'witch' founded church. (2004, June 5). *The Toledo Blade*. Retrieved from https://www.toledoblade.com/news/deaths/2004/06/05/Toledo-witch-founded-church/stories/200406050050

2 Toledo 'witch' founded church, *The Toledo Blade*.

3 Toledo 'witch' founded church, *The Toledo Blade*.

4 Toledo 'witch' founded church, *The Toledo Blade*.

5 Toledo 'witch' founded church, *The Toledo Blade*.

Chapter 25: Revisiting the Transcripts
[1] Baessler, Sheriff's Dept. starts dig, *The Toledo Blade*.

[2] Sifford, D. (1985, March 29). Anxiety ripe for rumors. *The Columbus Dispatch*, p. 32.

Chapter 26: An Interview with Dr. G. Micheal Pratt
[1] Breiner, J. (1985, June 22). Stripped earth yields no bodies. *The Columbus Dispatch*, p. 7A.

[2] Breiner, Stripped earth yields no bodies, *The Columbus Dispatch*.

[3] Brown, Satanism in Ohio, *The Akron Beacon Journal*.

[4] Breiner, Stripped earth yields no bodies, *The Columbus Dispatch*.

Chapter 27: Riding a White Horse
[1] Hill, M.D. (2008) *Spotlight: Dr. Dale. W. Griffis*. Jivepuppi. Retrieved October 19, 2021, from https://www.jivepuppi.com/dale_griffis.html

[2] Griffis, D.W. (n.d.) *Dale Griffis – West Memphis Three Case Information*. SMART Ritual Abuse Pages. Retrieved October 19, 2021, from https://ritualabuse.us/ritualabuse/articles/dale-griffis-west-memphis-three-case-information/

[3] Opperman, E. (Host). (2015, July 21). Dr. Dale Griffis West Memphis Three [Audio podcast episode]. In *The Opperman Report*. Opperman Investigations. http://www.oppermanreport.com/archive/dr-dale-griffis

[4] Opperman, E. (Host). (2015, July 24). William Ramsey, Dr. Dale Griffis WM3 Occult Experts [Audio podcast episode]. In *The Opperman Report*. Opperman Investigations. https://www.spreaker.com/user/oppermanreport/william-ramsey-dr-dale-griffis-wm3-occul_1

[5] Opperman, William Ramsey, Dr. Dale Griffis, *The Opperman Report*.

[6] *Testimony of Dale Griffis*. (2017, February 15). West Memphis Three Case Document Archive. Retrieved October 25, 2021, from http://www.callahan.mysite.com/wm3/ebtrial/dalegriffis.html

[7] *Testimony of Dale Griffis*, West Memphis Three Case Document Archive.

[8] *Testimony of Dale Griffis*, West Memphis Three Case Document Archive.

[9] Griffis, *Dale Griffis – West Memphis Three Case Information*, SMART Ritual Abuse Pages.

[10] Hill, *Spotlight: Dr. Dale W. Griffis*, Jivepuppi.

[11] Griffis, *Dale Griffis – West Memphis Three Case Information*, SMART Ritual Abuse Pages.

[12] Petit, Z. (2007, March 11). Cop story: Ohio. *The Tiffin Advertiser-Tribune*, pp. 1C, 5C.

[13] Griffis, *Dale Griffis – West Memphis Three Case Information*, SMART Ritual Abuse Pages.

[14] United Press International. (1984, July 12). Ohio police captain battles cults. *Tyrone Daily Herald*, Tyrone, Pennsylvania.

[15] United Press International, Ohio police captain battles cults, *Tyrone Daily Herald*.

[16] Associated Press. (1985, August 5). Officer's cult work gets mixed reaction. *The Columbus Dispatch*, p. 2D.

[17] Ricks, W.S. (1985, August 4). Tiffin's 1-man Satan squad draws fire. *The Cleveland Plain Dealer*, p. 1.

[18] Ricks, Tiffin's 1-man Satan squad draws fire, *The Cleveland Plain Dealer*.

[19] Associated Press, Officer's cult work gets mixed reaction, *The Columbus Dispatch*.

[20] Ricks, Tiffin's 1-man Satan squad draws fire, *The Cleveland Plain Dealer*.

[21] Associated Press, Officer's cult work gets mixed reaction, *The Columbus Dispatch*.

[22] Associated Press, Officer's cult work gets mixed reaction, *The Columbus Dispatch*.

[23] Ricks, Tiffin's 1-man Satan squad draws fire, *The Cleveland Plain Dealer*.

[24] Ricks, Tiffin's 1-man Satan squad draws fire, *The Cleveland Plain Dealer*.

[25] Ricks, Tiffin's 1-man Satan squad draws fire, *The Cleveland Plain Dealer*.

[26] Ricks, Tiffin's 1-man Satan squad draws fire, *The Cleveland Plain Dealer*.

[27] Ricks, Tiffin's 1-man Satan squad draws fire, *The Cleveland Plain Dealer*.

[28] Ricks, Tiffin's 1-man Satan squad draws fire, *The Cleveland Plain Dealer*. And United Press International. (1985, April 16) Overthrow captain. *Defiance Crescent News*.

[29] Ricks, Tiffin's 1-man Satan squad draws fire, *The Cleveland Plain Dealer*.

[30] Petit, Cop Story: Ohio, *The Tiffin Advertiser-Tribune*.

[31] United Press International, Ohio police captain battles cults, *Tyrone Daily Herald*.

[32] Ellis, Legend-tripping and satanism, p. 290.

[33] Baird, Sympathy for the devil, *The Columbus Dispatch*.

[34] Griffis, *Dale Griffis – West Memphis Three Case Information*, SMART Ritual Abuse Pages.

[35] Griffis, *Dale Griffis – West Memphis Three Case Information*, SMART Ritual Abuse Pages.

[36] Baird, Sympathy for the devil, *The Columbus Dispatch*.

[37] Opperman, Dr. Dale Griffis West Memphis Three, *The Opperman Report*.

[38] Breiner, Satanic Murders: A great story that just wasn't there, *The Columbus Dispatch*. And Breiner, Stripped earth yields no bodies, *The Columbus Dispatch*.

[39] Breiner, Satanic Murders: A great story that just wasn't there, *The Columbus Dispatch*.

[40] Breiner, Satanic Murders: A great story that just wasn't there, *The Columbus Dispatch*.

[41] Breiner, Satanic Murders: A great story that just wasn't there, *The Columbus Dispatch*.

[42] Breiner, Satanic Murders: A great story that just wasn't there, *The Columbus Dispatch*.

[43] *Testimony of Dale Griffis*, West Memphis Three Case Document Archive.

[44] *Testimony of Dale Griffis*, West Memphis Three Case Document Archive.

[45] *Testimony of Dale Griffis*, West Memphis Three Case Document Archive.

[46] Petit, Cop Story: Ohio, *The Tiffin Advertiser-Tribune*.

[47] Opperman, Dr. Dale Griffis West Memphis Three, *The Opperman Report*.

[48] Opperman, William Ramsey, Dr. Dale Griffis, *The Opperman Report*.

[49] Opperman, Dr. Dale Griffis West Memphis Three, *The Opperman Report*.

[50] Petit, Cop Story: Ohio, *The Tiffin Advertiser-Tribune*.

[51] Petit, Cop Story: Ohio, *The Tiffin Advertiser-Tribune*.

[52] *Testimony of Dale Griffis*, West Memphis Three Case Document Archive.

[53] Hill, *Spotlight: Dr. Dale W. Griffis*, Jivepuppi.

[54] Griffis, *Dale Griffis – West Memphis Three Case Information*, SMART Ritual Abuse Pages.

[55] Opperman, Dr. Dale Griffis West Memphis Three, *The Opperman Report*.

[56] *Testimony of Dale Griffis*, West Memphis Three Case Document Archive.

[57] Griffis, *Dale Griffis – West Memphis Three Case Information*, SMART Ritual Abuse Pages.

[58] Opperman, Dr. Dale Griffis West Memphis Three, *The Opperman Report*.

[59] *Testimony of Dale Griffis*, West Memphis Three Case Document Archive.

Chapter 28: Bibles and Badges

[1] Hicks, The police model of satanic crime, p. 182.

[2] Hicks, The police model of satanic crime, p. 182.

[3] Crouch, B. & Damphouse, K. (1991). Law enforcement and the satanism-crime connection: A survey of cult cops. In J.T. Richardson, J. Best, & D.G. Bromley (Eds.), *The Satanism Scare*. Aldine De Gruyter, p. 195.

[4] Hicks, The police model of satanic crime, p. 185.

[5] Hicks, The police model of satanic crime, p. 177.

[6] Beck, *We believe the children*, p. 122.

[7] Hicks, The police model of satanic crime, p. 185.

[8] *Testimony of Dale Griffis*, West Memphis Three Case Document Archive.

[9] Nathan & Snedeker, *Satan's Silence*, p. 130.

[10] Hicks, The police model of satanic crime, p. 182.

[11] Hicks, The police model of satanic crime, p. 185.

[12] Crouch & Damphouse, Law enforcement and the satanism-crime connection, p. 196.

[13] Hicks, The police model of satanic crime, p. 184.

[14] Hicks, The police model of satanic crime, p. 180.

[15] Hertenstein & Trott, *Selling Satan*, p. 284.

[16] Beck, *We believe the children*, p. 244.

[17] Beck, *We believe the children*, p. 242.

[18] Beck, *We believe the children*, p. 241.

[19] Beck, *We believe the children*, p. xxi.

Chapter 29: Rumor Has It

[1] Frankfurter, *Evil Incarnate*, pp. 1-2.

[2] Frankfurter, *Evil Incarnate*, pp. 1-2.

[3] Victor, The dynamic of rumor-panics, p. 221.

[4] DiFonzo, N. (2008). *The watercooler effect: An indispensable guide to understanding and harnessing the power of rumors*. Penguin Group, p. 38.

[5] DiFonzo, *The watercooler effect*, p. 18.

[6] Victor, The dynamic of rumor-panics, p. 222.

[7] Beck, *We believe the children*, p. 267.

[8] Victor, *Satanic Panic*, p. 55.

[9] Nathan & Snedeker, *Satan's Silence*, p. 30.

[10] Balch, R. & Gilliam, M. (1991). Devil worship in western Montana: A case study in rumor construction. In J.T. Richardson, J. Best, & D.G. Bromley (Eds.), *The Satanism Scare*. Aldine De Gruyter, p. 256.

[11] Bordia, P. & DiFonzo, N. (2005). Psychological motivations in rumor spread. In G.A. Fine, V. Campion-Vincent, & C. Heath (Eds.), *Rumor mills: The social impact of rumor and legend*. Transaction Publishers, p. 97.

[12] Bordia & DiFonzo, Psychological motivations in rumor spread, p. 89.

[13] Bordia & DiFonzo, Psychological motivations in rumor spread, p. 90.

[14] Bordia & DiFonzo, Psychological motivations in rumor spread, pp. 89-91.

[15] Campion-Vincent, From evil others to evil elites, p. 256.

[16] Bordia & DiFonzo, Psychological motivations in rumor spread, p. 92.

[17] Campion-Vincent, From evil others to evil elites, p. 256.

[18] Balch & Gilliam, Devil worship in western Montana, p. 250.

[19] Victor, The dynamic of rumor-panics, p. 222.

[20] DiFonzo, *The watercooler effect*, p. 98.

[21] Bordia & DiFonzo, Psychological motivations in rumor spread, p. 93.

[22] Bordia & DiFonzo, Psychological motivations in rumor spread, p. 95.

[23] Bordia & DiFonzo, Psychological motivations in rumor spread, p. 95.

[24] Balch & Gilliam, Devil worship in western Montana, p. 250.

[25] DiFonzo, *The watercooler effect*, p. 32.

[26] Victor, *Satanic Panic*, p. 117.

[27] Bromley, Satanism: The new cult scare, pp. 60.

[28] DiFonzo, *The watercooler effect*, p. 76.

[29] Victor, *Satanic Panic*, p. 4.

[30] Walker, *The United States of Paranoia*, p. 11.

[31] Victor, *Satanic Panic*, p. 60.

[32] Victor, The dynamic of rumor-panics, p. 228.

[33] Victor, The dynamic of rumor-panics, p. 222.

[34] Wall, J. (1985, June 21). Area residents skeptical of sacrifice stories. *The Toledo Blade*, p. 4.

[35] Victor, *Satanic Panic*, pp. 22-24.

[36] Evans & Wendling, Bedeviled searchers call it off, *The Plain Dealer*.

[37] Victor, *Satanic Panic*, p. 21.

[38] Blumenfeld, Procter & Gamble's devil of a problem, *The Washington Post*.

[39] Victor, *Satanic Panic*, pp. 22-24.

[40] Victor, *Satanic Panic*, p. 230.

[41] Hertenstein & Trott, *Selling Satan*, p. 404.

[42] Victor, *Satanic Panic*, p. 292.

[43] DiFonzo, *The watercooler effect*, p. 18.

[44] Bergstrom, C.T. & West, J.D. (2020). *Calling bullshit: The art of skepticism in a data-driven world*. Random House, p. 286.

Chapter 30: The Real Enemy

[1] Brotherton, R. (2015). *Suspicious minds: Why we believe conspiracy theories*. Bloomsbury Sigma, p. 80.

[2] Campion-Vincent, From evil others to evil elites, p. 104.

[3] Campion-Vincent, From evil others to evil elites, p. 110.

[4] Victor, *Satanic Panic*, p. 199.

[5] Victor, *Satanic Panic*, p. 200.

[6] Grey Faction. (n.d.) *QAnon: Facts and Fiction.* Grey Faction. Retrieved on December 2, 2021, from https://greyfaction.org/resources/qanon-facts-and-fiction/

[7] DiFonzo, *The watercooler effect*, p. 25.

[8] Brotherton, *Suspicious Minds*, p. 73.

[9] Brotherton, *Suspicious Minds*, p. 74.

[10] Campion-Vincent, From evil others to evil elites, p. 105.

[11] Brotherton, *Suspicious Minds*, p. 77.

[12] Brotherton, *Suspicious Minds*, p. 225.

[13] Brotherton, *Suspicious Minds*, p. 66.

[14] Brotherton, *Suspicious Minds*, p. 70.

[15] Brotherton, *Suspicious Minds*, p. 70.

[16] Bromley, Satanism: The new cult scare, pp. 61.

[17] Bromley, Satanism: The new cult scare, pp. 62.

[18] Best, Endangered children in antisatanist rhetoric, p. 96.

[19] Bromley, Satanism: The new cult scare, pp. 64.

[20] Best, Endangered children in antisatanist rhetoric, p. 104.

[21] Victor, *Satanic Panic*, p. 198.

[22] Beck, *We believe the children*, p. 115.

[23] Associated Press, Officer's cult work gets mixed reaction, *The Columbus Dispatch*.

[24] Victor, *Satanic Panic*, p. 199.

[25] Victor, *Satanic Panic*, p. 201.

[26] Victor, *Satanic Panic*, p. 209.

[27] Frankfurter, *Evil Incarnate*, p. 80.

[28] Frankfurter, *Evil Incarnate*, p. 85.

[29] Frankfurter, *Evil Incarnate*, p. 125.

[30] Frankfurter, *Evil Incarnate*, p. 11.

[31] Victor, The dynamics of rumor-panics, p. 231.

[32] Frankfurter, *Evil Incarnate*, p. 165.

[33] Frankfurter, *Evil Incarnate*, p. 12.

[34] Skvarla, When 1980s Satanic Panic targeted Procter & Gamble, *Atlas Obscura*.

[35] Walker, *The United States of Paranoia*, p. 333.

[36] Walker, *The United States of Paranoia*, p. 338.

Epitaph

[1] Associated Press. (1985, October 13). Special unit formed to protect Northwest Ohio from terrorists. *The Plain Dealer*. p. 41A.

Works Cited

Albrecht, B. (1984, December 30). Rumors swirl over animal mutilations in rural Ohio county.
The Plain Dealer, pp. 1, 8.

Associated Press. (1976, August 5). Vigilantes seek 'sect' in animal mutilations. *The Akron Beacon Journal*, p. 20.

Associated Press. (1985, April 15). Deputy says Union County is a satanic center. *AP News*. Retrieved from https://apnews.com/article/d7221d0cca4265edb63afe91e7b892ae

Associated Press. (1985, May 30). Devilish contest upsets Procter & Gamble. *The Akron Beacon Journal*, p. 7.

Associated Press. (1985, June 24). Sheriff to continue probe of alleged satanic deaths despite criticism. *AP News*. Retrieved from https://apnews.com/article/7f8380666eaf1d86d25970379ef376ff

Associated Press. (1985, June 25). Spencer Twp. official upset by cult search. *The Plain Dealer*. p. 15.

Associated Press. (1985, July 11). Spencer told it can't halt dig for Satan. *The Plain Dealer*. p. 1B.

Associated Press. (1985, July 12). Sheriff explains devil dig to township. *The Plain Dealer*. p. 10C.

Associated Press. (1985, July 27). Satanic search victims sue for $1.52 million. *The Plain Dealer*. p. 1B.

Associated Press. (1985, August 5). Officer's cult work gets mixed reaction. *The Columbus Dispatch*, p. 2D.

Associated Press. (1985, October 13). Special unit formed to protect Northwest Ohio from terrorists. *The Plain Dealer*. p. 41A.

Associated Press. (1986, June 22). Fruitless dig for victims of cult leaves family angry. *The Plain Dealer*. p. 22.

Associated Press. (2007, March 20). Procter & Gamble wins satanic civil suit. *CBS News*. Retrieved from https://www.cbsnews.com/news/procter-gamble-wins-satanic-civil-suit/

Baessler, J. (1985, June 20). Sheriff's Dept. starts Spencer Twp. dig for 50 reported killed by Satanic cult. *The Toledo Blade*, pp. 1, 7.

Baessler, J. (1985, June 21). Dig resumes for alleged victims of Satanic cult: Initial search uncovers eight-inch dagger, doll associated with occult. *The Toledo Blade*, pp. 1, 4.

Baird, D. (1984, July 15). Sympathy for the devil. *The Columbus Dispatch*, pp. 338-342. Available from NewsBank: Access World News – Historical and Current database.

Baird, D. (1985, April 14). Satanists suspected in animal mutilations. *The Columbus Dispatch*, p. 1.

Baird, D. (1985, April 14). Unmasking the devil. *The Columbus Dispatch*, p. 2B.

Baird, D. (1985, May 13). OSU professor says satanism is an escape from the turmoil. *The Columbus Dispatch*, p. 26.

Baird, D. (1985, May 22). Viewers who saw... *The Columbus Dispatch*, p. 19.

Baird, D. (1985, June 21). Satanic ritual murders aren't witches' style. *The Columbus Dispatch*, p. 18.

Balch, R. & Gilliam, M. (1991). Devil worship in western Montana: A case study in rumor construction. In J.T. Richardson, J. Best, & D.G. Bromley (Eds.), *The Satanism Scare*. Aldine De Gruyter. pp. 249-262.

Beck, R. (2015). *We believe the children: A moral panic in the 1980s*. PublicAffairs.

Belkin, L. (1985, April 18). Procter & Gamble fights Satan story. *The New York Times*. Retrieved from https://www.nytimes.com/1985/04/18/garden/procter-gamble-fights-satan-story.html

Bergstrom, C.T. & West, J.D. (2020). *Calling bullshit: The art of skepticism in a data-driven world*. Random House.

Best, J. (1991). Endangered children in antisatanist rhetoric. In J.T. Richardson, J. Best, & D.G. Bromley (Eds.), *The Satanism Scare*. Aldine De Gruyter. pp. 95-106.

Blumenfeld, L. (1991, July 15). Procter & Gamble's devil of a problem. *The Washington Post*. Retrieved from https://www.washingtonpost.com/archive/lifestyle/1991/07/15/procter-gambles-devil-of-a-problem/36f27641-e679-40f4-ac02-9d12c59a2f3b/

Bordia, P. & DiFonzo, N. (2005). Psychological motivations in rumor spread. In G.A. Fine, V. Campion-Vincent, & C. Heath (Eds.), *Rumor mills: The social impact of rumor and legend*. Transaction Publishers. pp. 87-101.

Bowling Green speaker mixes comedy, religion [Advertisement]. (1984, January 30). *Defiance Crescent News*, p. 19.

Breiner, J. (1985, June 21). No bodies found yet in cult probe. *The Columbus Dispatch*, p. 18.

Breiner, J. (1985, June 22). Stripped earth yields no bodies. *The Columbus Dispatch*, p. 7A.

Breiner, J. (1985, June 23). Satanic murders: A great story that just wasn't there. *The Columbus Dispatch*, p. 9C.

Bromley, D.G. (1991). Satanism: The new cult scare. In J.T. Richardson, J. Best, & D.G. Bromley (Eds.), *The Satanism Scare*. Aldine De Gruyter. pp. 49-71.

Brotherton, R. (2015). *Suspicious minds: Why we believe conspiracy theories*. Bloomsbury Sigma.

Brown, M. (1985, June 21). Satanism in Ohio – is it horror or hoax: Lucas County clues vague. *The Akron Beacon Journal*, pp. A1, A9.

Campion-Vincent, V. (2005). From evil others to evil elites: A dominant pattern in conspiracy theories today. In G.A. Fine, V. Campion-Vincent, & C. Heath (Eds.), *Rumor mills: The social impact of rumor and legend*. Transaction Publishers. pp. 103-122.

Canfield, D. (2015). Confessions of a creature feature preacher: Or, how I learned to stop worrying about satanism and love Mike Warnke. In K. Janisse & P. Corupe (Eds.), *Satanic panic: Pop-cultural paranoia in the 1980s*. FAB Press. pp. 263-273.

Canterbury, W. (1985, June 19). Animal mutilation probe stepped up in Kenmore. *The Akron Beacon Journal*, pp. D1, D4.

Case, G. (2016). *Here's to my sweet Satan: How the occult haunted music, movies, and pop culture, 1966-1980*. Quill Driver Books.

Christian comedian will entertain. (1985, April 20). *New Castle News*, p. 8.

Churm, S. & Carlton, J. (1988, October 23). Ohio girl, 13, found in Southland after 6-year search. *Los Angeles Times*. Retrieved from https://www.latimes.com/archives/la-xpm-1988-10-23-mn-463-story.html

Clements, C. (1985, June 24). Political notebook. *The Toledo Blade*, p. 3.

Comedian-evangelist scheduled [Advertisement]. (1985, October 26). *East Liverpool Evening News*.

Cross, Sue. (1985, July 15). Rural township tries to return to normal after search for bodies. *AP News*. Retrieved from https://apnews.com/article/adb05be6c18665cca0b640ba6613260b

Crouch, B. & Damphouse, K. (1991). Law enforcement and the satanism-crime connection: A survey of cult cops. In J.T. Richardson, J. Best, & D.G. Bromley (Eds.), *The Satanism Scare*. Aldine De Gruyter. pp. 191-204.

De Boer, R. (1985, June 21). Area witches express doubt of sacrifices by Satanic cult. *The Toledo Blade*, p. 4.

Denisoff, R. (1988). *Inside MTV.* Transaction, p. 289

Dental records confirm identity of slain woman. (1974, October 15). *The Toledo Blade*. Retrieved from: https://news.google.com/newspapers?id=o_NOAAAAIBAJ&sjid=HgIEAAAAIBAJ&pg=5661%2C645080

DiFonzo, N. (2008). *The watercooler effect: An indispensable guide to understanding and harnessing the power of rumors*. Penguin Group.

Elizabeth, L. (2018, July 18). *CHILLING: Cult Activity* [Video]. YouTube. URL https://www.youtube.com/watch?v=rGpBbHMt1_I

Ellis, B. (1991). Legend-tripping and satanism: Adolescents' ostensive traditions as 'cult' activity. In J.T. Richardson, J. Best, & D.G. Bromley (Eds.), *The Satanism Scare*. Aldine De Gruyter. pp. 279-295.

Erb, R. (2004, April 27). Area authorities no strangers to cult, ritual probes. *The Toledo Blade*. Retrieved from https://www.toledoblade.com/Police-Fire/2004/04/27/Area-authorities-no-strangers-to-cult-ritual-probes.html

Evans, C., & Wendling, T. (1985, June 21). Hunt near Toledo fails to find human sacrifices. *The Plain Dealer*, pp. 1, 16.

Evans, C., & Wendling, T. (1985, June 22). Bedeviled searchers call it off. *The Plain Dealer*, pp. 1, 14.

Frankfurter, D. (2006). *Evil incarnate: Rumors of demonic conspiracy and satanic abuse in history*. Princeton University Press.

Grey Faction. (n.d.) *QAnon: Facts and Fiction.* Grey Faction. Retrieved on December 2, 2021, from https://greyfaction.org/resources/qanon-facts-and-fiction/

Griffis, D.W. (n.d.) *Dale Griffis – West Memphis Three Case Information.* SMART Ritual Abuse Pages. Retrieved October 19, 2021, from https://ritualabuse.us/ritualabuse/articles/dale-griffis-west-memphis-three-case-information/

Haferd, L. (1985, June 21). Satanism in Ohio – is it horror or hoax: Devil worship feeds on fear. *The Akron Beacon Journal*, pp. A1, A9.

Hatton, L. (2015). All hail the acid king: The Ricky Kasso case in popular culture. In K. Janisse & P. Corupe (Eds.), *Satanic panic: Pop-cultural paranoia in the 1980s*. FAB Press. pp. 127-145.

Heller-Nicholas, A. (2015). "The only word in the world is mine": Remembering 'Michelle remembers.' In K. Janisse & P. Corupe (Eds.), *Satanic panic: Pop-cultural paranoia in the 1980s*. FAB Press. pp. 19-31.

Hertenstein, M. & Trott, J. (1993). *Selling Satan*. Cornerstone Press.

Hicks, R. (1991). The police model of satanic crime. In J.T. Richardson, J. Best, & D.G. Bromley (Eds.), *The Satanism Scare*. Aldine De Gruyter. pp. 175-189.

Hill, M.D. (2008) *Spotlight: Dr. Dale. W. Griffis*. Jivepuppi. Retrieved October 19, 2021, from https://www.jivepuppi.com/dale_griffis.html

Jenkins, P. & Maier-Katkin, D. (1991). Occult survivors: The making of a myth. In J.T. Richardson, J. Best, & D.G. Bromley (Eds.), *The Satanism Scare*. Aldine De Gruyter. pp. 127-144.

Johnson, R. (Ed.) (1985, June 25). The great cult caper. *The Toledo Blade*, p. 16.

Ladouceur, L. (2015). The filthy fifteen: When Venom and King Diamond met the Washington wives. In K. Janisse & P. Corupe (Eds.), *Satanic panic: Pop-cultural paranoia in the 1980s*. FAB Press. pp. 159-171.

LeRoy, M. & Haddad D. (2018). *They must be monsters: A modern day witch hunt*. The Manor Publishing House.

Mason, D. (1987, February 20). Ex-addicts may try satanism. *The Columbus Dispatch*, p. 3C.

McGruder, R. (Ed.). (1985, July 3). Lucas sheriff resumes dig for alleged sacrifice victims: Eight hours of excavation finds no evidence of foul play. *The Plain Dealer*, p. 1B.

Miller, W.C. (1985, June 21). Satanic worship is no joke: Lucas County officials praised for taking occult seriously. *The Plain Dealer*, p. 19.

Mills, D. (1985, June 18). *Criminal Report for Franklin J. Frazier*. Record Sections Number 002960-85. Lucas County Sheriff's Department Record Bureau.

Mulhern, S. (1991). Satanism and psychotherapy: A rumor in search of an inquisition. In J.T. Richardson, J. Best, & D.G. Bromley (Eds.), *The Satanism Scare*. Aldine De Gruyter. pp. 145-172.

Nathan, D. (1991). Satanism and child molestation: Constructing the ritual abuse scare. In J.T. Richardson, J. Best, & D.G. Bromley (Eds.), *The Satanism Scare*. Aldine De Gruyter. pp. 75-94.

Nathan, D. & Snedeker, M. (1995). *Satan's silence: Ritual abuse and the making of a modern American witch hunt*. BasicBooks, HarperCollins Publishers.

Nichols, J. (1985, June 21). Lights, camera, action! Media flurry catches residents by surprise. *The Toledo Blade*, pp. 1, 4.

Ofshe, R. & Watters, E. (1994). *Making Monsters: False Memories, Psychotherapy, and Sexual Hysteria*. Charles Scribner's.

Opperman, E. (Host). (2015, July 21). Dr. Dale Griffis West Memphis Three [Audio podcast episode]. In *The Opperman Report*. Opperman Investigations. http://www.oppermanreport.com/archive/dr-dale-griffis

Opperman, E. (Host). (2015, July 24). William Ramsey, Dr. Dale Griffis WM3 Occult Experts [Audio podcast episode]. In *The Opperman Report*. Opperman Investigations. https://www.spreaker.com/user/oppermanreport/william-ramsey-dr-dale-griffis-wm3-occul_1

Phillips, P. (1986). *Turmoil in the toybox*. Starburst Publishers.

Petit, Z. (2007, March 11). Cop story: Ohio. *The Tiffin Advertiser-Tribune*, pp. 1C, 5C.

Price, M. (2012, October 29). Local history: Akron's devilish rumor causes national scandal in 1970s. *The Akron Beacon Journal*. Retrieved from https://www.beaconjournal.com/article/20121029/NEWS/310299420

Rhoden, Y. (1985, June 11). Cult warning is sounded in Kenmore: animal mutilations spur information session. *The Akron Beacon Journal*, pp. C1, C2.

Richardson, J.T., Best, J., & Bromley D.G. (1991). Satanism as a social problem. In J.T. Richardson, J. Best, & D.G. Bromley (Eds.), *The Satanism Scare*. Aldine De Gruyter. Pp. 3-17.

Ricks, W.S. (1985, August 4). Tiffin's 1-man Satan squad draws fire. *The Cleveland Plain Dealer*, p. 1.

Rusnak, S. (2015). Scapegoat of a nation: The demonization of MTV and the music video. In K. Janisse & P. Corupe (Eds.), *Satanic panic: Pop-cultural paranoia in the 1980s*. FAB Press. pp. 173-199.

Scott, D. (1985, June 23). A cult in Kenmore – or just 'ornery kids?' *The Akron Beacon Journal*, pp. A1, A4.

Searcey, D. (2006, January 9). Behind the music: Sleuths seek messages in lyrical backspin. *The Wall Street Journal.* Retrieved from https://www.wsj.com/articles/SB113677367081541303

Shaw, D. (1990, January 20). Reporter's early exclusives triggered a media frenzy. *Los Angeles Times*. Retrieved from https://www.latimes.com/food/la-900120mcmartin_lat-story.html

Sielicki, J. (1985, June 22). Report could have been 'fairy tale'. *UPI Archives*. Retrieved from https://www.upi.com/Archives/1985/06/22/Report-could-have-been-fairy-tale/2901488260800

Sifford, D. (1985, March 29). Anxiety ripe for rumors. *The Columbus Dispatch*, p. 32.

Skeleton is discovered in Spencer Twp field. (1974, October 14). *The Toledo Blade.* Retrieved from: https://news.google.com/newspapers?id=ovNOAAAAIBAJ&sjid=HgIEAAAAIBAJ&pg=6513%2C96606

Skvarla, R. (2017, July 13). When 1980s Satanic Panic targeted Procter & Gamble. *Atlas Obscura*. Retrieved from https://www.atlasobscura.com/articles/procter-gamble-satan-conspiracy-theory

Smith, L. (1988, October 26). Family of man held in kidnapping of granddaughter flees apartment. *Los Angeles Times*. Retrieved from https://www.latimes.com/archives/la-xpm-1988-10-26-me-38-story.html

Stevens, P. (1991). The demonology of satanism: An anthropological view. In J.T. Richardson, J. Best, & D.G. Bromley (Eds.), *The Satanism Scare*. Aldine De Gruyter. pp. 21-39.

Surprise, K.R. (1985, June). *Affidavit for search warrant*. RB002113-85. Lucas County Sheriff's Department Record Bureau.

Surprise, K.R. (1985, June 8). *Investigation into local cult activities*. RB002113-85. Lucas County Sheriff's Department Record Bureau.

Testimony of Dale Griffis. (2017, February 15). West Memphis Three Case Document Archive. Retrieved October 25, 2021, from http://www.callahan.mysite.com/wm3/ebtrial/dalegriffis.html

The Satan Seller Christian comedian will entertain [Advertisement]. (1985, April 20). *New Castle News*, p. 8.

Toledo 'witch' founded church. (2004, June 5). *The Toledo Blade*. Retrieved from https://www.toledoblade.com/news/deaths/2004/06/05/Toledo-witch-founded-church/stories/200406050050

United Press International. (1984, July 12). Ohio police captain battles cults. *Tyrone Daily Herald*, Tyrone, Pennsylvania.

United Press International. (1985, April 16) Overthrow captain. *Defiance Crescent News*.

United Press International. (1988, December). Grandfather pleads guilty in kidnapping. *UPI Archives*. Retrieved from https://www.upi.com/Archives/1988/12/14/Grandfather-pleads-guilty-in-kidnapping/9629598078800/

Victor, J.S. (1991). The dynamics of rumor-panics about satanic cults. In J.T. Richardson, J. Best, & D.G. Bromley (Eds.), *The Satanism Scare*. Aldine De Gruyter. pp. 221-236.

Victor, J.S. (1993). *Satanic panic: The creation of a contemporary legend*. Open Court Press.

Walker, J. (2013). *The United States of paranoia*. Harper Perennial.

Wall, J. (1985, June 21). Area residents skeptical of sacrifice stories. *The Toledo Blade*, p. 4.

Wall, J. (1985, June 22). Sheriff calls off digging at site in Spencer Twp. *The Toledo Blade*, p. 1.

Wendling, T. (1985, July 7). The devil, you say: begone, sheriff! Dig for bodies infuriates trustee. *The Plain Dealer*, pp. 1, 19.

Whitfield, C.L, Silberg, J.L., & Fink P.J. (2001). *Misinformation Concerning Child Sexual Abuse and Adult Survivors*. Haworth Press. pp. 55–56.

Wooden, K. & Kunhardt, P.W. (Producers). (1985, May 16). *20/20: The Devil Worshippers* [Television broadcast]. ABC News.

Yonke, D. (2006). *Sin, shame, secrets: The murder of a nun, the conviction of a priest, and cover-up in the Catholic church*. Continuum International Publishing Group.

Printed in the USA
CPSIA information can be obtained
at www.ICGtesting.com
LVHW062339251223
767339LV00038B/1034